C000050480

THE BUMPER BOOK OF
CRICKET
USELESS INFORMATION

THE BUMPER BOOK OF
CRICKET
USELESS INFORMATION

ASTOUNDING FACTS AND FEATS BOTH
ON AND OFF THE PITCH

MARK DAWSON

metro

Published by Metro Publishing
an imprint of John Blake Publishing Ltd
3 Bramber Court, 2 Bramber Road,
London W14 9PB, England

www.johnblakepublishing.co.uk

First published in hardback in 2009

ISBN: 978-1-84454-735-7

All rights reserved. No part of this publication may be reproduced, stored in a
retrieval system, or in any form or by any means, without the prior permission
in writing of the publisher, nor be otherwise circulated in any form of binding
or cover other than that in which it is published and without a similar condition
including this condition being imposed on the subsequent publisher.

British Library Cataloguing-in-Publication Data:

A catalogue record for this book is available from the British Library.

Printed in the UK by CPI William Clowes Beccles NR34 7TL

3 5 7 9 10 8 6 4 2

© Text copyright Marc Dawson, 2009

Papers used by John Blake Publishing are natural, recyclable products made from
wood grown in sustainable forests. The manufacturing processes conform to the
environmental regulations of the country of origin.

CONTENTS

FOREWORD

Cricket is one of the great measures of my life.

Every significant moment I have experienced in the thrilling tapestry of Test and one-day history reminds me of who I was and where I was at the time.

Allow me to indulge …

When Dennis Lillee kicked then shaped up to Javed Miandad like Les Darcy at the WACA in 1981, I was at my nana's place after school cheering D.K. on for all it was worth. After all, he was my hero and if he had to knock Javed's block off with a sledgehammer to win the Test then that'd do me.

When Adam Gilchrist removed the bails, running out Lance Klusener to tie a match that ultimately thrust Australia into the 1999 World Cup final, I hugged my wife then charged jubilantly around the lounge room of my first house. Muted jubilation on this occasion though, after all, it *was* the middle of the night and my first-born baby daughter was in the next room dreaming her own dreams.

A shattered 22-year-old, sitting in his first car – that old grey Mazda 626 – listening in horror as Craig McDermott was dismissed one run short of taming the mighty West Indian supermen – a feat he considered impossible for most of his growing years.

A triumphant rent-paying patriot and his footy housemates, riding Stephen Roger Waugh all the way to his first Test two-hundred in the Caribbean a couple of years later, extracting revenge with every back foot punch.

A confused 11-year-old standing silently in his backyard after an Aussie captain asked his younger brother to bowl underarm.

The permutations are endless and the magic rolls on. It shines through the pages that you are about to read and the knowledge that you are about to absorb. The ammunition with which you are about to arm yourself to combat and conquer the trivia-loving tribes of your social circles is enormous. Don't take it for granted.

One of my first sporting memories is assembling in a school library during a junior cricket camp and watching Rick McCosker drag his bat and his bandages bravely to the middle of the MCG only to duck his broken jaw beneath the next bouncer of big bad Bobby Willis. It was the Centenary Test and I must have been seven. Skinny and apprehensive, I was unsure about so many things on my radar but certain of one – that cricket would forever remain in my veins.

A cavalcade of folklore stretches back before this and how much is still to come?

Cricket will answer that question and answer it well I suspect … and this book pays a wonderful tribute to that glorious notion.

RUPERT MCCALL, AUSTRALIAN POET

HIT & RUN

● Appearing in his seventh first-class match, Madhya Pradesh batsman Amay Khurasiya fell one run short of his maiden first-century *twice*. Playing against Vidarbha at Nagpur in 1991-92, Khurasiya was dismissed for 99 in the first innings, and was left stranded on 99 in the second when his side gained victory. His unbeaten 99 was scored in 88 minutes off 62 balls and included seven fours and three sixes.

Khurasiya's maiden century came four matches later – 132 against Hyderabad – one that was quickly followed by another, in his next match, against Mumbai. In 1998-99, he became the eighth Indian batsman to mark his one-day international debut with a half-century, scoring 54 against Sri Lanka at Pune.

● After indicating a preference to bat in the middle order, in-form opening batsman Lou Vincent was dropped from the New Zealand Test squad to take on the West Indies in 2005-06. Vincent had scored 52, 224, 13 and 92 in his four Test innings prior to the West Indies series, but the NZ coach John Bracewell couldn't accommodate his apparent wish to move down the order: **"Lou continually said that he didn't see himself as an opener and would prefer to bat in the middle order. We weren't prepared to play guys who were reluctant."**

"It was just a preference, I wasn't insisting on anything. I'd love to play for New Zealand as much as anyone. I'd play anywhere in the team – I don't think there's ever been any doubt over that. I can't understand it. I just want to play the game."

Lou Vincent

● Australia's Dean Jones began his captaincy for English county side Derbyshire in 1996 with a century (103*) and victory in a one–day match against Leicestershire. Opening the batting with Kim Barnett, Jones witnessed the curious sight of a prankster, decked out in a replica Derbyshire outfit, striding to the crease after his partner's dismissal. The intruder was even allowed to face one joke ball, before being escorted from the field.

● After Sri Lanka's openers had both been dismissed for a duck in the first Test against South Africa at Durban in 2000-01, Kumar Sangakkara (74) and Mahela Jayawardene (98) set about repairing the damage by posting a third-wicket stand of 168. With Sri Lanka all out for 216, their partnership represented 77.78 per cent of the total, a record-high in Test cricket.

The previous best in a Test match was 76.54 per cent, by Alec Bannerman (70) and Percy McDonnell (147) who put on a fourth-wicket stand of 199 in Australia's first-innings total of 260 against England at Melbourne in 1881-82. No other Australian reached double figures in the innings, the next best being an unbeaten seven by the No.10, Sammy Jones.

"I am not very aggressive. I play a more boring kind of cricket."

Kumar Sangakkara

● Responding to a reader's question in 2005, the *Cricinfo* website set about determining who was the most 'boring batsman' of all time. Despite being hampered by a lack of statistics regarding balls faced by batsmen in early Test matches, the website concluded that of all the batsmen with at least 1000 Test runs, England wicket-keeper Bob Taylor possessed the slowest rate of scoring – 1156 runs from 4260 balls for a strike rate of 27.14. The next two on the list were also English – Mike Brearley with a strike rate of 29.80 and Chris Tavaré, 30.60.

Melbourne statistician Charles Davis came up with a different set of names when he studied some of the earlier Test matches, calculating that Australia's Alec Bannerman was even slower than Bob Taylor. Estimating the number of balls that batsmen may have faced, he concluded that Bannerman, who played in 28 Tests between 1878-79 and 1893, scored his 1108 runs at a rate of 22 to 23 per 100 balls. Second on the list was England's Trevor 'Barnacle' Bailey (26-27 balls).

● Herbie Collins launched his Test career for Australia in fine style, peeling off four consecutive fifties, including a century on debut at the ripe 'old' age of 31. In his first Test series, against England in 1920-21, Collins made 70 and 104 at Sydney, 64 in Australia's innings-victory at Melbourne and 162 in the first innings of the third Test at Adelaide.

Statistically, Collins' two centuries and two fifties in consecutive innings remains the best start by a batsman in Test cricket, closely followed by India's Sunil Gavaskar who made 65, 67 not out, 116 and an unbeaten 64 against the West Indies in 1970-71. In the third Test at Bridgetown he was out for just one in the first innings, but made amends with 117 not out, and then struck gold in the fifth Test at Port-of-Spain with a double of 124 and 220. Gavaskar's four hundreds and total of 774 runs in four matches – average 154.80 – remains the best performance by a batsman in his debut Test series.

● A Dutch batsman struck a double-century of boundaries in a limited-overs match in 2002, taking part in a world-record partnership for the sixth wicket. Marnix van der Gun scored an unbeaten 245 for HCC against Quick Haag at The Hague, in which he plundered 21 sixes and 20 fours, a total of 206 runs in boundaries. He shared in a 285-run partnership with H. Maalderink (56), as HCC made 508 for 6 off its 40 overs.

● West Indies batsman Gordon Greenidge created history in 1982-83 when he brought to an end his own innings against India at St John's upon discovering his daughter was gravely ill. Greenidge became the first batsman in Test history to end an innings as 'retired not out' with his score on 154, shortly after taking part in a record opening stand against India of 296 with Desmond Haynes, who made 136.

● After making his Test debut in 1953, Australia's Alan Davidson went 51 innings without making a duck. His *only* Test-match duck in his 61 innings came at Manchester in 1961, falling to the bowling of England batsman Ted Dexter. Michael Slater and Ricky Ponting each played

44 Test innings before they scored their first nought – Ponting then made another two successive ducks – while Jim Burke played out his entire Australian Test career of 44 innings without ever recording a blob.

In one-day international cricket, Australia's Graeme Wood also played 51 innings before was he was dismissed without scoring. After making his debut, against India at Adelaide in 1977-78, Wood didn't taste his first duck until 1984-85, at New Delhi.

● Faoud Bacchus, who played in 19 Test matches for the West Indies during the 1970s and early '80s, had a highest score of 250, but an average of just 26.00. It was his only Test-match century, scored against India at Kanpur in 1978-79, his career also including as many as seven ducks in 30 innings. Curiously, every one of Bacchus' 19 Tests was played on a different ground.

● The West Indies' Garry Sobers had a relatively lean year with the bat in 1957, scoring just 320 Test runs at 32.00 in ten innings. He turned things around the following year in sensational style, blasting 1299 runs, with six centuries, from 13 innings at an average of 144.33.

● Two stars of the past in Viv Richards and Doug Walters were big hits at the 2004 Shanghai International Sixes tournament in China, with the former West Indies skipper scoring two not-out fifties. Richards retired upon reaching the half-century mark in both of his matches for the Shanghai President's team.

"I just want everyone to know that the masseuses have arrived to give free massages. Everybody is entitled to one."

ground announcer during the 2005 Shanghai Sixes

● South Africa's Peter Kirsten made history in a one-day international at Port Elizabeth in 1992-93 when Kapil Dev ran him out for backing up too far before delivering the ball. Kirsten was later pinged by match officials and fined half of his match fee for initially refusing to leave the crease as a result. The incident caused further acrimony, with the Indians claiming Kirsten's partner, the South African captain Kepler Wessels, had deliberately hit Kapil on the shins with his bat later in the same over.

● Wollongong-born batsman Phil Jaques enjoyed an impressive first-class debut in 2000-01, sharing the honours for the highest individual score after his team New South Wales had been routed for 140 by Queensland on the opening day of their Pura Cup match in Brisbane. Batting down the order at No.10, Jaques made 40 off 55 balls to match the 114-ball 40 made earlier in the innings by Matthew Phelps, the only two batsmen to reach double figures.

In 2004, Jaques was in commanding form in the English County Championship, hitting a quick-fire double-century in the match against Hampshire at Southampton. Opening the batting with Matthew Wood, the New South Welshman stuck 243 – with 33 fours and six sixes – out of Yorkshire's total of 395. In doing so, Jaques became the first batsman to score a first-class double-century both for and against Yorkshire, having struck 222 for Northamptonshire against the Tykes, at Northampton, in 2003.

● Batting in a club match against Awsworth in Nottinghamshire in 1997, Chris Knott hit 160 runs in boundaries in a record-breaking innings of 205 not out for Old Dalby. He reached 50, 100, 150 and 200 with sixes, hitting 14 in all, plus another 19 fours.

● Oxford University batsman Dan Fox, who struck a hundred in his only first-class match in 2004, played in just two matches the following year and marked one with a record-breaking 400-run third-wicket partnership. Fox struck a career-best 184 in the match against Cambridge at Fenner's, and in company with the Delhi-born Rhodes Scholar Salil Oberoi moulded a match-winning stand of 408, at the time the 15th-highest for the third wicket in first-class history.

Oberoi went to the top of the class that day, with his 247 breaking a 74-year old record surpassing the Nawab of Pataudi snr's 238 not out in 1931, previously the highest individual innings in Oxford-Cambridge cricket.

● Unlucky for some, the number 13 has worked in Mark Butcher's favour, with the England opener scoring his maiden Test century in his 13th Test. He brought up his first three-figure innings in 1998, making 116 against South Africa at Leeds. His opening partner on the day, Mike Atherton ended his career three years later with the most number of innings of 13 in Test cricket. Atherton was dismissed for 13 on seven occasions in his 115 matches, including one such dismissal in his final Test – against Australia at The Oval in 2001.

● After putting together a record-breaking innings with the bat and sealing the best player award as a result, Ireland's Eoin Morgan had his one-day international debut in 2006 slightly tarnished, when he was reprimanded for using obscene language.

Morgan became the first batsman to be dismissed for 99 on his one-day international debut, and upon being run out – in the match against Scotland at Ayr – let loose with a few choice words as he departed. He became just the fourth batsman to be run out for 99 in 2396 one-day internationals, after Graeme Smith, Sanath Jayasuriya and Adam Gilchrist, but the first to suffer the fate on his debut.

● After beginning the calendar year of 2004 in sumptuous style, producing consecutive unbeaten innings of 241, 60 and 194, India's Sachin Tendulkar then suffered the biggest slump of his Test-match career. In his next eight innings, Tendulkar was able to reach double figures on just one occasion, falling for scores of two, eight and one against Pakistan and – coming back from injury – eight, two, five and 55 against Australia and then three against South Africa. Things were back to normal, though, not long afterwards with Tendulkar scoring another double-century – 248 not out, against Bangladesh at Dhaka.

Tendulkar finished what turned out to be a topsy-turvy year with the highest average for his country, scoring 915 runs in ten Tests at 91.50:

"2004 was full of ups and downs. There have been some big disappointments in the year. I never thought I would have such a terrible injury. The injury was such a big setback. However, it has made me a tougher person and helped me fight back and get back to where I am supposed to be."

His unbeaten 248 was the 250th double-century scored in Test cricket. In 2000-01, Tendulkar had registered the 200th Test-match 200, an innings of 201 not out against Zimbabwe at Nagpur.

● Despite ending up on the losing side, Sri Lankan import Aravinda de Silva won the man-of-the-match award in the final of the 1995 Benson & Hedges Cup at Lord's. Chasing a target of 275 to beat Lancashire, de Silva led the Kent assault with a dazzling century (112), while the next best contribution was just 25 by both David Fulton and Graham Cowdrey. De Silva, who came into the match without a single fifty in his previous 15 one-day innings for the county made history by becoming the first player in a losing team to win the Gold Award in a B&H final.

● Somerset batsman Graham Rose was in sparkling form in the year 1990, twice reaching 100 in a limited-overs match in fewer than 50 balls. He set a world record against Devon at Torquay, blasting his way to a century off just 36 balls, and against Glamorgan at Neath made it to the century-mark off 46 deliveries, reaching his fifty in 16.

Kent batsman Matthew Fleming, who appeared in 11 one-day internationals in the late 1990s, also had a penchant for quick scoring in one-day matches. Twice he reached 50 off just 16 deliveries, once against Scotland at Glasgow in 1991 and then against Gloucestershire at Canterbury in 1996.

● After Australia had amassed an even 600 in its first innings at Melbourne in 1924-25, England's Jack Hobbs (154) and Herbert Sutcliffe (176) replied in spectacular fashion with a first-wicket stand of 283. The pair batted throughout the third day, the first time this had happened in Test cricket, with Sutcliffe adding 127 in the second innings, becoming the first batsman to achieve two hundreds in a Test against Australia. With two sizeable knocks in the previous Test at Sydney, Sutcliffe's first four innings against Australia were 59, 115, 176 and 127, while his first three partnerships with Hobbs against Australia were 157, 110 and 283. Their stand of 283 remains the highest-ever response by an opening pair to an opposition's total of over 500.

● In the first Test against Pakistan at Faisalabad in 2004-05, Sri Lankan opener Marvan Atapattu made a pair, while his partner Sanath Jayasuriya posted a history-making double-century. His knock of 253 was the first score of 253 in Test history, and along the way the 35-year-old became the first-ever batsman to reach 100 and 200 in the same innings with a six. Earlier in the year, batting against the same opposition, Pakistan, at Multan, Indian opener Virender Sehwag (309) became the first to reach the landmarks of 100 and 300 in the same innings with sixes.

● Appearing in just his eighth first-class match, New South Wales batsman Dominic Thornely produced a dynamic maiden double-century in 2004-05, an innings that included a record number of sixes. On his way to a massive 261 not out against Western Australia at Sydney, Thornely smashed 21 fours and 11 sixes, engineering a last-wicket partnership of extraordinary proportions with Stuart MacGill. Thornely's innings, spanning 405 minutes and 367 deliveries, broke Bob Simpson's 1963-64 record of 247 not out for the highest score by a Blues batsman against Western Australia, while his 11 sixes eclipsed the Australian record held by David Hookes, who hit ten in his innings of 243 in the South Australia–New South Wales match at the Adelaide Oval in 1985-86.

Thornely was on 76 at the fall of the ninth wicket on the opening day, and even reaching a century seemed highly unlikely with the No.11 MacGill at the other end. But to the amazement of all, the pair went on to reach the magical milestone of 100 runs for the final wicket, of which MacGill contributed just one. Their partnership was eventually broken the following morning when MacGill, who batted for 168 minutes and faced 70 deliveries, was out for 27, leaving Thornely unbeaten on 261. Their union of 219 runs – which has greater than either of WA's innings (137 & 148) – was the seventh-highest tenth-wicket alliance in all first-class cricket and the second-best in Sheffield Shield/Pura Cup history.

Within a matter of weeks of the Thornley-MacGill partnership, the

Lahore Whites' pair of Aqeel Arshad (105) and Ali Raza (126*) dominated the Quaid-e-Azam Trophy match against Hyderabad in Lahore sharing a colossal 239-run last-wicket stand. Aqeel, batting at No. 9, and Ali, the wicket-keeper, both scored their maiden first-class centuries, with Ali's 126, the highest undefeated century by a No.11 batsman in first-class cricket.

● After taking just one wicket between them in the first innings of the New Zealand Test at Brisbane in 2004-05, Jason Gillespie and Glenn McGrath set about inflicting some damage with the bat. The opening fast bowlers, batting at nine and eleven, each scored their maiden Test-match 50 and shared in a tenth-wicket stand of 114, only the third 100-run last-wicket partnership for Australia. Gillespie finished unbeaten on 54, while McGrath made 61 – the highest Test score by an Australian No.11, overtaking the previous best of 52 by Rodney Hogg against the West Indies in 1983-84.

McGrath's maiden fifty came in his 102nd match, the most Tests anyone has taken before reaching the milestone, easily surpassing Sri Lanka's Muttiah Muralitharan who got his first fifty (67 v India at Kandy 2000) in his 64th Test. Gillespie was next on the list at the time, needing 59 Tests.

In Queensland, an umpire had just completed his on-field duties, and when he came off the ground and was told that McGrath had scored a fifty, he fainted.

"It's a good laugh, but I probably got more pleasure out of Glenn getting his [half-century] than mine, because it was totally unexpected."

Jason Gillespie

● In between carrying his bat for 156 against Pakistan at Bulawayo in 1997-98 and 106 not out against India at Nagpur in 2000-01, Zimbabwe's Grant Flower went a record 33 Test-match innings without a fifty. Flower – the first Zimbabwean to score five Test centuries – managed just 433 runs at an average of just 13.53 with 16 single-figure innings and a top score of 49. Team-mate Alistair Campbell was also struggling with the bat at the same time, going for 26 innings without a fifty.

Flower and Campbell share the dubious distinction of being the only top-order batsmen to have played in as many as 60 Test matches, yet fail to attain an overall career-average of at least 30.00. Campbell played in 60 Tests, with 113 innings, scoring 2858 runs at 27.21, while Flower appeared in 67 Tests, with 3457 runs in 125 innings, average 29.54.

● During a one-day international against Sri Lanka in 2004, Australia's Andrew Symonds was surprisingly recalled to the crease after he was given out leg-before-wicket. In the same year, in England, it happened to one batsman on three occasions, twice in the same match. Appearing for Exmouth against South Devon, James Hope was recalled to the crease twice after being dismissed lbw, once by the umpire realising he'd made a mistake; the other time by the opposing captain, who admitted that the batsman had hit the ball. Hope went on to make an unbeaten 73, with his team claiming victory by seven wickets. Remarkably, it happened to him again … in a match against Exeter – given out leg-before, he was recalled to the crease and proceeded to make a match-winning unbeaten century.

● The two-match Test series between Bangladesh and India in 2004–05 featured two history-making knocks by the opposing number elevens. The first Test at Dhaka saw India's Zaheer Khan obliterate the record for the highest score by a No.11 batsman, hitting 75, an innings littered with ten fours and two sixes.

Bangladesh's Talha Jubair – who made his Test debut aged 16 years and 223 days – made his highest score in first-class cricket in the second Test at Chittagong. Jubair's 31, which came off 24 balls with five fours and a six, was Bangladesh's highest score of the innings. This was only the sixth time that the No.11 had top-scored in a Test innings, while earlier in the match, team-mate Mohammad Ashraful (158*) made Bangladesh's highest individual score to date, while passing the milestone of 1000 Test runs, aged just 20, second only to Sachin Tendulkar.

● India's Sunil Gavaskar (97) and Chetan Chauhan (93) fell eight runs short of a double-century partnership against Pakistan at Lahore in 1978-79, with both openers dismissed in the nineties, a first in Test-match cricket. Not until 1997-98 did another set of opening batsmen fall in the nineties in the same innings, and again it happened to India, with V.V.S.

Laxman and Navjot Sidhu both narrowly missing out on a century in the second Test against Australia at Kolkata. The pair put on 191 for the first wicket as India assembled a match-winning total of 633 for 5 declared, with the top six in the order all passing 50 – Laxman 95, Sidhu 97, Rahul Dravid 86, Sachin Tendulkar 79, Mohammad Azharuddin 163 not out and Sourav Ganguly 65.

● In his long and illustrious career, Mark Taylor was stumped on just seven occasions in his 186 Test-match innings. Remarkably, three of them came in consecutive Test matches on his first overseas tour in 1989, a few months after making his Test debut. On his way to accumulating a record tally of 839 runs in the six-match Ashes series, Taylor was stumped in the first innings of three successive Tests – for 43 at Birmingham, for 85 at Manchester and for 219 at Nottingham.

● Top-order batsman Andrew Jones appeared in 87 one-day internationals for New Zealand and never scored a century, despite passing fifty on 25 occasions. He entered the nineties twice during his career with a highest innings of 93 – scored in 93 minutes – against Bangladesh at Sharjah in 1989-90.

● After his first half-a-dozen one-day internationals, England's Kevin Pietersen boasted a record double-century batting average. After 12 innings, his average was still over 100. The Natal-born batsman scored his maiden one-day international hundred against South Africa at Bloemfontein in 2004-05, reaching the 100-mark in 91 balls with five fours and two sixes. His unbeaten 108 in the match, which ended in a tie, boosted his career-average after five innings to a stunning 234.00 – more than double that of the previous record-holder, Australia's Michael Clarke, who averaged 104.50 after his first five outings.

In the fifth one-day international at East London, Pietersen made another hundred, bringing up his century with a six. He compiled his runs off a mere 69 balls and crowned the series with another century at Centurion. His 116 saw him pass the milestone of 500 runs in record-equalling time, with his average at 139.50, and a strike rate at a smidgeon over the hundred-mark (100.72).

In a portent of things to come, Pietersen had begun the tour of his homeland with a match-winning 97 off 84 balls against South Africa A at Kimberley: **"I knew I was going to cop a lot of stick, but it will be like water off a duck's back. I expected stick at the start of the innings, but I just sat back and laughed at the opposition, with their swearing and 'traitor' remarks. Some of them can hardly speak English."**

● Zimbabwe batsman Mark Dekker appeared in a total of 14 Test matches and was never once bowled. The left-hander set a world record by being dismissed 21 times without losing his wicket in such fashion, and on the one occasion he remained not out established another world-first. Playing against Pakistan at Rawalpindi in 1993-94, Dekker became the first batsman to carry his bat in a completed Test innings in which he didn't make the highest score. Alistair Campbell made 75, while Dekker carried his bat for 68 not out, which, coincidentally, followed a first-innings score of 68 – the only two half-centuries of his Test career.

In the one-day international arena, Dekker played in a similar number of innings (22), which again spawned just two half-centuries, again coming in consecutive innings. On his debut – against New Zealand at Bulawayo in 1992-93 – Dekker hit 79, making 55 in his next match, against the same opposition, at Harare.

● In between making a Test-match duck at Cape Town in 2000-01 and another nought at Colombo in 2002, Sri Lanka's Mahela Jayawardene put together a string of 29 consecutive double-figure innings. His run included a highly productive sequence of 139, 150 and 99 – against three different opponents, India, Bangladesh and West Indies – breaking the previous record of 25 consecutive double-figure scores held by England's Len Hutton and the West Indies' Rohan Kanhai. After his Colombo duck of 2002, Jayawardene made 39 and one against South Africa at Johannesburg before marching onwards with another run of 24 double-figure scores, culminating in just two dismissals of under ten in 35 Tests.

● During the 2004-05 VB one-day international series, Pakistan's Shahid Afridi scored at better than a run a ball, hitting a total of 16 sixes in the seven matches in which he batted. The holder of the record for the fastest one-day international century, Afridi was the only batsman in the competition to achieve a strike rate in excess of 200 in a match, and he did so twice. He began the tournament with an audacious knock of 56 not out against Australia at Hobart, an innings encompassing 26 balls with four fours and four sixes. He then hit 48 off 37 balls against Australia in Sydney, 17 off 16 against the West Indies in Adelaide, 30 off 13 against Australia in Perth and finally, 23 off ten deliveries against the Windies, again in Perth.

He continued his uncanny run in the finals against Australia, scoring 26 off 15 deliveries with three sixes at the MCG, an effort that saw him claim the world record for most sixes in one-day internationals. Afridi overtook the record of Sri Lanka's Sanath Jayasuriya with incredible gusto, beating his mark of 188 career sixes in a whopping 138 fewer matches. The second final in Sydney – his 199th match – featured a 21-ball 31 with two sixes, ending the series with a strike rate of 167.39.

"I like hitting the ball into stands and want to hear the cracking sound that comes out of my bat. I don't know why, but that sound and sight of seeing the ball land in enclosures gives me immense pleasure and satisfaction."

Shahid Afridi

In 1996-97, Afridi had marked his first innings in a one-day international by reaching 100 against Pakistan at Nairobi in 37 deliveries. Aged just 16 at the time, Afridi smashed a record-equalling 11 sixes, and with a further six fours, made 102 in 50 minutes to demolish the previous record of 48 balls, set by Sanath Jayasuriya, against Pakistan at Singapore, earlier in the year. Afridi brought up his 50 off 18 balls – one shy of Jayasuriya's record – producing a similar rollicking knock against The Netherlands in the 2002-03 Champions Trophy at Colombo. Batting at No. 3, he made an unbeaten 55, of which 52 runs came in boundaries (four fours & six sixes).

● Promoted up Pakistan's batting order for the 2004-05 Test series against India, Shahid Afridi became the first opener from any country to score a half-century in under 30 balls. Opening the second innings with

Yasir Hameed at Bangalore, Afridi made 58 – with eight fours and two sixes – reaching his 50 in just 26 balls, a Pakistani record.

The Indian opening bowling attack felt the full force of Afridi's onslaught, with Irfan Pathan and Lakshmipathy Balaji both conceding over eight runs per over. Pathan went for 45 runs in five overs, the worst bowling performance in a Test match by any player bowling exactly five overs in an innings.

Afridi upped the ante in the one-day internationals that followed, with a scorching hundred in the fifth match at Kanpur, becoming the first player in the history of the game to twice reach the century-mark off less than 50 balls and the first to reach the milestone of 200 sixes. His innings of 102 – in which he reached his century off 45 deliveries – included ten fours and nine sixes – a staggering 94 of his runs coming in boundaries, or 92.15 per cent, another world-record performance. His opening partner Salman Butt contributed just 21 runs in a first-wicket stand of 131 that came off 14.2 overs.

AFRIDI – PLEASE SPARE US FOR FRIENDSHIP'S SAKE

Indian crowd banner at India-Pakistan one-day international,

Kanpur 2004-05

● In 2005, Nandu Patil scored an unbeaten 403 for the P.D. Hinduja Hospital XI in the *Times Of India* Shield competition. Patil indicated he was keen to press on and challenge the tournament's long-standing individual record of 515, but the opposition, Central Excise, had had enough and tossed in the towel.

● Mike Hussey made his one-day international debut for Australia in 2003-04 after Michael Bevan had suffered a cracked rib. Fast forward to 2005-06 and a case of déjà vu, with Hussey making his Test debut – against the West Indies at Brisbane – after a cracked rib had forced Justin Langer to sit on the sidelines.

Hussey had served the longest apprenticeship of any batsman in the history of Australian first-class cricket before making his Test debut, with a record number of runs (15,313) and matches (176) under his belt. The second Test, at Hobart, saw the debut of another batsman with a ton of runs in the bank. Victoria's Brad Hodge – replacing the out-of-form Simon Katich – debuted with over 12,500 runs – and 167 first-class matches – behind him, second only to Hussey.

Hussey went on to make back-to-back centuries in the series, the first scored as an opener in the second Test at Hobart, the other at No. 5 in Adelaide. His aggregate of 361 runs came at an average of 120.33, a record for an Australian batsman in his first series, eclipsing Albert Trott's 102.50 against England in 1894-95.

Batting against South Africa at Perth – in the series that followed the West Indies' visit – Hodge brought up his maiden Test century, an unbeaten 203, becoming only the second Australian batsman, after Don Bradman (212) against England at Adelaide in 1936-37, to score a double-century in the second innings of a Test match. Hodge's double-ton came in just his fifth Test-match innings, and 32 days after making his debut, beating the previous record of 196 days set by Mark Taylor in 1989.

"I feel the same as when I got my first call-up – a bit nauseous, but excited."

Mike Hussey – on the eve of his Test debut in 2005-06

MOST FIRST-CLASS RUNS & MATCHES BEFORE AUSTRALIAN TEST DEBUT

Runs	Matches		Season of First-Class Debut	Test Debut
15,313	176	Mike Hussey	1994-95	1st Test v West Indies at Brisbane 2005-06
12,679	167	Brad Hodge	1993-94	2nd Test v West Indies at Hobart 2005-06
10,571	166	Andrew Symonds	1994-95	1st Test v Sri Lanka at Galle 2003-04
10,267	123	Darren Lehmann	1987-88	3rd Test v India at Bangalore 1997-98
10,255	129	Martin Love	1992-93	4th Test v England at Melbourne 2002-03

"It has been a long, hard road and I honestly believe if anyone deserves to play cricket for Australia, it's me."

Brad Hodge – prior to his first Test in 2005-06

"When I got the message, I was devastated."

Brad Hodge – on being dropped from the Test squad four months later, after five Tests and 409 runs, average 58.42

● Zimbabwe fast bowler Christopher Mpofu made history with the bat in 2005-06 when he became the first batsman to be stumped for nought in each innings of a Test match on the same day. Mpofu was stumped by New Zealand's Brendon McCullum for a duck in both innings off the bowling of Daniel Vettori on the second, and final, day of the first Test at Harare. He was only the second batsman ever to be stumped for a pair on the same day, after England's Bobby Peel suffered the misfortune in the fourth Test against Australia at Sydney in 1894–95.

In a rare two-day Test match, both McCullum and Vettori were New Zealand's stars with the bat, each scoring a century in under 100 balls. McCullum, batting at No. 7, made 111 reaching 100 off 94 balls, while Vettori, at No. 8, struck 127, his century coming off 82 deliveries.

Following his history-making pair at Harare, Mpofu suffered further humiliation in the second Test at Bulawayo when he was run out for three by McCullum after nonchalantly wandering down the pitch to congratulate his partner Blessing Mahwire, who had just reached his maiden Test-match fifty (50*).

● In the same innings that Sri Lanka's Kumar Sangakkara struck a double-century against South Africa at Colombo in 2006, his team-mate Mahela Jayawardene (374) trumped him with a triple. Sangakkara's effort of 287 is the highest score not to be the highest in a Test-match innings.

● In 2006, an English club cricketer went one better than Garry Sobers and Ravi Shastri, an illustrious pair that shares the first-class record for scoring 36 runs in an over. Batting in an Aire-Wharfe League match for North Leeds, Jonathan Hughes hit 42 runs against Hall Park. In an over – that included two no-balls – sent down by medium-pacer Craig Hobson, Hughes clobbered six sixes, a four and a two on his way to an unbeaten 126.

Later in the same summer, Rob Ellis faced the final over of a Yorkshire league match and progressed from 90 to his century in two balls, and ended up unbeaten on 138. The Evening League Reserve quarter-final between Glasshouses and Blubberhouses had been reduced to 14 eight-ball overs because of rain, and Ellis went the tonk, hitting eight consecutive sixes off Tim Hendry to finish the match.

● Steve Waugh occupied a number of positions in the Australian batting order during his lengthy career, becoming the first batsman to top 5000 Test runs at No. 5. Waugh built up 6754 runs at No. 5 from 142 innings – scoring 24 centuries and 29 fifties – with India's Mohammad Azharuddin, second on the list with 4346 runs from 94 innings. Waugh also displayed a certain flair further down the order, becoming the first to top the 3000-run mark at No. 6, hitting a total of 3165 in 79 Test innings.

● In his 128 Test matches, Mark Waugh made 8029 runs, but never scored a double-century, an Australian record. His highest innings was an unbeaten 153 against India at Bangalore in 1997-98, the only occasion he exceeded the 150-mark in his 209 Test-match innings.

● Chasing a victory-target of 140 against Bangladesh at Old Trafford in 2005, openers Matthew Hayden and Adam Gilchrist knocked off the required number of runs in 19 overs and 73 minutes giving Australia its first ten-wicket victory in a one-day international overseas. Both batsmen made an unbeaten 66, the first occasion when both openers had identical undefeated scores of over 50 in the same one-day international innings.

At the 'Gabba in 2005-06, Gilchrist fell to the opening ball of the VB Series match against South Africa, and with his new partner Simon Katich also failing to score, provided the first instance of an Australian opening combination both making a duck in a one-day international. On their return to the 'Gabba later in the summer in a finals match against Sri Lanka, the pair then became the first set of Australian openers to both score a century in a ODI in Australia, Gilchrist posting a ripsnorting 122 off 91 balls, and Katich an unbeaten 107.

● During the summer of 2005-06, Andrew Symonds became the first batsman in world cricket to pass 150 in a day-day international twice in the same season. After scoring 156 against New Zealand at Wellington in December, he then scored 151 – his first ODI hundred in Australia – in the second VB Series final against Sri Lanka at the SCG in February. Symonds reached his 150 at Wellington off just 125 balls, hit 12 fours and eight sixes and shared in a record 220-run fifth-wicket partnership with Michael Clarke (82*). He was then a part of an even bigger stand at the SCG, an Australian-record 237, for the fourth wicket, with Ricky Ponting (124).

He reached his 150 from exactly the same number of balls as he did in Wellington, hitting 13 fours and three sixes, but was involved in an unpleasant incident after his dismissal. Going up the stairs to the dressing rooms, he used his bat to push away a spectator: "**I was just exhausted. I had my head down. As I looked up, the bloke had his arms in the air and I thought he was going to hug me. I just would have collapsed because I had nothing left. I just put my bat in his chest so he couldn't jump on me**." In his defence, the spectator denied he had attempted to make contact with Symonds, merely attempting to offer his congratulations: "**I was not going to jump on Andrew Symonds as he has stated. I opened my arms in sheer delight at his fantastic innings and in the most joyous and happy tone I said to him, 'Give this man a hug'. I am not a yobbo … I was just happy for Andrew and his great innings**."

● After his first half-a-dozen ING Cup innings in 2005-06, New South Wales opener Phil Jaques had scored 483 runs, with three centuries, at an average of 120.75. In his first six innings for his Sydney club side Sutherland, Jaques had identical figures – 483 runs with three centuries, average 120.75. Jaques was the star of the domestic one-day summer scoring three hundreds in a row and back-to-back unbeaten 150s. After scoring a neat 100 against WA in Perth, he then hit 152 not out off 141 balls against Queensland at Sydney, followed by an undefeated 158 – again off 141 deliveries – in his next innings, against South Australia at Adelaide. He became the first batsman to record two consecutive unbeaten innings of 150-plus in domestic one-day cricket.

With a bagful of runs in the Pura Cup to match, his irresistible form earned him a call-up to the national Test team, thanks to an injured Justin Langer, making two and 28 on debut against South Africa at the MCG. With an injury to Simon Katich, he then made his first appearance in a one-day international, scoring 94 against the same opposition at Melbourne's Docklands Stadium, the highest score by an Australian batsman on his debut since Kepler Wessels made 79 against New Zealand at Melbourne in 1982-83.

Despite his record-breaking 94, Jaques was unable to keep his place in the national one-day team making way for the return of Katich. Back in his New South Wales uniform, Jaques promptly scored 138 – off 137 balls – against Tasmania at Hobart, becoming the first batsman to score four domestic limited-overs centuries in a season.

● On the day Phil Jaques reached the 200-mark against India A at Cairns in 2006, the Sydney-based *Daily Telegraph* newspaper suggested the incumbent Test opener Justin Langer was vulnerable with the New South Wales batsman in such sparkling form. And while Jaques scored another century (117) in the same match to add to his 240, Langer was busy rewriting the record books at the same time with the highest-ever first-class score for Somerset. His 342 against Surrey at Guildford overtook Viv Richards' 21-year-record 322 and was one boundary shy of breaking Charlie Macartney's 1921 tour-score of 345 as the highest first-class innings made by an Australian in England: **"Three-hundred ... it's been written in my diary for the last eight years, so I was never sure whether I would achieve that milestone, but it's one that's kept driving me for a long time."**

Prior to competing in the 'Top End Series', which involved A teams from Australia, India, Pakistan and New Zealand, Jaques had been in scorching form for English club Worcestershire, hitting double-centuries in two consecutive matches – 244 against Essex at Chelmsford and 202 against Northamptonshire at Worcester. He plundered three double-hundreds in four matches, six half-centuries in seven successive innings and scored 1000 first-class runs in just six weeks: **"I'm in the form of my life. It's quite incredible. I haven't had a month of cricket quite like it."**

● During a Central Lancashire League match in England, Rochdale batsman Hartley Wilson smashed a mighty six off Walsden's Peter Green that sailed out of the ground and through the window of a nearby house, landing on the bed of – believe it or not – the bowler. Wilson, who was making a comeback after a spell in the second XI, was just as surprised as everyone at the ground that day: **"I slammed it as hard as I could. But I hadn't the faintest idea it would finish up in his bed. We'll be talking about this one for the next 20 years. The trouble is**

it couldn't have happened to a nicer fellow. Peter is a friend of mine." Green's club insurance policy covered the two-pound cost of replacing his bedroom window.

● Two Maharashtra batsmen, who share the initials S.S. and were both born in 1966, scored over 6500 first-class runs and averaged over 55.00, yet never played in a Test. Shantanu Sugwekar made his first-class debut in 1987-88 and went on to gather 6563 runs in 85 matches at 63.10, while team-mate Surendra Bhave played the first of his 97 first-class matches in '86-87, accumulating 7971 runs at an average of 58.18.

Sugwekar hit 19 centuries in first-class cricket, while Bhave collected 28 hundreds, both finishing with a highest score between 290 and 299. Although a long way off the record for the most runs by batsmen who never played Test cricket, their averages are right at the top.

The pair proved to be a big hit in English club cricket in 1999, with Bhave hitting 1246 runs for the Settle club and Sugwekar 1051 runs for Great Harwood in the Ribblesdale League. Bhave, who topped his club's run-scoring feats for the summer – as did Sugwekar – had a rather unsettling habit while batting, for which he later apologised. He was known to constantly shout out "four" the second he hit a ball he knew would be a boundary: "**I don't do it to annoy anybody. I'm just concentrating and a few words come out spontaneously. It just happens ... it is in my game unknowingly.**"

When Maharashtra made 700 against Madhya Pradesh at Pune in the 1988-89 Ranji Trophy, Sugwekar was left unbeaten one run shy of a maiden triple-century. He retired from first-class cricket in 2001-02 as the only batsman with 299 not out as his highest score.

● In his only innings in the 2002 Test series against New Zealand, Imzamam-ul-Haq scored a triple-century, breaking a long-standing record held by Australia's Bob Simpson in the process. After the Test series in Pakistan was reduced to a single match – the second Test was cancelled following a bomb blast in Karachi – Imzamam became the first batsman to top 300 runs in a one-Test 'series', with 329 in his only innings, at Lahore. The previous record had been held by Simpson who hit 268 runs – 153 & 115 – in the one-off Test against Pakistan at Karachi in 1964-65.

● During his record-breaking innings of 173 against the West Indies at Melbourne in 2000-01, Mark Waugh became the first Australian batsman to score 500 runs in a one-day international series twice. He finished the 2000-01 Carlton Series with 542 runs in just seven innings, to match exactly the same aggregate – from 12 innings – in the corresponding series in 1998-99.

● One of the more tension-packed 99s in the history of the game was played out in South Australia in 2004-05, when Mark Benbow was involved in three consecutive run outs trying to reach 100. Representing West Augusta in a 50-overs match against Central Stirling, Benbow ran out two partners and then himself seeking that elusive run which would have taken him to a maiden A-grade century.

● For the final Test of its ill-fated Australian tour in 2000-01, which they lost 5-0, the West Indies tried a new opening combination after partnerships of 21, 0, 1, 7, 45, 26, 5 and 1 from Sherwin Campbell and Daren Ganga. The change paid off with Campbell and his new partner Wavell Hinds producing the West Indies' only two 50-run Test-match partnerships of the entire summer – 147 and 98 at the SCG. It was the only occasion that the two opened the West Indies' batting, with their first-innings stand beating the previous best opening partnership by a West Indian pair in Australia – 135 by Gordon Greenidge and Desmond Haynes at Brisbane in 1988-89.

● Glamorgan tail-ender Don Shepherd, who collected a staggering 149 ducks in first-class cricket, once scored a blinding half-century against the might of the touring Australian side of 1961. Coming to the crease with his side in trouble at 94 for 8, Shepherd, smacked 51 in just 11 scoring shots, hitting spinners Lindsay Kline and Richie Benaud three times each over the fence.

● Sussex batsman Ken Suttle, who, between 1954 and 1969, played in a record 423 consecutive County Championship matches, retired from first-class cricket in 1971 with 30,225 runs to his credit, the exact same number as Leicestershire's Les Berry. The two county stalwarts are amongst just four in the world to have scored 30,000 runs in the first-class game, but never to have played in a Test.

BATSMEN WITH THE MOST FIRST-CLASS RUNS WHO NEVER PLAYED IN A TEST

	Major Teams	Career Span	M	Runs	HS	100s	Avge
Alan Jones	Glamorgan, Natal, Northern Transvaal, Western Australia	1957-1983	645	36,049	204*	56	32.89
John Langridge	Sussex	1928-1955	574	34,378	250*	76	37.44
Les Berry	Leicestershire	1924-1951	609	30,225	232	45	30.25
Ken Suttle	Sussex	1949-1971	612	30,225	204*	49	31.09

● Dean Jones possessed one of the best overall records in one-day internationals, commanding an average of 44.61 from 164 matches. But against Sri Lanka, Jones went up a gear, with his average sky-rocketting to a massive 109.87 from 17 appearances. The difference of 65.25 is unmatched by any batsman against a particular opposition, although when pitted against the West Indies, his average plummeted to 23.75 from 41 matches, a difference of 20.86.

● England fast bowler James Anderson began his Test career in 2003 without being dismissed in his first six innings. After making his debut against Zimbabwe at Lord's, Anderson played in four Tests (4*, 12*, 0*, 21*, 4*, 0*) before losing his wicket, for the first time, to South Africa's Shaun Pollock at Nottingham. He then put together a further three unbeaten knocks (0*, 0*, 0*) to record just two dismissals in his first ten Test innings.

● Kaushalya Weeraratne, who made his one-day international debut for Sri Lanka in 2000, struck the fastest fifty in limited-overs history during a provincial match in 2005-06, reaching his half-century off just 12 deliveries. Representing Ragama against the Kurunegala Youth Cricket Club in Colombo, Weeraratne struck one four and seven sixes on his way to 50, finishing with 66 not out off 18 balls. Weeraratne hit five straight sixes off 40-year-old slow left-armer Ajith Ekanayake in a single over that cost him 34 runs.

● Amjad Khan made two first-class appearances in India's Ranji Trophy tournament in 1988-89, and later became one of the few batsmen in the world to score a triple-century in a limited-overs match. The Kashmiri-born Khan hit 304 not out – with 28 fours and 19 sixes – in a quarter-final match in the Northern California Cricket Association at Fairmede Park, Richmond in 1999, going on to represent the United States in a series of domestic one-day matches in the West Indies in 2000-01.

In 2006, Shabir Mohammed struck an undefeated 353, off 156 deliveries, for the United Cricket Club on the very same ground. Scored on the day of Don Bradman's birthday – August 27 – Shabir struck 310 runs in boundaries, with 25 sixes and 40 fours, reaching his first hundred off 46 balls, his 200 off 94. He went into the 45-overs match with an average for the season of 18.60, and a top score of just 41 in nine innings, and walked away with a world record.

● During the second Test against the West Indies at Multan in 2006-07, Pakistan's Younis Khan was twice dismissed for 56. His batting mate Mohammad Yousuf also fell for 56 in the first innings, and was unbeaten on 56 at stumps on the penultimate day.

Yousuf went on to make 191, following 192 in the previous Test at Lahore. It was his third Test innings to end in the 190s in the calendar year of 2006, having already posted an innings of 192 against England at Leeds. He became the first batsman to fall in the 190s three times in Tests, passing Mohammad Azharuddin, Ian Chappell, Herschelle Gibbs, Brian Lara, Marcus Trescothick, Michael Vaughan, Everton Weekes and team-mate Younis Khan.

The third Test at Karachi saw Yousuf star yet again, this time with a pair of centuries (102 & 124), becoming the first batsman to score eight, and then nine, hundreds in a calendar year. Alongside his 665 runs, at 133.00, in the three-match series, Yousuf set a new benchmark for the most Test runs in a calendar year – 1788 – overtaking Viv Richards' 30-year record of 1710 runs in 1976: "**I am extremely happy and proud for my country because whenever the record is discussed now, it will be with the name of a Pakistani batsman.**"

Brian Lara was also in record-breaking form in the Multan Test, scoring his fourth hundred in four consecutive appearances against Pakistan and breaking Don Bradman's record of 18 scores of 150-plus in Test-match cricket. On his way to 216, Lara also broke Bradman's record of most double-centuries (4) by a Test captain, having already become the first batsman to twice achieve the feat of 24-plus runs off a single over. Facing spinner Danish Kaneria, Lara smacked him for 26 runs (4-0-6-6-6-4), reaching his first hundred off just 77 balls:**"He is such a great batsman that it is an exciting challenge for me to bowl to him. I don't think getting hit by the world's number one batsman is a failure on my part. I am actually happy that a player as great as Lara hits me around. I learn from that, but he has hit everyone from around the world."**

● A country cricketer collected 40 runs and then 28 off consecutive overs from the same bowler while playing for Werribee South in a Victorian district competition in 2002-03. Simon Williams hit six sixes and a four off a no-ball in the over which brought him 40 runs, on his merry way to a neat 100 in the match against Wyndhamvale.

● After gaining a pair of ducks on his Test debut, Sri Lanka's Chamara Silva bounced back with a pair of fifties in his next match. Having scored a half-century (55) on debut in a one-day international in 1999, Silva's first Test came much later in 2006-07, suffering the ignominy of two ducks against New Zealand at Christchurch. In the second Test, at Wellington, Silva became the first batsman in history to follow a pair of ducks on his Test debut with a century in his next. Silva piled on 200-plus runs in the match, with a first-innings 61 followed by an unbeaten 152.

Kumar Sangakkara was the only other batsman to score a century in the two-match series, unearthing two gems with 100 not out in the first Test and 156 not out in the second. His even 100 at Christchurch came in a team total of just 170, the second-lowest all-out total on record to include a century, after John Reid's 100 in New Zealand's second-innings 159 against England, at the same ground, in 1962-63.

Apart from Silva's two blobs in the first Test, there were 16 others ducks in the two matches, with both captains, Mahela Jayawardene and Stephen Fleming recording two in a row.

A FAMILY AFFAIR

● When Surrey took on Kent in a limited-overs match at The Oval in 1996, the club fielded two sets of brothers. Darren and Martin Bicknell and Adam and Ben Hollioake became the first sets of brothers to appear together in the same match in England since 1957, when Alec and Eric Bedser and Derek and Ron Pratt turned out for Surrey against Oxford University.

● Anirudh Srikkanth, the son of former Indian Test opener Kris Srikkanth, scored a match-winning 143 in a junior one-day international against the England Under-19s at Siliguru in 2004-05. In the first match of the series, Srikkanth's innings was terminated when he was caught by Ben Harmison, brother of England fast bowler Steve Harmison. In 2006, the junior Harmison joined his brother at Durham, and marked his first-class debut with a century (110) in the match against Oxford at The Parks.

● On the 24th of October 1969, Hanif Mohammad marked his last Test match for Pakistan by opening the batting against New Zealand at Karachi with his brother Sadiq, who was playing in his first Test. They became only the second set of brothers to open the batting in a Test – after E.M. and W.G. Grace against Australia at The Oval in 1880 – and with Mushtaq at No. 4 in the order, they provided the third instance of three brothers appearing in the same match.

The 24th of October seven years later marked another historic milestone in the Mohammad story when Sadiq and Mushtaq became just the second pair of brothers, after Australia's Ian and Greg Chappell, to score centuries in the same Test – Sadiq making 103 not out and Mushtaq 101 in the first innings of the second Test against New Zealand at Hyderabad in 1976-77.

● A pair of brothers made their debuts in the same one-day international in 2006, with both opening the batting, but for different sides. The occasion was Ireland's first-ever official ODI, at Belfast, which saw Dominick Joyce make a duck, while his elder brother Ed made ten on his debut for England.

Brothers in arms – Dominick and Ed Joyce

The double-debut signalled a unique quadrella for the Joyce clan, with their twin sisters Cecilia and Isobel already having played one-day international cricket for the Irish women's team. In 2004, the identical twins had celebrated the day of their 21st birthday by appearing together in a one-day international against New Zealand at Dublin. The sisters were among only three of Ireland's players to reach double figures in the match, Cecilia top-scoring with 33, and Isobel making 18. They played together for their country for the first time in 2001, in a one-day international against Australia, also in Dublin.

Another brother, Gus, also played first-class cricket, appearing in a single match for Ireland in the year 2000, opening the batting against Scotland at Ayr.

"There are nine children in our family so we all used to play in the back garden. Our brothers used to teach us how to bowl because they thought it was funny, but then we got quite good at it."

Isobel Joyce

● A young Don Bradman and one of his uncles, George Whatman, both scored double-centuries in a partnership worth 374 that brought their team victory in the Berrima District Cricket Competition final of 1925-26. Don, aged just 17, made a record 300 while George, the Bowral captain, made 277 in the match against Moss Vale. Don's brother, Vic, also played as did another uncle, Richard Whatman.

The match lasted five Saturdays, which Bowral won by an innings, a performance noted by the Sydney *Sun* newspaper: "**At last! Yes, it is really over. The final match in the Berrima District Cricket Competition has been brought to a conclusion. It was the easiest win in the history of Berrima District cricket, but it took Bowral five weeks to vanquish their persevering rivals.**"

● Queensland's Andy Bichel marked the opening match of the domestic program in 2004-05 by achieving his best figures in first-class cricket to date, dedicating the feat to his uncle who had just died at the age of 69. A minute's silence was held on the opening morning of the match against New South Wales at the 'Gabba as a mark of respect for Don Bichel, an off-spinner, who appeared in three first-class matches for Queensland during the seasons of 1963-64 and '64-65.

Bichel took 7 for 77 in the first innings, finishing with a match-haul of 10 for 127: "**No doubt it did inspire me having that minute's silence and it really meant a lot for me doing well in this game. I was really emotional in the first day and I really wanted to implement something from that to say 'There you go mate, I've done that for you'.**"

● Two brothers were dismissed on the same day in club cricket in England in 2002 for the same score, dismissed in the same fashion, while both were captaining their side and opening the batting. John and Andy Lyne were each dismissed for 101, bowled leg-stump, in separate matches for the Anston club against Whitwell – John for the first XI, and his brother for the second.

● Mark Waugh made two appearances in limited-overs matches for Ireland in 2000, top-scoring with 38 on his debut against the touring Zimbabweans at Dublin. Mark followed in the footsteps of his brother Steve, who had played first-class cricket for Ireland in 1998.

● The County Championship fixture between Lancashire and Gloucestershire at Manchester in 1884 was abandoned following the death of Martha Grace, the mother of W.G. and E.M. Grace, both of whom were playing in the match. The cancellation signalled the first and only occasion a first-class match had ended in such circumstances. Thirty years later, in 1914, a 66-year-old W.G. Grace commemorated the date of his mother's death on 25 July by scoring 69 not out in his final innings in club cricket.

● Trinidad & Tobago advanced to the final of the West Indies one-day tournament in 2004-05, thanks mainly to the batting of two brothers. Opener Sherwin Ganga (64) and his brother Daren (50), the captain, were the only ones to reach fifty in the Trinidad total of 256 for 5 as they defeated Barbados by 11 runs.

● Tehzib-ul-Ghani, who had four brothers who also played first-class cricket, hit a century on his debut at the age of 44. Born in 1929, the right-hander hit 104 – in the first of just two innings he played at first-class level – for Pakistan's Commerce Bank against Khaipur at Karachi in 1973-74.

In 1957-58, his brother Nasim-ul-Ghani made history by becoming the youngest player to appear in a Test match when he debuted against the West Indies at Bridgetown at the age of 16. And appearing in his first Test at Lord's, he became the first Pakistani to score a century against England, his 101 being his maiden hundred in first-class cricket.

● A son and four grandsons of former Yorkshire skipper Stanley Raper all captained Harrow against Eton at Lord's. Raper played three times for Yorkshire between 1936 and 1947, and was captain in his final first-class match, against Nottinghamshire at Sheffield.

● Twenty-nine-year-old Richard Smith collapsed and died during a club match in Yorkshire in 2003, having just scored 98 for Queensbury against Bridgeholme. Eighteen years earlier, his father had suffered the same fate while bowling.

● Identical male twins played together in an international match for the first time in 2005, with each dismissed in identical fashion. Making his debut against Australia at Auckland in 2004-05, James Marshall joined his brother Hamish in the New Zealand XI, signalling the first occasion twins had played together since Steve and Mark Waugh in 2001-02. Hamish was run out by Andrew Symonds for 55, while James went for 14 in the very next over, also run out by Symonds.

The first time the two had played side-by-side on the international stage came during the 1997-98 Under-19 World Cup match against Si Lanka at Port Elizabeth, with each dismissed for 17. The twins marked their first appearance together in a first-class match with a pair of half-century opening stands (80 & 60) for Northern Districts versus Wellington at Hamilton in 1998-99. Also in the ND XI playing alongside Hamish and James was another set of brothers in Robbie and Matthew Hart.

● The Hussey brothers, Mike and David, played in the same match for an Australian XI for the first time in 2004-05 with each top-scoring for either side in successive appearances. Playing for Australia A against the touring West Indians in two one-day matches in Hobart, David made the highest score, 128, in the first match, while Mike took the honours, with 70, in the following match.

In 2005, the Husseys dominated the county scene in England, each topping their county's first-class batting averages. In the year of his Test debut, Mike was No. 1 at Durham, hitting 1074 County Championship runs at 76.71, while David took the honours at Nottinghamshire with 1231 runs, average 68.38. Mike was No. 2 on the overall Championship averages, while David came in at No. 4.

"We had massive blues in the backyard – big punch-ups and fights. We were very competitive and probably a bit temperamental and if things didn't go our way we'd certainly get flustered. Dave would nick one behind and say he didn't hit it, and he'd refuse to go, so I'd have to clip him around the ear. I don't really remember the cricket so much as I do the fights."

Mike Hussey

● Shaun Tait, who was named 'Young Cricketer of The Year' in 2003-04, once played in a grade match against his father. In a C-grade fixture, a 12-year-old Shaun was called up to act as 12th man, but ended up playing – with his dad in the other team. He proudly boasts that he helped his father get a century, when, on 94, he smashed a ball towards him fielding on the boundary, and rather than catch it, helped the ball over the fence to bring up his hundred: "**The blokes I was playing with were stoked**."

● Afghanistan pulled off a notable victory over the MCC at Mumbai in 2005-06 with a pair of brothers combining to dismiss former England great Mike Gatting for a duck. Jalalabad fast bowler Hafti Gulabid claimed Gatting's wicket, caught behind by his wicket-keeping brother Karim Khan Sadiq. The Afghanis put on a hefty 356 for 7 off 40 overs, and then disposed of the MCC XI for just 185 to win the match by 171 runs.

● History was created at the Fenner's Ground at Cambridge in 2003 when twin brothers made their first-class debuts in the same match. All-rounders Adnan Akram and Arfan Akram both debuted for Cambridge University against Essex, although neither shone with either bat or ball. Both, however, went on to score their maiden century within their first five first-class matches. In just his second game, Arfan made 110 against Kent at Canterbury in 2003, while Adnan followed a 98 in his third appearance with an innings of 128 – against Middlesex in 2004 – in his fifth match.

● In a Logan Cup match at Mutare in 2003-04, Andre Soma hit his maiden half-century in first-class cricket, going on to make 204, while his brother Leon claimed his maiden five-wicket haul (5-58) in first-class cricket. Despite their fraternal feats, Manicaland went down by 16 runs to Matabeleland.

● Two brothers made their first-class debuts in the same match for Namibia in 2004, each marking their first game with a duck. Appearing against Uganda in the ICC Intercontinental Cup at Windhoek, Sarel and Louis Burger – both of whom had already appeared in one-day internationals at the 2003 World Cup – are the sons of Hennie Burger, who had represented South-West Africa for many years and at the time of his sons' first-class debuts was still playing club cricket in South Africa.

● Ryan Sylvester, who once scored 73 for Wales in a limited-overs match, became, in 2004, the first batsman to score a double-century in the South Wales Premier League. His unbeaten 216, for Sully Centurions against Chepstow, overtook the previous record of 166, scored by his brother Jamie.

● Fond memories of a bygone era in English cricket were rekindled in Middlesex's opening first-class fixture in 2006, when grandchildren of two batting legends both scored centuries in the same match. Opening the innings against Oxford at The Parks, Len Hutton's grandson Ben hit 100, while Denis Compton's grandson Nick hit 101 in a first-wicket stand of 192.

● Oxford wicket-keeper John Abell, whose father, brother and great-uncle all played first-class cricket, claimed eight dismissals in his brief career behind the stumps, six of which were stumpings. In his final first-class match – at Oxford in 1953 – Abell stumped both of the Richardson brothers, Peter and Dick, who were playing for his father George's old county Worcestershire.

● When the Cayman Islands took on the USA in Ontario in the America's Cup one-day tournament in 2000, they had in their team four members of the one family. History was made at the Maple Leaf Cricket Club when brothers Michael (2), Chris (2), David (4) and Phillip Wight (5) all played in the XI against the Americans, a match the USA won by one wicket.

● A pair of brothers made their Test debuts for Pakistan in 2001 within the space of just three matches. Opening batsman Imran Farhat played in his first Test against New Zealand at Auckland in the 2000-01 series, while his brother, the wicket-keeping Humayun made his debut in the third Test at Hamilton. Together they contributed exactly half of Pakistan's first-innings total of 104 in the Hamilton match, Imran making 24 and Humayun 28.

● In 1996, Brighton College in England had a set of twins, Chris and James Sell, playing cricket for its school XI. Both brothers dislocated a shoulder in the very same match that year, against Old Brightonians.

● Ian Botham played the part of guest umpire in a charity match at The Rose Bowl in 2006, a game held for his son Liam. Botham snr retired from first-class cricket in 1993 and vowed at the time he would never take part in a cricket match again: "**If I can't reappear on a cricket field on behalf of my own flesh and blood, when could I ever make a comeback. But I won't be doing that again in a hurry. Umpiring is far too much like hard work for grandfathers like me.**"

Decked out in a bright pink shirt, Botham had a ten-over stint as umpire in a match that saw the Liam Botham's Legends go down to the Hampshire Legends XI. Liam had burst onto the first-class cricket scene as a teenager in 1996, taking 5 for 67 in his debut innings for Hampshire against Middlesex at Portsmouth, but played in just two more matches before pursuing his other great sporting love, rugby union and league.

● Hitesh Modi, who briefly captained Kenya, is the son of a one-day international umpire. When Kenya hosted Bangladesh in a ODI at Nairobi in 2006, Modi was adjudged out lbw, for one, by his dad, Subhash Modi.

● When Pakistan's Bazid Khan made his Test debut in 2004-05, he joined his father, Majid Khan, and grandfather, Jahangir Khan, in providing only the second instance of three generations of the same family playing Test cricket. George Headley and his son, Ron, who played for the West Indies, and England's Dean Headley, were the first. Majid and Bazid Khan also provided just the third instance of a father and son – after New Zealand's Lance and Chris Cairns and India's Yograj and Yuvraj Singh – playing both Test and one-day international cricket.

During Bazid's first Test match – against the West Indies at Bridgetown – in which he made nine and 23, his team-mate Shahid Afridi came close to breaking one of his father's greatest records. On his way to 122 in the second innings, Afridi made it to the century-mark in just 78 balls – at the time, the Pakistan record for the fastest Test-match hundred belonged to Bazid's dad. In 1976-77, Majid Khan blasted his way to 100 in the third Test against News Zealand at Karachi off 74 deliveries. Out for 112, Majid became the first non-Australian batsman to score a century before lunch on the first day of a Test match.

Two of Bazid's uncles – Javed Burki and Imran Khan – also played Test cricket: "**I didn't see my grandfather much because when he died in 1988 I was just seven. What I know of my father was that he was majestic and awe-inspiring. It would be very tough to emulate his achievements**."

● During his innings of 23 not out against England at Christchurch in 2001-02, New Zealand all-rounder Chris Cairns extended his career-tally of sixes to 72. His father, Lance Cairns, was a similarly-renowned big-hitter with 28 sixes to his credit, and Chris's one six at Christchurch saw the pair combine to reach the milestone of 100 sixes in Test-match cricket, a unique family feat. They were also the first father and son to both take 100 Test wickets, with Chris reaching the milestone during the third Test against Sri Lanka at Colombo in 1998.

● A Hampshire League match in England in 2002 saw both sets of opening batsmen forge an unbeaten double-century partnership. Almost 500 runs were scored on the day without a single wicket falling, with brothers Kieron and Chris Hall both hitting centuries in a first-wicket stand of 243 for Wildern Mansbridge. But, Mark Williams and Jason Murdoch responded in spectacular style, taking Farehaven to a ten-wicket victory.

● A family-oriented cricket club was formed in England in 1982 to give fathers and sons the chance to play cricket together in a competitive environment. The Fathers & Sons Cricket Club was set up in Gloucestershire and even though fathers and sons dominate club membership, others are not precluded.

SPEED & SPIN

● In the third Test between Pakistan and the West Indies at Karachi in 1997-98, both teams were captained by opening bowlers, with each dismissing the other for a duck. Rival captains capturing each other's wicket in the same Test had occurred on six previous occasions, but this was the first time that the captains involved – Wasim Akram and Courtney Walsh – had opened the bowling with each dismissing the other for nought.

● On two occasions during the 2000-01 Test series against Australia, Indian spinner Harbhajan Singh collected more than 12 wickets in a match, yet failed to bowl a single batsman. His first haul, in the second Test at Kolkata, of 13 for 196 (7-123 & 6-73) included a hat-trick, while his second big bag came in the following match at Chennai, where he took 15 for 217 (7-133 & 8-84). Apart from claiming India's first-ever Test-match hat-trick, Singh became the first bowler in the history of the game to *twice* take more than 12 wickets in a Test without bowling out a batsman.

Singh came close to repeating the feat in the first Test against Australia in the 2004-05 series, at Bangalore, with a match-haul of 11 for 224 (5-146 & 6-78). He made history by claiming ten wickets in three consecutive Tests against Australia in India, and taking five wickets in six successive innings. With five wickets in the second Test at Chennai, Singh went past the milestone of 50 wickets against Australia in just his seventh match, equalling the record of England's Tom Richardson, who achieved his 50th wicket against the old enemy in his seventh Test, at Lord's in 1896.

● When Victoria hosted New South Wales at the MCG in 1859-60, only six bowlers were used in the entire match, with four claiming five wickets in an innings. Victoria's captain Tom Wills and his opening partner Gideon Elliott both returned figures of 6 for 23, while Richard Murray, in his final first-class match, claimed 5 for 13, and George Richardson, on his debut, 6 for 42 for New South Wales.

Richardson only played in one more first-class match, and ended his career with 15 wickets at an average of 7.00, while Murray appeared in just four first-class matches, ending his career with nine wickets at a 7.66-average.

● During his school's cricket tour of Australia in 2005-06, 17-year-old Theo Bossom took six wickets in six balls against a Bathurst Under-16 XI in country New South Wales. The Eton College schoolboy finished with 7 for 4 off five overs, his first-ever five-wicket haul in an innings: **"It was easily the best I've ever bowled. Once I got a hat-trick I was pretty satisfied, I wasn't really thinking about much else. I definitely wasn't thinking about getting all six."** After Bossom's double hat-trick, Bathurst crashed from 38 for 1 to 38 for 7.

● Pakistan's Wasim Akram opened proceedings in the 2002 PSO Tri-Nations Tournament by taking three Kenyan wickets in the match at

Nairobi, but conceded as many as ten wides in just seven overs. He also sent down another seven no-balls in taking 3 for 30.

When Pakistan played Scotland at Chester-le-Street in the 1999 World Cup, Wasim had six wides beside his name, with a total of 43 in the match. The Scots were responsible for 29 of the indiscretions and a further 15 no-balls, for a record total of 44 such extras. In a latter match in the same tournament, Scotland was at it again giving away 26 wides and 11 no-balls in the match against Bangladesh at Edinburgh. Both opening bowlers, John Blain and Asim Butt, each had seven wides, with the former also chipping with in eight no-balls.

● Tasmanian Shane Jurgensen made history in 2001-02, when he attained two consecutive hauls of ten wickets in a match, becoming the first bowler to achieve ten in a Sheffield Shield/Pura Cup final. The right-armed quick – who also played for the state of his birth, Queensland, and Western Australia – opened the bowling against the Bulls in the 2001-02 final at Brisbane, capturing 5 for 68 and 6 for 104. His match-figures of 11 for 172 bettered the previous best return in a final of 9 for 84 by Queenslander Adam Dale and Wayne Holdsworth for New South Wales in the 1990s. In Jurgensen's previous match – against New South Wales in Hobart – he took 5 for 38 and 6 for 65, which included Tasmania's second first-class hat-trick, the first since Peter Clough's in 1982-83.

● When Sri Lanka thumped the West Indies at Colombo in 2001-02, Chaminda Vaas took seven wickets in each innings, claiming a wicket in his opening over in both innings. West Indies firebrand opener Chris Gayle was dismissed for a pair by Vaas, who claimed his wicket with the second ball of the Test match, and with his last ball of the opening over in the second innings. Vaas took 14 for 191 (7-120 & 7-71) in the match, the best figures by a Sri Lankan fast bowler as the West Indies went down by ten wickets. Earlier in the match, Windies captain Carl Hooper dismissed Russel Arnold, his 100th wicket, achieved in his 90th Test – the most matches taken by any bowler to reach the landmark.

● In the 2001-02 domestic season in Pakistan, Wasim Akram and Fazl-e-Akbar ripped through the Habib Bank XI at Lahore, robbing them of all ten wickets in one of the shortest completed innings in the history of first-class cricket. Opening the bowling for PIA, Wasim took 3 for 14, while Fazl claimed 7 for 13, which included four wickets in four balls during his eighth over. Habib Bank was all out for just 27 in 15.5 overs, with as many as five of its batsmen making ducks.

● Sam Marshman enjoyed a dream debut in Sydney grade cricket in 2004-05 when he took a hat-trick for the North Sydney second-XI. He claimed his prize with the first three balls of the innings, a feat unique in the competition.

● Pakistan's Abdul Razzaq is one of those rare breeds who made his international debut before he had played any first-class cricket. In his first one-day international – in 1996-97 – Abdul took 2 for 29 against Zimbabwe at Lahore, making his first-class debut three weeks later in the final of the Quaid-e-Azam Trophy. Playing for Lahore City, Abdul was one of the stars, taking a match-winning nine wickets against Karachi, including a second-innings haul of 7 for 51.

● Although he ended up on the losing side, Kent fast bowler Dean Headley provided a rare bowling treat for the crowd at Canterbury in 1996, when he claimed a hat-trick, his second in consecutive first-class matches. The feat had only been achieved four times in the history of first-class cricket – by Yorkshire's George Freeman in 1868, by Sid Pegler for the South Africans in England in 1912, by Joginder Rao for Indian Services in 1963-64 and by Gloucestershire's Mike Procter in 1979. Headley's consecutive hat-tricks came against Derbyshire at Derby and against Worcestershire at Canterbury, adding a third, against Hampshire, again at Canterbury, the following month, to equal the world record for most hat-tricks in a season.

● In 2004, Shane Warne publicly derided the quality of the Test-match wickets secured by Muttiah Muralitharan, as a fair proportion had been at the expense of the lesser likes of Zimbabwe and Bangladesh. Not two years later, and appearing in the first Test against the Bangladeshis at Fattulah, Warne went wicketless in the first innings with figures of none for 112. It signalled the first time in his lengthy Test career that he had recorded an economy rate in excess of 5.00 from ten overs or more in a Test innings. Off 20 overs, Warne went for 5.60 runs per over, eclipsing the 4.94-run rate he established against New Zealand at Brisbane in 2001-02, where he had figures of 3 for 89 off 18 overs.

● In his 50 one-day internationals for Zimbabwe, Henry Olonga twice took five wickets in an innings, and each was a six-wicket haul. The first of 6 for 19 against England at Cape Town in 1999-2000 was followed by 6 for 28 against Kenya at Bulawayo in 2002-03.

● At The Oval in 1976, West Indies speedster Michael Holding carved through England, achieving match-winning figures of 14 for 149. In the first innings, he took a career-best 8 for 92 without assistance from the field – bowling six batsmen and having two out lbw. He bowled another three batsmen in the second innings on his way to 6 for 57 and a match-total of nine batsmen bowled. His performance, although a record for a Test match in the 20th century, is a long way off the all-time record – 14 by England's Johnny Briggs against South Africa at Cape Town in 1888-89. His match-haul of 15 for 28 included 8 for 11 – all bowled – in the second innings.

● Appearing in Zimbabwe's inaugural Test match, and in his first for 22 years and 222 days, the Egyptian-born off-spinner John Traicos celebrated the occasion by claiming his one-and-only five-wicket haul at the highest level. Having made his Test debut for South Africa in 1969-70, Traicos re-emerged in 1992-93 and played in Zimbabwe's first four Tests, taking a career-best 5 for 86 against India at Harare, where the wily 45-year-old dismissed a 19-year-old Sachin Tendulkar for a duck.

● New South Wales left-arm quick Mike Whitney appeared in 12 Tests for Australia twice taking seven wickets in an innings. The first occasion came against the West Indies at Adelaide in 1988-89 where he took 7 for 89, his maiden five-wicket haul in Test cricket. His second, and final, five-wicket haul was a personal-best at first-class level – 7 for 27 against India at Perth in 1991-92.

● After scoring just ten with the bat, West Indian Phil Simmons mesmerised Pakistan in a 1992-93 World Series Cup match at Sydney by taking a world-record four wickets for three runs off ten overs with eight maidens. Opening the bowling with Curtly Ambrose, Simmons' medium-paced swing disposed of Asif Mujtaba for one, Aamer Sohail for six, Salim Malik for a duck and Javed Miandad for two to have Pakistan reeling at 14 for 5. His match-return of 10-8-3-4 bettered Bishan Bedi's 12-8-6-1 in the 1975 World Cup as the most economical figures ever recorded in a one-day international.

● Appearing in his fifth match for Australia, Queenslander Andy Bichel claimed his first five-wicket haul at Test level. His bag of 5 for 60 came in the fourth Test against the West Indies at Melbourne on 2000-01, and improved markedly on his previous returns where he had only ever taken one wicket in an innings (1-31 & 0-16 v West Indies at Adelaide 1996-97, 0-79 & 0-17 v West Indies at Perth 1996-97, 1-103 & 0-51 v South Africa at Adelaide 1997-98, 1-25 & 1-21 v West Indies at Brisbane 2000-01).

● There was some champagne bowling in the ING Cup at Canberra's Manuka Oval in 2004-05, when New South Wales left-arm Doug Bollinger dismissed three South Australian batsmen for a duck in a rare limited-overs hat-trick. Bollinger, playing in his first match of the summer, ended the innings on a high with four wickets – all gained without assistance from the field – and only the fourth instance of a hat-trick in domestic one-day cricket.

The previous hat-trick in the competition was achieved by his opening partner Nathan Bracken, who also disposed of three batsmen for a duck, against Victoria at Melbourne in 2001-02.

Despite Bollinger's feat, there was no celebratory bubbly at day's end as he ended up on the losing side: "**It would have been better had we won, but it didn't work out that way**." New South Wales also lost the match at the MCG in which Bracken claimed his hat-trick.

● In his 400 first-class matches, Lancashire's Len Hopwood claimed 673 wickets with a best innings-return of 9 for 33, but failed to claim a victim at Test level. The medium-pacer sent down 462 balls in his two matches – against Australia in 1934 – the most delivered by a bowler in Test cricket without taking a wicket.

● On his Test debut, England left-arm spinner Monty Panesar only took three wickets, but each was a top-quality batsman to be proud of. His very first wicket was that of India's Sachin Tendulkar, which came at Nagpur in 2005-06, followed by Mohammad Kaif, and then Rahul Dravid. To mark his Test debut, Panesar was presented with the ball that gave him his first Test wicket, and was inscribed with a special message from Tendulkar: "To Monty. Once in a blue moon. Never again mate – Ha Ha – Well done!"

● Pakistan international Yasir Arafat equalled a world record with the ball in 2004-05 by claiming five wickets in six balls for Rawalpindi against national champions Faisalabad in the Quaid-e-Azam Trophy. He became only the fourth bowler to achieve the feat after Bill Copson for Derbyshire against Warwickshire at Derby in 1937, North Eastern Transvaal's William Henderson against Orange Free State at Bloemfontein in 1937-38 and Pat Pocock for Surrey against Sussex at Eastbourne in 1972. He did become, however, the first to achieve the feat over two innings. Yasir took nine wickets – including a hat-trick – in the match, claiming 5 for 22 in the first innings with the Faisalabad Region XI all out for just 64.

● During a Ranji Trophy match at Indore in 1999-2000, Madhya Pradesh left-arm spinner Manish Majithia conceded just three runs from his 32.3 overs. He sent down a total of 136 consecutive balls in the match against Railways without conceding a run, one off the world record held by South Africa's Hugh Tayfield, achieved in the third Test against England at Durban in 1956-57. Majithia's match figures were 12.3-9-3-1 and 20-20-0-1.

● The cricketing career of Oxford University spinner Stephen Moreton was launched in inauspicious circumstances in 2005 when he conceded the most expensive maiden over by a player on his first-class debut. Playing against Gloucestershire at The Parks, Moreton's only over in the match cost 34 runs, with New Zealander Craig Spearman hitting him for 6, 6, 6, 6, 4 and 6 during his knock of 216.

● Appearing in his 17th Test match for Australia, the New Zealand-born Clarrie Grimmett took his 100th wicket, becoming, at 39 years and 25 days, the oldest Australian bowler to reach the milestone. Grimmett celebrated the achievement – in the third Test against the West Indies at Brisbane's Exhibition Ground – by taking 5 for 49 in Australia's innings-and-217-run victory.

● With the wicket of Sri Lanka's Chaminda Vaas in the third Test at Colombo in 2003-04, Shane Warne became the first slow bowler to claim 100 Test-match wickets lbw. At the time of reaching the milestone, only three bowlers had preceded him – Pakistan's Wasim Akram (119) and Waqar Younis (111) and India's Kapil Dev (112).

● When Shane Warne captured Brendon McCullum's wicket at Auckland in 2004-05, he became the first Australian bowler to take 100 Test wickets against New Zealand and the first to take 100 Test wickets against three countries, having already achieved the feat against England and South Africa. Previously, only the West Indian pair of Courtney Walsh and Curtly Ambrose had claimed 100 wickets against two opponents, each doing so against Australia and England.

In 2006-07, Warne became the first bowler to capture 50 Test wickets at four different venues. Of his 708 wickets, 68 came at Brisbane, 64 at Sydney, 56 at Adelaide and 56 at his home ground, the MCG.

● Glamorgan's Alex Wharf celebrated his call-up to England's one-day squad in 2004 by producing the remarkable figures of 6 for 5 in a one-day match, yet ended up on the losing side. Playing at Cardiff, Wharf claimed his first-ever five-wicket haul in limited-overs cricket, but his efforts weren't enough on the day, as Kent, chasing 143, hung on to achieve a miraculous one-wicket win off the last ball.

Wharf took his sparkling form onto the international stage, claiming the man-of-the-match award on his England debut, despite one of his team-mates claiming a hat-trick. Wharf took 3 for 30 against India at

Nottingham, snaring the deluxe wickets of Sourav Ganguly, V.V.S. Laxman and Rahul Dravid. Later in the match, Steve Harmison wrapped up the Indian innings, taking England's second hat-trick in one-day international cricket, after James Anderson's, achieved in 2003.

● Shaun Tait, who made his Test debut for Australia as a 22-year-old in the 2005 Ashes series, was once described as possibly the worst overseas professional to ever play county cricket. In 2004, Tait played in just two first-class matches for Durham, returning figures of 12-0-113-0 against Somerset at Chester-le-Street and 6-0-63-0 against Essex at Colchester. His two stints at the bowling crease included two wides and 26 no-balls.

"You don't go out there and aim to kill the batsman, but there's times when you need to hit the batsman to put him off his game and put the rest of the blokes coming in off their game. If the guys on the sidelines are seeing their blokes with heads cut open and that sort of stuff, they're not going to want to come out there."

Shaun Tait

● Sri Lanka was denied victory in a one-day international at Adelaide in 2005-06 when South Africa's Andrew Hall bowled a maiden over to finish off the match. The Sri Lankans required ten runs off the last over to win, but Hall did what no other bowler had done in 750 previous one-day internationals. Delivering the 100th over of the match, Hall sent down six dot balls to conclude proceedings, with South Africa gaining victory by nine runs.

● Muttiah Muralitharan marked his 100th Test match by becoming the first bowler to reach the milestone of 1000 international wickets. In the first Test against Bangladesh at Chittagong in 2005-06, Murali's dismissal of Khaled Mashud was his 589th wicket at Test level, to go with his 411 in one-day internationals: "**I am delighted. When I played my first Test I never thought I would have all these records. All I wanted was to play a few games. It is a dream for me to play 100 Tests and to take 1000 international wickets. I never expected it.**"

During the second Test at Bogra, Murali, with figures of 5 for 79, became the first bowler to achieve five wickets in an innings on 50 occasions, and later the first bowler to take 50 Test wickets against all Test-playing countries. With his dismissal of Khaled Mashud in the second innings, Murali became the first Sri Lankan to pass the coveted milestone of 600 Test wickets.

● Vidarbha's Manohar Agasti claimed only wicket in his career, doing so with the only ball he bowled in first-class cricket. An opening batsman, Agasti – on his debut – bowled Railways' Ashok Sharma for 14 in a Ranji Trophy match at Yavatmal in 1985-86.

● Despite a Test bowling average of 318.00, and not having played international cricket for seven years, leg-spinner Rawl Lewis was recalled by the West Indies for the tour of New Zealand in 2005-06. The Windward Islands captain got the nod after a successful season in the Carib Beer Cup, but his comeback to Test-match cricket, at Wellington, bore no fruit returning figures of none for 70 off 29 overs and extending his world-record career average to 388.00.

● Shane Harwood, who celebrated his first-class debut for Victoria by uniquely claiming a hat-trick, made his mark in England's Northern League in 2005 by becoming only the second bowler in its 53-year history to take 100 wickets in a season. Harwood took exactly 100 wickets at an average of 7.68 in his first season for Andrew Flintoff's old club St Annes, emulating Colin Hilton who took 113 wickets for Morecambe in 1968.

Back home in Victoria, Harwood warmed-up for his domestic summer by taking four quality wickets in a World XI one-day match at Melbourne's Junction Oval. With figures of 4 for 37, Harwood dismissed a bunch of renowned big-hitters in India's Virender Sehwag (32), South Africa's Jacques Kallis (6), the West Indies' Brian Lara (9) and England's Kevin Pietersen (5).

"I have been working a lot on my core strength but I still haven't got the Brett Lee arse yet ... I'm just talking about my little behind. If you have a look at Bichel, Kasprowicz, Brett Lee and Flintoff ... the powerful lads, they seem to have the big arse."

Shane Harwood

● Yorkshire's Ryan Sidebottom finished a limited-overs National League match against Glamorgan at Leeds in 2003 with the bizarre bowling figures of 0.1-0-11-0. After bowling two wides, being hit for six and then sending down another three wides, Sidebottom left the field with a hamstring injury.

● Victorian fast bowler Walter Dudley only appeared in four first-class matches, but made a name for himself on Christmas Day in 1940 when he had Don Bradman out first-ball on the opening morning of the Sheffield Shield match at the Adelaide Oval. The prized scalp of the Don for a duck came off the third ball of the match, after Ken Ridings had been dismissed for nought off the previous delivery.

● After marking his 100th Test with a duck, Allan Border celebrated his 101st with his first-ever haul of five wickets in a first-class innings. Captaining Australia against the West Indies at Sydney in 1988-89, Border took 7 for 46 and came closing to capturing a second consecutive haul of five, content with 4 for 50 and a match-total of 11 for 96. No player had taken quite so long in securing a maiden haul of five wickets in a Test innings, with Sri Lankan batsman Sanath Jayasuriya second on the list, with 5 for 43 against Zimbabwe at Galle in 2001-02 in his 69th match. Coincidentally, for Jayasuriya his 'five-for', like Border's, was his first in first-class cricket, and he also took four wickets (4-31) in the second innings of the Test.

Border's average of 47.18 coming into the match was also one of the highest by a bowler – who had played in at least five Tests – going on to take ten wickets. For Australia, only spinner Bob Holland had a higher average, one of 48.75 coming into the second Test against New Zealand at Sydney in 1985-86, where he took 10 for 174.

● Slow left-armer Jimmy Allen began his first-class career in 1953 returning figures of 7-7-0-1 for Oxford University against Yorkshire, with five of the maidens bowled to Len Hutton. In his second match – against the touring Australians – he dismissed Keith Miller and Ian Craig in his opening over, and it wasn't until his fourth over of the game, and his 11th in first-class cricket, that a batsman finally took a run off his bowling.

● In one of his rare first-class appearances for Victoria, Shane Warne took 7 for 100 and 3 for 64 against Queensland at Melbourne's Junction Oval in 2005-06. It was the first time Warne had taken ten wickets in a first-class match for Victoria, having made his debut – at the same venue – back in 1990-91.

"When I was at kindergarten someone jumped on my back and broke my legs. I was getting around on a trolley like that for twelve months, lying down with broken legs. That might have something to do with why my wrists are good and have helped me bowl leg-spin."

Shane Warne

● In 2000-01, Pakistan's Saqlain Mushtaq marked his first Test match against England with a first-innings haul of 8 for 164 at Lahore, becoming the first bowler to take five wickets in an innings on his debut against four different countries. Saqlain took 5 for 129 in his first Test against South Africa, 5 for 54 against the West Indies and then 5 for 94 – *and* 5 for 93 – on debut against India.

Saqlain's ten-wicket haul against India, at Chennai in 1998-99, was followed by another batch of ten in the second Test at Delhi, topping the Pakistani averages with 20 wickets at 20.15, pipped at the post by Anil Kumble, who finished the series with 21 wickets, average 14.85. Kumble's lot included the taking of all ten wickets, for 74, in the second innings of the second Test at Delhi, in which Saqlain matched his Chennai effort with another haul of 5 for 94, and then 5 for 122.

● Appearing in just his third first-class match, a Queensland-born fast bowler sliced through Kenya in the semi-finals of the 2004 ICC Intercontinental Cup, returning the eye-popping figures of 5 for 5 off 5.5 overs. Peter Hoffman, a club cricketer from Rockhampton, helped Scotland dismiss the Kenyans for just 95 in the three-day match played at Abu Dhabi.

In 2005, he blew away Oman (83) in an ICC Trophy match at Belfast, taking 6 for 12 off eight overs, with none of his victims reaching double figures. He then opened the batting for Scotland, top-scoring with 39 belting five fours and two sixes.

● Upon being released from the South African Test side in 2004-05 due to a broken hand, Charl Langeveldt turned out for his domestic club and opened the bowling. Playing for Lions against the Warriors at Port Elizabeth in the first-class Supersport Series, he was unable to hold a bat and was listed as 'absent hurt' in both innings, but with the ball took 1 for 46 and 3 for 61.

● New Zealand's Shane Bond made a triumphant return to Test-match cricket on home soil during the summer of 2005-06, taking eight wickets in two Tests against the West Indies. Back in the team after recovering from a back operation, and playing in his first home match in three years, Bond bowled two balls to Brian Lara in the first Test at Auckland and dismissed him both times.

● After recuperating from an injured ankle in 2006, Andrew Flintoff marked his return to competitive cricket in a blaze of glory, collecting a record for the best-ever figures in a Twenty20 match. Representing Lancashire at Old Trafford, Flintoff sliced through Nottinghamshire's top order, taking 3 for 4 off three overs. Former England bowler Dominic Cork was also in top form, picking up 4 for 16 and beating off Flintoff to be named man-of-the-match.

● Former Australian fast bowler Wayne Clark, who coached Yorkshire to the County Championship victory dais in 2001, never took five wickets in an innings in his Test-match career, but did take a 'four-for' seven times. In ten Tests for Australia – he got his start during the World Series days – Clark took 44 wickets at 28.75, with five lots of four wickets in his first series, against India in 1977-78, with two such hauls on his Test debut at Brisbane.

England's Mike Hendrick, who appeared in a total of 30 Tests, left the international scene in 1981 with the most wickets (87) of any bowler who never took five wickets in an innings. He captured four five times, with a best return of 4 for 28 against India at Edgbaston in 1974.

● When Surrey piled on 668 for 7 declared at The Oval in 2006, four Leicestershire bowlers were carted for 100 or more runs in the innings.

The South African Test-match spinner Claude Henderson took 3 for 235, the greatest number of runs conceded in a County Championship innings since Gloucestershire's Charlie Parker took 6 for 231 off 61 overs against Somerset at Bristol in 1923.

● In the same match that Australia's Andrew Symonds marked his County Championship debut for Lancashire with a century, Essex import, the Pakistani leg-spinner, Danish Kaneria sent down over 400 balls in an innings without claiming a single wicket. With Symonds scoring 134 and Mal Loye 194, Lancashire chalked up a total of 655 for 6 declared in the 2005 match at Old Trafford in which Kaneria bowled the third-longest spell in first-class cricket without success. When the match finally came to a close, Kaneria had figures of 70.2-10-208-0 in the innings.

● New South Wales bowler Stuart Clark stormed into Test-match cricket in 2006, taking over 20 wickets in his first two Test series. Clark was the leading Australian bowler with 20 wickets at 15.85 in three Tests against South Africa in 2005-06, including 5 for 55 and 4 for 34 at Cape Town − the third-best match figures by an Australian debutant behind Bob Massie and Clarrie Grimmett.

Following one Test against Bangladesh, Clark then picked up 26 wickets, average 17.04, in the 2006-07 Ashes series, the most by any bowler on either side. He was one of four Australians to exceed 20 wickets in the series, the others being Shane Warne (23), Glenn McGrath (21) and Brett Lee (20), while only two England bowlers − Matthew Hoggard (13) and Andrew Flintoff (11) − managed more than ten.

MOST WICKETS IN FIRST YEAR OF TEST CRICKET

			5wi	BB	M	Avge
54	Terry Alderman (A)	1981	4	6-135	10	22.63
49	Curtly Ambrose (WI)	1988	1	5-72	11	23.20
44	Roy Tattersall (E)	1951	3	7-52	12	26.68
43	Ted McDonald (A)	1921	2	5-32	11	33.28
42	Dominic Cork (E)	1995	2	7-43	8	25.31
42	Stuart Clark (A)	2006	1	5-55	8	17.76
42	Jack Saunders (A)	1902	3	7-34	10	19.31

● During the 1967-68 series against New Zealand, Abid Ali earned the dubious distinction of becoming the first Indian bowler to be no-balled for throwing in a Test match. It came, though, in the most unusual of circumstances. Convinced that Kiwi fast bowler Gary Bartlett was a chucker and had not been called during the second Test at Christchurch, he went on to imitate his opponent's action, and was himself no-balled for throwing.

● At the 'Gabba ground in Brisbane in 2004-05, Shane Warne and Glenn McGrath made history by becoming the first pair of bowlers to reach the landmark of 1000 Test wickets. The duo went into the first Test against New Zealand with 995 wickets between them, Warne having collected 541 and McGrath 454: **"It is pretty amazing when you sit there and think about it. It has been something special. We've always bowled well in a partnership, building pressure from both ends, and things seem to happen when we're bowling together."**

"This sounds strange, but have you ever been in one of those MRI machines in hospitals? It feels like you're in a coffin and you get claustrophobic. Well, that's what it feels like when you face the best bowlers in the world. It feels like you're in a coffin and you can't score runs. It's like they've got a fishing net around you."

Justin Langer – on Shane Warne and Glenn McGrath

The following summer when the West Indies spluttered to 129, and defeat, in the first Test at the same ground, it signalled the first occasion in 155 innings that the McGrath-Warne combination had failed to take a wicket in an all-out total. While Brett Lee took 5 for 30 – his best figures since taking 5 for 47 on his Test debut in 1999-2000 – McGrath returned figures of 11-3-22-0 and Warne 2-1-1-0. In the next Test at Hobart, Warne took 0 for 48, the first time in 50 Tests he had failed to take a wicket in two consecutive innings.

The 'Gabba Test match in 2006-07, against England, provided yet another significant milestone for the pair when they appeared in their 100th Test match together. Despite Australia prevailing in the following Test at Adelaide, McGrath, with none for 107, conceded more runs without taking a wicket than in any time in his career, while Warne's 1 for 167 off 53 overs were his most expensive set of Test figures. Their combined return of 1 for 274 was also the worst of their careers, with Warne enduring one of the most barren spells of his life, sending down 46.1 overs before he collected his first wicket of the match.

Both Warne and McGrath announced their retirements from Test cricket during the series, with the Sydney Test match against England their last. They ended their remarkable partnership during the SCG match becoming the first pair of bowlers to take 1000 Test wickets together, and after 104 Tests in tandem had savoured 71 victories, another world record.

The MCG, 2006-07 – in his final Test match at his home ground, Shane Warne became the first bowler to reach the milestone of 700 Test wickets. Glenn McGrath also bowed out of Test cricket on a high, taking a wicket with his final delivery, at his home ground, the SCG. At the same venue later in the summer, he repeated the feat in his final one-day international in Australia

● In the fifth Test against England at The Oval in 1948, Australia's Ray Lindwall took nine wickets for the match, seven of which were bowled. His seven bowled victims followed on from six such-dismissals obtained in the second Test at Lord's. In his 61 Test-match career, Lindwall came close to bowling out 100 batsmen – 98 out of 228, almost 43 per cent of his total number of wickets.

● Ross Hiern only made a dozen appearances in first-class cricket, but took wickets with his first delivery in his first two matches. On his debut for South Australia, at Melbourne in 1949-50, he bowled Victorian opener Colin McDonald for a duck with his first ball, and repeated the feat in his second match, accounting for another top-quality Test player. With his opening delivery in the Sheffield Shield match at Brisbane a week later, he had Ken 'Slasher' Mackay out for a duck, going on to produce the best figures of his career, 5 for 49.

● Josephat Ababu, a medium-pacer, only claimed a single wicket in his international career, but it was one to remember. Appearing in the first of his three one-day internationals for Kenya, at Nairobi in 1999-2000, the teenaged Ababu claimed the wicket of Zimbabwe opener Neil Johnson with his very first ball.

● Australian spinner Jack Saunders, who took 79 wickets in 14 Tests in the early part of the last century, never claimed a wicket lbw. England's Willie Bates was another to take 50 wickets in Test cricket without an lbw. His total of exactly 50 wickets in 15 Tests all came in Australia during the 1880s, with his finest moment coming at Melbourne in 1882-83 taking 7 for 28 – including the first hat-trick by an England bowler – and 7 for 74.

Dead by the age of 44, Bates' career was cruelly cut short after a bowling mishap during England's 1887-88 tour of Australia. Bowling in the nets, he was hit in the eye by a cricket ball, an injury from which he never fully recovered.

● At Kandy in 2003-04, Stuart MacGill finished the Test match against Sri Lanka with figures of none for 20 and none for 69. This was the first occasion MacGill had gone wicketless in a match in his Test career that began in 1997-98. In his first 31 appearances, MacGill had taken at least one wicket, his record run coming to an end in the second Test against the Sri Lankans.

Fred Trueman played in 67 Tests for England and he claimed a wicket in every single Test he appeared in, from beginning to end, a world-record performance. His worst performance came in 1961 during the fourth Test against Australia at Manchester, where he took 1 for 55 and none for 92.

PERSONAL MATTERS

● The Australian cricket team was named in the High Court in London in 2004 during a high-profile case brought on by two feuding lawyers, Lawrence Jones and his former fiancée Kerry Cox. The former lovers' court action involved accusations by Ms Cox of drunken violence, and by Mr Jones, of her 'outrageous advances' of a sexual nature towards members of Australia's cricket team during a Governor-General's reception at Grenada in the West Indies.

● In 2001, former England Test star Ian Botham issued a public apology to his wife and family after revelations of an affair with an Australian waitress he met in Sydney in 1998. Claims concerning Botham's trysts with the 31-year-old were splashed over the pages of the *News Of The World* newspaper, detailing trips the pair had taken to Scotland and France, and how she had purchased wrist straps, ankle ties and a leather whip to spice up their affair: **"This is obviously a very difficult time for my family and friends. I am extremely sorry for the distress and embarrassment I have caused them and in particular to my wife."**

● Megan McKenzie, the younger sister of South African batsman Neil McKenzie, was named the sexiest woman in the country in 2003. The previous year, the title went to Kerry McGregor, a model romantically linked to the South African middle-order batsman, while in 2004 the title went to a model dating the national captain Graeme Smith. Minki van der Westhuizen came a close second to singer Britney Spears in the magazine *FHM*'s '100 Sexiest Women in the World' poll, earning the title of 'Sexiest Woman in South Africa'. A famous jeans model in her country, she was also a favourite pin-up girl for American troops serving during the Iraqi war.

Jacques Kallis made it a hat-trick of sorts when during the 2003-04 Test series against the West Indies, it was revealed that he, too, had hooked up with a model, Cindy Nel, a former Miss South Africa, who came third in the 2003 Miss Universe contest.

● West Indies batsman Brian Lara was reported to the police in 2001 for allegedly assaulting his model-girlfriend, only to have his accuser declare, two days later, that it was nothing more than a 'lovers' tiff'. Lindsey Ward told police she had fled Lara's home after being hit several times, but not long afterwards all was forgiven and she returned to his Trinidad mansion: **"He's my hero. We had a misunderstanding but it was just a lovers' tiff, just like a lot of couples have. I feel great being with him. I want to be with him forever ... I would like to marry him."**

● A Pakistani cricketer on tour of Australia in 2004-05 was front-page news in Melbourne after he was accused of the sexual assault of a woman in a city hotel. The woman – also of Pakistani origin – reported the alleged rape to a sexual assault centre, but it was later revealed the pair had been an 'item' on a previous tour of Australia. An Indian newspaper claimed the woman had falsely accused the cricketer of rape to 'teach him a lesson', after being informed he would not marry her as she'd been hoping.

● Coinciding with the 2005 Ashes, Shane Warne found himself front-page news battling a series of damaging sex scandals that ultimately contributed to the break-up of his marriage. Under the headline 'SHANE'S SHAME', the British *Sunday Mirror* newspaper detailed, over a two-page spread, claims by a 25-year old London student who said she'd met up with Warne and Hampshire team-mate Kevin Pietersen at a London nightclub earlier in the year: **"My friend was dating Kevin and they invited me out. They introduced me to their friend Shane, but I don't follow cricket and had no idea who he was. The first thing he said was 'How about a foursome?' I thought ... who was this creep?"**

Labelled a 'serial sex cheat' by the British tabloids, Warne faced another scandal on the opening day of the 2005 Ashes series. A 20-year-old student, identified as Rebecca Weeden, claimed Warne had begged her to seduce his then-wife, Simone, into a having a threesome, saying it could help save his marriage: **"It was his fantasy, something he'd always wanted, but never done, and he wanted me as the other woman."**

"I'm not going to sit and defend myself every time some silly person makes up lies and

talks rubbish. What am I supposed to do, call a press conference? You've got to live your life. The public are not dumb, the public understand what is absolute lies and rubbish when it happens. They know exactly what the truth is."

Shane Warne

● South African fast bowler Andre Nel had to push back his wedding by two hours in 2004 after finding himself an indispensable part of his country's Test line-up. Nel and his partner, Deanne Weitz, had, ten months beforehand, set January 17 as their wedding day, which turned out to be the Saturday afternoon of the fourth Test against the West Indies at Centurion. At the time the big day was selected, Nel was not a permanent member of the team: **"It's been a pretty confusing and difficult time, but I am very pleased we were able to find an alternative time. Deanne has been very understanding and supportive throughout the whole issue."**

Nel made it to the altar on time, an hour after stumps on the second day, and returned to the field the following morning where he went on to twice dismiss Brian Lara, as South Africa wrapped up the match by ten wickets: **"Getting married is a special feeling, a bit like getting your first five wickets in an innings. But getting Brian Lara out twice in a day is also a special feeling."**

● During a stint on Australian radio in 2004-05, Kiwi cricket commentator Bryan Waddle was inundated with a flurry of rather unusual phone calls of a sexual nature. A Sydney newspaper had accidentally placed his mobile phone number in a personal ad from a couple seeking a threesome. Waddle received up to 30 enquiries before realising what was up: "**I can assure you, I have nothing to do with it. I think a digit's been left off somewhere and it's all roads to me.**"

● 2004 was a big year for Stephen Fleming, becoming New Zealand's most-capped Test player and highest run-scorer, while off the field the identity of his father was revealed to the public for the first time. In a book penned by sportswriter Richard Boock, Gary Kirk is named as Fleming's father, the NZ batsman the result of a brief affair his parents had in Christchurch: "**I have pretty much lived in quietness about it. A very good friend kept an eye on him from a distance. He was telling me how good he was and I knew he got in the 1st XI at school. But I was pretty amazed when my friend said, when Stephen was 14 or 15, 'This kid will play for New Zealand'. I remember when I watched Stephen play against India in his debut. He scored 92 and I'm sitting in the boardroom at work with some colleagues and I couldn't actually say anything because no one knew. But I'm sitting there thinking, 'This is my son'.**"

● While he was a member of the Pakistan squad competing against the touring New Zealanders in 2002, all-rounder Shoaib Malik took time out to get married. But his was a wedding with a difference – while Shoaib was in Pakistan, his bride was in Saudi Arabia, the pair taking part in a 'nikah' (marriage ceremony) over the telephone while his parents listened in. Shoaib celebrated the event by scoring a century in his next match – 115 in the third one-day international at Lahore.

● When Ricky Ponting blew a kiss to his wife, Rianna, upon reaching 200 against India at Adelaide in 2003–04, his grade cricket club in Launceston 'fined' him $25 for publicly showing signs of affection. The Mowbray Cricket Club promptly received a cheque from the Australian captain, not for $25, but for $250. On the 1989 Ashes tour, Ponting's uncle, Greg Campbell, who appeared in four Test matches, had led the way in publicly declaring his love when he unfurled a banner over the Lord's balcony asking his girlfriend to marry him.

"I had no idea who he was. I hate cricket with a passion."

Rianna Ponting – recalling her first meeting with her future husband in

Melbourne in 2000

● South African batsman Gary Kirsten was nicknamed Tom Cruise by Shane Warne in 1993-94 after an awkward incident while on tour of Australia. Kirsten earned the sobriquet after he was found chatting up a group of women, which he later discovered were the wives and girlfriends of the Australian cricket team: **"That night I had great difficulty sleeping. The abuse I was sure to get on the field the next day chilled me to the bone."**

● In 1997, New Zealand all-rounders Chris Cairns and Chris Harris both tied the knot in the same church in Christchurch on consecutive days in the month of April. First to go down the aisle was Harris with Linda Farrell at the St Barnabas Church, followed by Cairns, who married Ruth Leslie.

● New Zealand fast bowler Daryl Tuffey was fined $NZ1000 in 2005 after being exposed in a sex tape scandal. Tuffey was filmed by two British teenagers – identified as Archie Curtis and Paddy Brookband – allegedly having sex with a woman at a flat in Christchurch in 2004. An independent inquiry, conducted by a leading QC, found that Tuffey had engaged in conduct with a 'sexual element' with the woman, who later, though, denied that sex had taken place.

An eyewitness, who was allegedly present at the gathering where the filming occurred, claimed the event had been blown out of all proportion: **"I was there on the night, I know exactly what happened. They had probably been there a minimum of ten minutes to a maximum of a quarter of an hour before Paddy and Archie walked in. They were quite both drunk and when they walked into the bedroom, I walked in straight after them, and all they caught was them on the bed."**

"There was nothing happening, there was no physical contact at that stage. They were just lying on the bed. She was naked and Tuffey still had his pants on, but his shirt off. There would only

have been a couple of minutes of videoing going on, saying 'Did you shag her? ... rada, rada, rada ...' because I walked in right after them. That's when I realised 'Oh, its Daryl Tuffey' and I said to them 'Paddy, Archie, let's go and leave them to it'. Then they walked out a couple of minutes later."

The incident also resulted in the official cricket program for the summer – titled *Uncovered* – being withdrawn from sale and pulped. It featured Tuffey on the front cover.

● England captain Michael Vaughan made history of sorts in 2004 when he left the field during the second Test against New Zealand at Leeds to attend the birth of his child. Three hours later, a daughter, Tallaluh, was born at a hospital in the nearby city of Sheffield.

● At the conclusion of two consecutive one-day internationals at Perth in 2004-05, two Pakistan players were informed of the death of their father. The first was Younis Khan who came off the field celebrating a three-wicket victory over Australia only to be told his father had passed away back home in Pakistan. Two days later, another Pakistan victory at the WACA – this time against the West Indies – was soured when it was discovered that the father of opening fast bowler Rana Naved-ul-Hasan had died during the match.

● Off-spinner Clyde Butts, who took over from Viv Richards as a West Indies selector in 2004, was married on the rest day of his Test debut, against New Zealand in Georgetown in 1984-85. The last of ten children, Butts was born in 1957 in the quaintly-named Guyanese village of Perseverance.

● Alan Hansford, who appeared in a handful of first-class matches for Sussex in the late 1980s-early 90s, claimed he was ostracised by his club when it became known he was gay. The seam bowler, who took 30 first-class wickets and 30 one-day wickets for the club, believes he was 'outed' by a former county colleague in whom he had confided: **"On the first occasion I went back to the county ground, my former second-team coach saw me from afar, turned, and walked away."**

● A gay cricket club was accused of insulting the memory of the legendary W.G. Grace in the year 2000 after naming themselves The Graces. Believed to be the first homosexual cricket club in the world, the team was founded in a gay bar in London, but upset the family of the pioneering W.G., including Morny Grace, the widow of his great-grandson: **"I and my family are horrified they should have called this team The Graces without asking us. We are not beastly to gays, but they could have found about the Grace family. We object to them using our family name."**

"A lot of people ask 'Why do you need a gay cricket team? There's nothing gay about cricket'. It's not about a pink clubhouse or meeting to discuss makeovers, or how we could rearrange the furniture. We are here because there is still prejudice. Some of our players have had to invent girlfriends at previous clubs they played at as they were uncomfortable saying they had a boyfriend. Here they a place they can be themselves."

Grace's Cricket Club press secretary Duncan Irvine

"One of our batsmen was abused once, but that was nothing to do with being gay. It was because he was fat. I'm afraid he threw a hissy fit and stormed off the pitch. It was the first and only time we recorded a dismissal as 'retired – hurt feelings'."

team chairman Shane McGing

● A former Miss Sri Lanka was sprung by security guards hiding in bushes outside a first-class hotel in Colombo in 1996 during the four-nation Singer World Series one-day international tournament. It was claimed she'd been in one of the players' rooms at the hotel, the Lanka Oberoi.

● England batsman Bill Edrich, who played the first of his 39 Tests in 1938, and South Africa's dominant off-spinner of the 1950s Hugh Tayfield are believed to be the co-holders of one the game's more obscure 'records', that of the most marriages for a Test cricketer. Both tied the knot on five occasions.

CRICKETING CONTRETEMPS

● A brawl involving nearly 20 people at a club cricket match in Lancashire in 2004 resulted in one man ending up in intensive care. The unsavoury incident erupted after a group left a village pub and began heckling players at a nearby cricket ground. Up to 18 people – including players and spectators – became embroiled in a mass fight on the field, with one man admitted to hospital after being hit with a stump.

● Australia's tallest first-class cricketer only appeared in two matches, making his debut against an England XI at Melbourne in 1998-99. Ashley Gilbert, a fast bowler who opened the Victorian attack, and who is 208 centimetres (6'10") tall, made headlines when he and the slightly shorter (175 cm) England batsman Mark Ramprakash had to be separated by one of the umpires after a mid-pitch confrontation. Things got out of hand when Gilbert apparently sledged fast bowler Dean Headley, a move that saw Ramprakash move in from his fielding position to remonstrate with Gilbert. The pair stood toe-to-toe, chest-to-chest until the intervention of umpire Terry Prue.

● The final Test match of the 1970-71 Ashes series at the SCG has its special place in history when crowd disturbances led to the England captain Ray Illingworth taking his team from the field. Objects – mostly beer bottles – were thrown onto the ground and one spectator famously leant over the boundary fence and grabbed England fast bowler John Snow by the shirt, which led to play being suspended.

In 1998, the identity of the spectator was finally revealed after ABC Radio made an appeal for him to come forward. Trevor Guy said he had deliberately grabbed at Snow, angry that he had felled Australian tail-end batsman Terry Jenner with a bouncer. Snow was in Australia when the 80-year-old made himself known, and said he had no hard feelings: **"I'd shake his hand if I met up with him. That was a long time ago."**

● On its way to its biggest loss in over 100 years, at Southampton in 2004, Hampshire's captain Shane Warne became involved in a heated exchange with Essex skipper Ronnie Irani, an incident that was later reviewed by the umpires. Although he later recanted an accusation that the Australian spinner had called his mother a 'whore', a slanging match erupted between the two, with Warne allegedly prodding Irani in the chest. Hampshire lost the match by 384 runs – its biggest defeat since 1896 – with Warne contributing a second-innings duck.

Later in the season, Warne was again in hot water, finding himself on report by the umpires following an incident in the County match against Somerset at Taunton. Warne and former Tasmanian batsman Peter Bowler were both reprimanded for a level-two breach of the ECB's discipline code that prohibits language or gestures deemed insulting to another player.

● An ICC Champions Trophy match in 2004 ended in slight mayhem at The Oval, with a drunken brawl erupting in the middle of the ground. A dozen-or-so alcohol-fuelled spectators invaded the pitch at the conclusion of the Australia-New Zealand match, followed by an equal number of ground stewards. The resulting melee lasted some 20 minutes with headlocks and high tackles, an incident downplayed by the Australian captain Ricky Ponting: **"I'm not sure how it started ... probably too many beers in the sun."**

● Although it's not known whether alcohol may have played a part, a cricket match between two hotels in Melbourne in 1961 resulted in one of the players spending two months in prison after attacking an umpire. W.J. Young, the captain of the High Bridge Hotel team, was charged after striking umpire E.J. Mangan, who spent over a month in hospital as a result of his injuries.

● Sebastianites club fast bowler Ajit Cooray was banned for assaulting an umpire during a first-class match in Sri Lanka in 2002-03. Cooray copped a five-year ban from the game after the incident which took place in a match against Air Force Sports Club at Moratuwa.

● A club umpire was lucky to escape serious injury when a Nottinghamshire club cricketer took out his frustration by almost running him over after a match in 1992. Bryn Derbyshire was given a three-month suspended jail sentence and ordered to pay £400 compensation to Joseph Purser after causing 'bodily harm by wanton furious driving'. The batsman, upset at having been dismissed lbw by Purser, reversed his car in the direction of the umpire, who suffered an injured elbow when he jumped out of the way.

● Indian batting star Ambati Rayudu was attacked with a stump during a Ranji Trophy match against Hyderabad in 2005-06, by one of his former team-mates. Rayudu, representing Andra Pradesh having played for Hyderabad since his debut in 2001-02, was involved in a heated scuffle with Arjun Yadav after the latter had been dismissed.

● An annual cricket match in Bermuda turned ugly in 2005 with one player allegedly punched by a member of the opposition. The incident occurred during the annual Bermuda Cup match, when St George fast bowler George O'Brien reportedly hit Somerset batsman Stephen Outerbridge after he'd been spat at.

● Tempers flared during a club match at Bayfield in the West Indies in 2000, with a mid-pitch confrontation involving up to four players. The incident erupted when Carlton's Ryan Clarke was bowling to St Catherine batsman Dale Mason, but failed to release the ball. Mason, seemingly upset, then advanced towards the bowler waving his bat, while the wicket-keeper Jason King pulled a stump from the ground and ran in the direction of the feuding pair. Mason's partner Terry Watson intervened and helped defuse a potentially violent incident, before play was halted for the day.

● Freshly reinstated as West Indies captain in 2006, Brian Lara was front-page news after overseeing a drama-packed drawn first Test match against India at St John's. Lara found himself centre-stage in a finger-waving, ball-snatching incident when India's Mahendra Singh Dhoni refused to walk after a disputed catch taken on the boundary rope by Daren Ganga.

After 15 minutes of inconclusive replays, TV umpire Billy Doctrove was unable to determine whether the catch was legal and decided to allow the on-field umpires to determine Dhoni's fate: "**Brian came up to me and said 'I'm taking the charge of my players', as in taking the responsibility of his players, and 'I think you should walk off. What they say is going to be the truth'. Then we decided that I should walk off. He came late to me. Daren came first and it was tough for him because it** [the boundary rope] **was on his back side. And it's hard to feel a piece of paper when it's behind you. So he was not entirely sure about it, he said 'I'm not really sure if I stepped on it'.**"

Dhoni accepted Lara's 'advice' and left the field with his score on 69, while Lara made a duck in the West Indies' subsequent run-chase of 392.

"At the end of the day, it's a sport you're playing and you got to trust the guy who you're playing against. There are situations where we can't come to decision. Of course, it's left to the umpires. But if we can't back each other as a team, it doesn't say much for the sport. I just felt that the spirit of the game was being tested. As human beings, we all make mistakes but we all want to see the betterment of the game. It took so long – 15 minutes for 24 big men to come to a decision. I thought it was ridiculous."

Brian Lara

● A Melbourne club cricketer received a ten-year ban from the game in 2006 as punishment for threatening to kill an umpire during a match against Old Mentonians. Heatherton captain Darryl Rose admitted to losing his temper after Gerard Pinto had given three of his batsmen out lbw. The umpire had to be escorted from the field following the confrontation and said it was the most frightening incident he had faced in 100 games of umpiring: "**He** [Rose] **said 'I know what sort of car** you've got. **I know where you live. I'll catch up with you and I'll get you'. They were personal and physical threats**." Rose said the ban was devastating: "**It's worse than going to jail for me.**"

● A series of controversial umpiring decisions during a village cricket match in Bangladesh in 2005 resulted in the stabbing death of a spectator and more than 200 people hospitalised. Police and paramilitary forces used rifles and tear gas in an attempt to control the frenzied crowd at a cricket facility 100 kilometres from the capital Dhaka. More than a dozen nearby properties were torched and destroyed during the disturbance.

● A one-day international at Leeds was brought to a halt in 2001 after unruly crowd behaviour resulted in a ground steward hospitalised with broken ribs. After Pakistan's captain Waqar Younis had taken a record haul of 7 for 36 in the NatWest Series match against England, his counterpart Alec Stewart conceded the match after a section of the crowd spilled onto the field with the steward set upon while attempting to protect the pitch.

● A group of Indian cricketers threatened to immolate themselves in 2006 if India's national cricket board didn't reinstate the first-class status of Bihar. The state had lost out in 2000 when Jharkhand, a new state carved out of Bihar, was granted first-class affiliation by the Board of Control at its expense. Six years after its demise, Bihar was brought back into the fold, but came after threats from Mrityunjay Tiwari, the president of the Bihar Players Association: "**If the recognition to Bihar cricket is not restored, 25 first-class cricketers of the state will immolate themselves.**"

● After commanding a sizeable first-innings lead over England at The Oval in 2006, Pakistan went to become the first team in history to lose a Test by forfeiture. On the fourth day of the match, Australian official Darrell Hair accused the Pakistanis of ball-tampering, becoming the first umpire to award a five-run penalty for the offence, an action that led the Pakistanis to protest by refusing to resume play on time after the tea break.

Law 21.3 states that a match is over if the umpires believe that one of the sides has refused to play, and as a result, Hair flicked off the bails, signalling an end to proceedings. Skipper Inzamam-ul-Haq eventually led the team back onto the field, but were back indoors within a few minutes with the umpires sticking to their guns insisting that the game was over.

Two days after the match had come to an end, and in the midst of the drama escalating seemingly minute-by-minute, Hair came up with a plan to extricate himself from the imbroglio by seeking a payment of $US500,000 in exchange for his resignation. Following a series of email exchanges between Hair and various ICC representatives, he later withdrew his request for a golden handshake: "**This correspondence was composed at a very difficult time and was revoked by myself two days after a period of serious consideration. There was no malicious intent behind this communication with the ICC. I wish to apologise to all my family, friends and supporters, because I somehow feel that I may have let them down, simply by sending an ill-advised but entirely confidential email. That has given other people the opportunity to question my motives.**"

Inzamam-ul-Haq was later cleared by the ICC of ball-tampering charges brought against him, but was found guilty of bringing the game into disrepute for failing to resume play on time. ICC chief referee Ranjan Madugalle banned the Pakistan skipper for four one-day internationals as a result, but dealt a blow to the decision of Hair to, essentially, accuse the Pakistanis of ball-tampering: "**Having regard to the seriousness of the allegation of ball-tampering – it is an allegation of cheating – I am not satisfied on the balance of probabilities that there is sufficiently cogent evidence that the fielding team had changed the condition of the ball. In my judgment, the marks were as consistent with normal wear and tear, and with the ball being pitched into the rough and contact with cricket equipment, as they are with deliberate human intervention.**"

"**The umpires should do everything possible to try to defuse tensions in the dressing room by explaining that a team is entitled to raise any grievance through the ICC but that it is not in their interests, or in the interests of the game, for the team to interrupt play. The umpires and other officials should do** everything possible to ensure the resumption of play. And they should not return to the field of play and then declare the match to be forfeited unless, and until, they are absolutely sure that the team is refusing to play the rest of the match."

The ICC then removed Hair as an elite international umpire, and although he returned to the fold in 2008, he retired shortly afterwards.

"Hair is one of those characters when he wears the umpire's coat, he matamorphoses into a mini-Hitler. Pakistan captain Imzamam-ul-Haq and the team were in their right to protest. The pride of an entire people has been tarnished by his ludicrous and highly insensitive decision."

former Pakistan captain Imran Khan

"This idea that umpires are always right is a load of old cobblers. What I want to know is, who umpires the umpires? The players suffer from their mistakes, but no one ever seems to get rid of the umpires themselves. Being an umpire is a people job. That's why 'Dickie' Bird was good at it. Yes, he was a loony, and he made mistakes – everyone does. But he knew how to deal with people, so they respected him."

former England opener Geoff Boycott

● A dispute within the hierarchy of the Himachal Pradesh Cricket Association in 2005-06 saw two separate teams selected for the same Ranji Trophy match against Tripura. One of the teams turned up for the match and locked all gates in order to prevent the other side gaining entry. The match official called off the game, describing the events as a farce.

● After being given his marching orders by an umpire in a Bulawayo cricket match against Emakhandeni in 2006-07, Metropolitan XI captain Bradley Ras took offence and punched him. Earlier in the season, Bulawayo Athletic Club wicket-keeper Dumisani Mankunzini lost his temper with an opposing batsman during a second-league match, with their differing point of view ending up in a fight.

● Former Zimbabwe batsman Mark Vermeulen had his *annus horribilis* in 2006, firstly banned from playing cricket in England and then arrested on charges of arson. His problems began when he threatened spectators during a match in the Central Lancashire League, an incident that occurred while he was bowling for his club Werneth. According to Ashton's Jon Selby, Vermeulen took offence at some light-hearted sledging from the crowd: **"He got hit for a boundary then bowled a wide and someone from the crowd shouted, 'If you take your sunnies off you'll be able to see where you are bowling.' At the end of the over he marched towards the boundary and appeared to hurl a ball towards the spectators. It hit the railings so missed everyone, but it was an end-of-season match with plenty of women and children watching. He then picked up a boundary marker, which are white discs with a steel spike, before being stopped by a Werneth member."**

In an effort to restrain him, Vermeulen was pinned to the ground by a club official and repeatedly punched in the head, before being escorted from the ground. Originally banned for ten years, it was reduced to three years – with the second and third suspended – on appeal. But things only got worse for Vermeulen.

Back in Zimbabwe and keen to resurrect his Test career, he was arrested in relation to two arson attacks that destroyed buildings and the pavilion at the Zimbabwe Cricket Academy, and caused damage to a room at the headquarters of the Zimbabwe cricket board in Harare. It was suggested he'd become disillusioned when he failed to gain immediate selection for Zimbabwe, and according to prosecution attorney Tawanda Zvekare: "**This did not go down well with the accused who verbally threatened that he was going to destroy Zimbabwe Cricket in two weeks**."

Prior to the fires, Vermeulen had been arrested after turning up to the gates of the president's residence demanding to see Robert Mugabe, while Zimbabwe's coach Kevin Curran spotted him acting in an unusual manner at a practice game at the academy ground: "**He tried to stop one of the matches at the academy. He was throwing boundary boards and bricks onto the field**." It was later claimed that Vermeulen went into the academy gym, poured whisky over himself, and announced to all present what he was going to do.

"He's always been a little ... what's the word, different. He's never reacted that well to authority or to adversity, and some of his actions in those situations have not been those of normal people. Everyone is allowed their idiosyncrasies and professional sport is full of oddballs. But they don't go around burning down buildings."

former Zimbabwe team-mate Alistair Campbell

● When an umpire raised his finger towards the heavens in a club fixture in England in 2006, all hell broke loose with the visiting team picking up their bats and going home. The incident took place during a heated County League match between Westbury and Walls when one of the umpires adjudged Walls' No. 9 batsman out lbw. Although the No.10 had taken his guard, another Walls batsman came onto the field and began arguing with a fielder, which led to the match ending prematurely and the maximum 22 points awarded to Westbury.

"They left the field while we stayed out in the middle. Their captain explained that they definitely would not be restarting the game and offered to pay for their teas. It was a strange decision which, I think, was led by a small element of their team. No words were exchanged and some of their players even shook our players' hands."

Westbury team captain Ian Martin

Another disputed lbw decision in England in 2006, this time in a Minor Counties match, saw an umpire abandoning his post on the opening day after failing to receive an expected apology from the aggrieved batsman. When Berskshire's captain Julian Wood was given out lbw for a duck in the match against Dorset at Bournemouth, he expressed his disgust at the decision of Guy Randall-Johnson as he made his way from the field. During the lunch break, an indignant Randall-Johnson packed his bags and left. Cliff Pocock, the other umpire, had to stand at both ends for the rest of the day's play, while Peter Kingston-Davey came out of retirement to officiate on the second.

● Greg Matthews found himself embroiled in a bit of a stink with a Sydney grade cricket club in 2005-06, with the former Australian Test all-rounder accused of 'revolting', 'reprehensible' and 'insulting' behaviour. During a second-grade match between Sydney University and Gordon, Matthews had scooped up a pile of dog excrement on the edges of Killara Oval, placing it in a glass on a drinks tray being carried by the secretary of the Gordon club Andrew Falk.

After a match report that condemned Matthews' behaviour, he claimed his act was in the best interests of all players on the field: "**I ran past a 'number-two' from a dog and thought 'How bad is this?' It's dangerous. One of the blokes dives on it with an open wound, he might get it in his mouth, in his eye. I put the turd in one glass and put the other glass on top of it. I did not give it a second thought.**"

"I had a turd posted to me, and then a bible packed with marijuana sent to me. I hurled it out the window and in ten minutes the cops came and said they were doing a drug search."

Greg Matthews on cricket 'fans' in New Zealand

● The Australian cricket team copped a pasting in the Indian press in 2006, accused of manhandling an official following their victory over the West Indies in the Champions Trophy one-day tournament. On the dais for the presentation of the trophy that had, up until then, eluded them, Australian captain Ricky Ponting and batsman Damien Martyn were accused of being rude and arrogant towards the main guest at the function, the BCCI president Sharad Pawar. It was reported that Ponting had requested Mr Pawar to leave the podium, and was then gently sent on his way by Martyn so that a team photo could be taken. Both players later apologised.

● A former Australian Test umpire got stuck into the Australian cricket team in 2006 after three of its players had been charged with various offences throughout the summer. During the Test series at home against South Africa, Brett Lee, Glenn McGrath and Adam Gilchrist were all summoned to appear before the match referee, which prompted unflattering comments from an array of commentators and former players and umpires.

Lou Rowan, who stood in 25 Tests during the 1960s and '70s, reserved most of his criticism for the Australian captain Ricky Ponting: "**Ponting is a smart arse and a disaster as leader. The conduct of him and his players is absolutely disgraceful. He has no control over his players. It is an insult to former players and people associated with the game**."

"While present-day cricketers promote the need for the spirit of cricket to be adhered to, many of them do not follow in action this norm, which they publicly endorse in words. This not only includes sledging but excessive appealing, disrespecting the umpiring decisions and using their well-paid, generally ghost-written columns to bait opposition teams and players. Public criticism of the opposition now seems to be part of the team tactics. All this reminds me of the behaviour of small children and the bravado they use to disguise their own fallibilities."

former Australian captain and national coach Bob Simpson

"The standard of conduct that was common-place in my time has been contemptuously trampled underfoot by certain Australian players who cannot grasp the significance of the honour bestowed on them by the baggy green cap. The ever-present and accepted practice of sledging, obscenities, excessive appealing, the questioning of umpires and the accompanying dissent leaves our Australian team quite correctly dubbed 'the ugly Australians'."

Lou Rowan

KEEPING UP APPEARANCES

● Of the 29 stumpings achieved by Ian Healy in his 119 Tests, two came in the fifth Test against England at Sydney in 1998-99. Not since 1881-82, when Jack Blackham accounted for England's Dick Barlow and George Ulyett, had a pair of openers in a Test match in Australia been stumped in the same innings. Healy was responsible for the second-innings demise of Mark Butcher and Alec Stewart, stumped off the bowling of Shane Warne and Stuart MacGill respectively.

● West Indies wicket-keeper Ridley Jacobs opened the batting and took five catches against Zimbabwe in a one-day international at Sydney in 2000-01, and also made a name for himself when he incurred a five-run penalty. Attempting to take a record-equalling sixth catch, off the bat of Brian Murphy, his cap fell off and hit the ball, which delivered the opposition five extra runs.

● In 2004, Surrey's captain Jonathan Batty starred in the County Championship match against Kent, scoring a century and taking eight catches in an innings. Having made 129 in the first innings of the match at The Oval, Batty then equalled the world record for most catches by a wicket-keeper in an innings, made it ten dismissals for the match, and was at the crease with another 18 runs beside his name as Surrey won the match by seven wickets.

Batty became only the fifth 'keeper to achieve eight catches in a first-class innings after Queensland's Wally Grout in 1959-60, Essex's David East in 1985, Kent's Steve Marsh in 1991 and Habib Bank's Tahir Rashid in 1992-93. Rashid also claimed a stumping and set a world-record nine innings-dismissals in the match against PACO at

Gujranwala, while Marsh scored a century (108*) in his match, against Middlesex at Lord's.

● Opening the batting and keeping wicket for the first time in his first-class career, Manicaland's Norbert Manyande scored both a century (148) and a duck. Playing against Matabeleland in the 2003-04 Zimbabwe Logan Cup series at Mutare, the first-time 'keeper scored his first fifty in first-class cricket and shared a double-century third-wicket partnership with Andre Soma (204). Matabeleland's wicket-keeper Wisdom Siziba also opened the batting in this match, scoring 66 and four. In 1999-2000, Siziba, then aged 19, had made history on his first-class debut by carrying his bat for 40 in the match against Manicaland at Harare. He became just the tenth player in the entire history of first-class cricket to carry his bat in a completed innings on debut.

● When the Papua New Guinean-born England wicket-keeper Geraint Jones made his Test debut, at St John's in 2003-04, he had to watch his opposition compile a first-innings total in excess of 700. Jones didn't let through a single bye until the 194th over, by which time the West Indies had amassed 730 runs. His opposite number, Ridley Jacobs, who reached the milestone of 200 Test dismissals during the match, was also in fine form – with the bat – scoring a century (107*) and sharing in a record sixth-wicket partnership of 282 with Brian Lara, who made Test cricket's highest individual score of 400 not out.

THERE'S ONLY ONE PAPUA NEW GUINEAN WELSH AUSSIE ENGLISH GERAINT JONES

crowd banner at the West Indies-England Test match at St John's in 2003-04

● Despite being thrashed by an innings at Bulawayo in 2004, Zimbabwe's five-foot-high wicket-keeper Tatenda Taibu held his head high by not conceding a single bye during the Sri Lankan total of 713 for 3 declared. His world-record performance followed another first in the preceding match at Harare, where he provided the first instance of a wicket-keeper bowling in a Test match taking the first wicket of the opposition. Bowling for the time in his Test career, Taibu grabbed a wicket with his third delivery, breaking the massive opening partnership of 281 between Marvan Atapattu (170) and Sanath Jayasuriya (157), finishing with figures of 1 for 27.

● During the 1999 World Cup, Sri Lanka's spritely little stumper Romesh Kaluwitharana became the first wicket-keeper not to concede a bye in a one-day international total of over 350 when India made 373 for 6 at Taunton. Kaluwitharana, the first wicket-keeper to achieve three stumpings in a one-day international on two occasions, marked his Test debut for Sri Lanka in 1992-93 with a century against Australia at Colombo, his unbeaten 132 being the highest score by a debutant in Test cricket batting at No. 7.

● India employed as many as four wicket-keepers for the five-match Test series against Pakistan in 1952-53, with one claiming four stumpings on his debut at Mumbai. For Vijay Rajindernath, this was his only Test match, in which he neither took a catch nor scored a run. The first and fifth Tests saw Khokan Sen behind the stumps, Nana Joshi in the second and Ebrahim Maka in the fourth – a world-record number of wicket-keepers for one side in a series.

In more recent times, England used three 'keepers – Paul Downton, Bob Taylor and Alan Knott – in the 1981 Ashes series, while South Africa also used three – Thami Tsolekile, A.B. de Villiers and Mark Boucher – against England in 2004-05.

In the Lord's Test against New Zealand in 1986, England famously used four wicket-keepers in the first innings of the match, after Bruce French had retired hurt when hit on the helmet while batting. Team-mate – England's No. 3 batsman – Bill Athey deputised behind the stumps for two overs, until he was replaced by former England 'keeper, the 45-year-old Bob Taylor, who happened to be at the ground working for the Test-match sponsor, Cornhill. The next day, another substitute was permitted to take to the field – Hampshire's Bobby Parks, who took over until French resumed duties for the final ball of the innings.

● New Zealand wicket-keeper Adam Parore was a good enough batsman to score ten hundreds in first-class cricket, two of which came in

Tests with a world-record gap in between. His first of 100 not out came against the West Indies at Christchurch in 1994-95 and his last, 57 Tests later, was an innings of 110 against Australia at Perth in 2001-02.

● Three wicket-keepers played in the first-ever Twenty20 match in Australia, with each scoring a half-century. The inaugural match, between Western Australia and Victoria at the WACA in 2004-05, was played in front of a sell-out crowd numbering some 20,000. Victoria's 'keeper Adam Crosthwaite scored the first domestic Twenty20 half-century, a 46-ball 57, while the only other fifties in the match came off the bats of West Australians Luke Ronchi (67) and Ryan Campbell (56*).

Ronchi, the designated 'keeper, and Campbell – WA's No. 1 man behind the stumps – opened the batting with a 101-run stand, an association that came to an end when Ronchi was stumped by Crosthwaite for a whirlwind 67 off just 24 balls.

● The second Test against Pakistan at Sydney in 2004-05 was a landmark match for Adam Gilchrist, breaking a number of significant records, with commentators-galore rapturous in their applause of his exploits with the bat. After surpassing Ian Healy's record for most consecutive Test-match appearances since debut (64), he then reached the milestone of 4000 Test runs in record time by a wicket-keeper, before scoring his 13th Test-match hundred, overtaking Andy Flower's record of 12 centuries by a 'keeper. In typical swashbuckling style, Gilchrist reached his century with a six – one of five in the innings – before he was out for 113, scored off just 120 balls: **"I'm going to sound like bit of a dickhead, but it didn't feel like one of my best innings. Certainly from 80 to 100, the way I struck the ball was as clean as I could ever want to, but its wasn't until I was on 49 and Shoaib [Akhtar] bowled me a bouncer that felt like a bullet with my name on it and I managed to play a wild hook shot, getting it right in front of my face, and was lucky not to get caught. That sort of woke me up. Prior to that, I didn't feel I was hitting the ball very well."**

● Adam Gilchrist matched the great Don Bradman in 2004-05 when he became just the sixth Australian batsman, and the first wicket-keeper, to score a century in three consecutive Test innings. After scoring 113 against Pakistan at Sydney, he then tortured New Zealand with two six-laden hundreds in a row. His 14th Test century, at Christchurch, featured 12 fours and six sixes – in his 66th Test – in a 126-ball innings of 121, batting at No. 8. He followed it up with 162 in his next innings – the second Test at Wellington – which included 22 fours and five sixes. He reached the century-mark off 86 balls, joining Jack Fingleton, Warren Bardsley, Charles Macartney, Arthur Morris and Bradman as the only Australian batsmen to score three Test centuries on the trot.

He was well on target for a fourth consecutive century in the third Test at Auckland, when he ran out of partners, finishing on 60 not out. Gilchrist topped the Australian batting averages in the three-match series, scoring 343 runs in three innings at 171.50.

● Adam Gilchrist achieved an unusual first in a one-day international in 2004-05, with a stumping off fast bowler Glenn McGrath. Decked out in a helmet and standing up to the paceman at Wellington, the ploy worked a treat, with Gilchrist stumping Craig McMillan.

Another world-first came Gilchrist's way in the following match at Christchurch, where he caught the first five wickets to fall. The previous record of four dismissals had been held by a number of 'keepers – the West Indies' Ridley Jacobs, South Africa's Mark Boucher, India's Nayan Mongia, England's Alec Stewart, Kenya's David Obuya and Sri Lanka's Kumar Sangakkara.

"You see the way Gilly throws the ball in the air. He tends to play on his walking, his honesty, but he still tries to burgle anyone and everyone."

former New Zealand batsman Mark Richardson on Adam Gilchrist

"I admire anyone who makes a living crouched on his haunches staring through three sticks at the sweaty buttocks of a boring batsman. That's what my mate Gilly does for his country."

Channel Ten's David Tench Tonight, *2006*

● In consecutive Test matches in the 2005-06 series between Pakistan and India, the two wicket-keepers both scored a century in under 100 balls, with both featuring in a record-breaking sixth-wicket partnership. Kamran Akmal (102*), the Pakistani 'keeper, hit his second consecutive century in a Test match after making 154 against England on the same ground just a month before. He brought up his hundred off 81 deliveries, and it was a fun-filled knock that included 11 fours and two sixes. He put on 170 runs for the sixth wicket with Shahid Afridi – in just 129 balls – a Pakistani record against India at Lahore, surpassing a stand of 146 between Zaheer Abbas and Mushtaq Mohammad in 1978-79.

In the following Test at Faisalabad, India's Mahendra Singh Dhoni scored 148 – his maiden century, in just his fifth match – reaching triple figures in 93 balls. His 210-run partnership with Irfan Pathan was India's highest for the sixth wicket against Pakistan, beating the previous best of 143 between Kapil Dev and Mohammad Azharuddin at Kolkata in 1986-87.

● When India hosted Sri Lanka at Jaipur in 2005-06, the only batsmen to score centuries were the opposing wicket-keepers, a first in one-day international cricket. Kumar Sangakkara opened Sri Lanka's innings with an unbeaten 138, while India's Mahendra Singh Dhoni smashed 183 not out, establishing a new high for a wicket-keeper in one-day internationals. Of the 601 runs scored in the match, 321, or more than half, came off the bats of the two 'keepers.

Sangakkara had the pads on for the entirety of the match, batting through 50 overs and then standing behind the stumps for 46.1, while the reverse applied for Dhoni, wicket-keeping for 50 and batting for all but a few balls of India's innings: "**Playing a long innings after keeping wickets for 50 overs is tough, but I am happy that I managed a pretty good innings**."

Dhoni's unbeaten 183 beat Brian Lara's 153 against Pakistan at Sharjah in 1993-94 as the highest century in the second innings of a one-day international, while it also overtook Lara's 169 against Sri Lanka at Sharjah in 1995-96 as the highest innings by a No. 3 batsman.

Dhoni finished the seven-match series against Sri Lanka with 17 sixes – a record number for a tournament – while his average of 115.33 was the best by a wicket-keeper in a series of five or more matches, beating West Indian Deryck Murray's 105.00 in the 1975 World Cup.

● In 2005, England's Geraint Jones became the first wicket-keeper to achieve 20 dismissals in a one-day international series in fewer than ten matches. Jones took 20 catches in just seven appearances in the NatWest Series, eclipsing the effort of Adam Gilchrist who finished the 2003 World Cup with 21 dismissals from ten matches.

In the final of the NatWest Series against Australia, Jones became the first 'keeper to record the all-round feat of a half-century (71) and five dismissals in a one-day international at Lord's, and only the third overall to achieve the double at any venue, after Gilchrist and the West Indies' Ridley Jacobs.

● Picked to lead New Zealand on his Test debut, Canterbury wicket-keeper Lee Germon led by example, top-scoring in both innings of his first match. In a low-scoring Test against India at Bangalore in 1995-96, Germon was the only Kiwi to reach 20, going on to make 48 out of 145, batting at No. 8. In the second innings, Germon matched Stephen Fleming's 41, hitting six boundaries in an 80-ball stay. Germon became only the second wicket-keeper in Test history to top-score in both innings of his debut, following in the foot-steps of England's Edmund Tylecote. Debuting against Australia at Melbourne in 1882-83, Tylecote became the first player to achieve the double, hitting 33, out of 177, and promoted to open the batting in the second innings, hit 38 in a total of 169.

In the previous season of '94-95, Germon marked his one-day international career by taking a catch off the very first ball he received. Standing in the first of his 37 ODIs, Germon took a catch off the bat of Sri Lanka's Roshan Mahanama at Bloemfontein, while the then specialist wicket-keeper Adam Parore played as a batsman. In his 49 international matches, including 12 Tests, Germon led his country in all but one, his first one-day international.

● Hailing from the same club in Perth as Rod Marsh, West Australian wicket-keeper Kevin Wright appeared in ten Tests during World Series Cricket days, shining in the series against Pakistan at home in 1978-79. Wright made 14 dismissals behind the stumps, a record for a two-match Test series, until 2004-05 when Pakistan's Kamran Akmal achieved 16 against the West Indies.

● Both wicket-keepers in the third Ashes Test at Perth in 2006–07 scored a duck in the first innings. And while one went on to make a pair, the other scored the fastest-ever century seen in a Test match in Australia. Up until the WACA Test, England's Geraint Jones had never been dismissed for a duck in the first 51 innings of his career – an England record – but marked his 52nd and 53rd with noughts, while his opposite number Adam Gilchrist became the second Australian, after Don Bradman, to record a duck and a century (102*) in the same Test match more than once.

Gilchrist reached his fifty in the second innings in 40 balls, but went from 50 to 100 off just 17, an all-Test record. It was the fastest hundred on record in Ashes cricket, the quickest by an Australian in any Test, and the second-fastest of all time, just behind Viv Richards' 56-ball hundred against England at St John's in 1985–86.

Given the flick for the following Test, Jones' replacement Chris Read became the first 'keeper in history to achieve six dismissals in consecutive Test innings. With six catches pouched in the fourth Test at Melbourne, he claimed another six dismissals in Australia's first innings in the fifth Test at Sydney. Gilchrist was also in top nick in Sydney, achieving a record-equalling nine dismissals in an Ashes Test, while also scoring a half-century (62) and passing the milestone of 10,000 first-class runs.

In the same season, Western Australia's other main wicket-keeeper Luke Ronchi broke team-mate Adam Voges' record for the fastest ton in domestic limited-overs cricket. Opening the batting against New South Wales at the WACA, the New Zealand-born Ronchi reached his maiden one-day century off 56 balls, clouting 11 fours and five sixes along the way. The previous fastest century in the competition was Voges' 62-baller against New South Wales at North Sydney in 2004–05. Ronchi was also in fine fettle behind the stumps, securing three catches and a stumping.

● Adam Gilchrist celebrated his final innings in a World Cup tournament with a match-winning knock of 149 in the final against Sri Lanka at Bridgetown in 2007. He reached his hundred off a record 72 balls – he also became the first wicket-keeper to effect 50 dismissals in World Cup matches.

FOOD & DRINK

● Two legends of English cricket, Allan Lamb and Ian 'Beefy' Botham, spearheaded a publicity drive in 2005 to encourage the population to eat more meat. The English Beef and Lamb Executive group invested over four million pounds in an initial advertising campaign, which featured animated caricatures of the two cricketers competing over who could make the tastiest meal using either beef or lamb.

● England's Marcus Trescothick, who had never eaten steak until he was 27, earned the nickname 'Bangers' because of his love of sausages. After England's 2005 Ashes success, national team-mate Kevin Pietersen had a snag named after him by a butcher in Somerset, while Andrew Flintoff was honoured with a special vanilla-flavoured ice-cream, called 'Freddie's Glory'.

● A club match in England was brought to a halt in unusual circumstances in 1997 when it was discovered during a drinks break that the team fielding had 12 players on the ground. The error was only revealed when a member of the Southampton Travellers side complained that he had not received a drink.

● Surrey batsman Richard Clinton had to make an emergency dash to the dentist during Sri Lanka's opening first-class tour match in England in 2006. Representing British Universities in the match at Cambridge, Clinton made the highest score in either innings with 44, but had to race off to the dentist after a mishap while chewing gum. According to a local newspaper one of Clinton's teeth "… **imploded under the strain of furious gum-chewing**."

● Former Test star Kapil Dev fulfilled a long-held ambition in 2004 when he opened his own hotel and restaurant in the Indian city of Chandigarh. 'The Kaptain's Retreat' is a boutique hotel, where its ten rooms have no numbers, identified instead by major landmarks in Kapil's cricketing career, such as 'Tied Test' and '432': "**It is my gift to the city. I always wanted to give something back to the city where I spent my formative years. It has always been my dream project and I must say it was my vision and my wife Romi's execution that helped me to realise my dream**." The hotel opened with a multi-cuisine restaurant called 'Elevens'.

Other Indian cricketers, including Sachin Tendulkar, Ajay Jadeja and Sourav Ganguly have also branched out into the restaurant-trade – Tendulkar became involved in two up-market establishments in Mumbai, Jadeja opened an Italian eatery-cum-bar 'Senso' in New Delhi in 2002, while Ganguly launched a so-called multiplex-restaurant in Kolkata in 2004. 'Sourav's: The Food Pavilion', officially opened by Tendulkar, is a multi-storied complex with each level accommodating a different-style fare. In 2006, the establishment was robbed of 80,000 rupees.

"Sachin [Tendulkar] … his hunger for runs finds a match in his appetite for dishes, especially when it is seafood."

Indian fast bowler Ashish Nehra

● Delia Smith, one of Britain's best-known celebrity chefs, used to prepare tea for her husband's village cricket team in Suffolk. But it was later revealed that she did not always use her own culinary skills in the preparation of meals: "**I would make the teas every now and then – but when I was really busy, I would get some sandwiches from Marks & Spencer**."

Miss Smith made her confession in 2004 as she opened a new pavilion at the Battisford Cricket Club near Stowmarket, where her husband was a founding member. The news came as a great shock to many, including one former player: "**The club was renowned as having fantastic teas because Delia often did them. But now it looks like she took a short cut**."

Durham added some spice to its stocks in 2004, with Philip Mustard and Graham Onions both appearing on the club's playing menu. The two turned out together for the first time for the county in a Twenty20 match against Nottinghamshire at Trent Bridge, Mustard hitting 64, while Onions, opening the bowling, took 2 for 25.

All-rounder Andrew Hall was given the added responsibility of standing behind the stumps in the final of the indoor one-day international series at Melbourne's Docklands Stadium in 2000 after South Africa's regular wicket-keeper was sidelined after suffering an unusual, and painful, injury. Mark Boucher had sliced through his hand with a knife while cutting some meat in his hotel room.

Nathan Bracken was sent fifty packets of Minties by Nestlé in 2005 to thank him for all the free publicity the Australian fast bowler had inadvertently provided the company. During a radio interview, Bracken remarked that county bowlers regularly used mints to polish the ball for reverse swing, a weapon used to great effect by England in its 2005 Ashes win.

"It is just a breath mint you put in your mouth, but it makes your saliva very sugary. Every team has lollies and things like that. We had all our lollies checked before the first game to make sure there was nothing illegal. When I was playing at Gloucester a couple of years ago as soon as we needed the ball to go 'Irish' the captain would call and they would bring out some of these mints and it would work."

Nathan Bracken

In the same year that a ten-year-old piece of cheese on toast containing an image resembling the Virgin Mary sold for $36,000, a dim sim that looked like Darren Lehmann was auctioned online and went for $254. According to the seller who advertised his unique 'cricketing item' on the *eBay* website in 2004, " ... **this unexplained deep-fried phenomenon bares an almost eerie likeness to the Australian cricket legend Darren 'Boof' Lehmann. This remarkable one-off piece captures Darren looking relaxed sometime during a recent lunch break. It should also be noted that although this dim sim may very well end up on a boardroom wall somewhere, it belongs in the National Museum.**"

"I've heard about all sorts of things being sold on *eBay*, but this takes the cake. All I can say is it must be a pretty good-looking dim sim if it's meant to be my look-alike."

Darren Lehmann

● Two of the game's sweetest-hitting batsmen, Lance and Chris Cairns launched a fudge-making business in New Zealand in 1999. The company, Cairns Fudge Limited, stemmed from a small franchise set up by son Chris in Christchurch in the mid-1990s: "**Our friendship has always been great and cricket has been such a great thing in both our lives. I just thought, why not transfer that respect, trust and relationship to the business. I have always felt our fudge is a great product, but we needed to get the whole company functioning smoothly before launching under the Cairns banner.**"

● A university lecturer dressed as a carrot was unceremoniously evicted from the Headingley cricket ground in 1997 during the fourth Ashes Test match. Brian Cheesman, who had regularly attended Test matches at the ground in fancy dress, was removed for 'drunken and abusive behaviour', an allegation he denied.

● Members of the Australian cricket team on tour of India in 2004-05 were left a little gobsmacked while dining one night in Nagpur when a cockroach appeared on their table. The story goes that the waiter attempted to assure the players it was not a cockroach, and to prove his point to the disbelieving diners popped the creature into his mouth and swallowed it.

● South African batsman Herschelle Gibbs put behind him a string of low scores in 2004, by posting a historic century in the ICC Champions Trophy tournament, declaring that a pizza had been responsible for reinvigorating his appetite for runs. After nine consecutive innings in one-day internationals in which he had failed to reach 50, Gibbs made 101 at The Oval, becoming the first batsman to make four centuries against the West Indies: "**I was quite relaxed. I had a pizza for the first time in a few months. Maybe it helped with the balance … it made me sleep a bit better. It was washed down with a bit of Jack Daniels**!" It was his first one-day hundred for South Africa in 17 months.

● In the 1995 edition of *Wisden Cricketers' Almanack*, the manager of the Lord's dining rooms was named in an 'Alternative Five' list that noted other exceptional cricketing personalities. Nancy Doyle, who started as a casual waitress at Lord's in 1961, was responsible for the serving of approximately a hundred meals for players and officials during Test matches, although she admitted to having never read a cook book in her life.

"The best thing about playing at Lord's is the food. Lord's makes me hungry. The grub in the pavilion there just can't be beaten."

England fast bowler Matthew Hoggard

● The West Indies' record-breaking fast bowler, and former captain, Courtney Walsh became a restaurant owner in 2004 when he opened 'Cuddy'z' in Kingston, Jamaica. Some of the dishes on the menu have included the 'Record-Breaking Pasta' and 'Chicken Howzat Salad', while drinks have been named the 'Bouncer', 'Silly Mid-Off' and 'Leg Slip'.

● Pakistan all-rounder Abdul Razzaq is referred to as Popeye by team-mates due to his unusual addiction to spinach. After falling ill while playing in New Zealand in 2003-04, Abdul was put on a strict diet of the green stuff, which he insisted should be on his menu wherever he tours.

● Australian all-rounder Tom Moody famously gained a world haggis-throwing record at Scotland's Highland Games in 1989. Australian fast bowler Fred Spofforth was similarly skilled, but more delicately so. Legend has it that Spofforth could throw an egg over a distance of some 45 metres without it breaking when it landed.

● A group of English cricket fans in Perth for the 2006-07 Ashes missed their favourite food so much that they placed ten takeaway orders from an Indian restaurant in Bath. Restaurant-owner Nasir Abdul agreed to fly from England to Perth to deliver the order of lamb tikka masala, lamb dansak, mushroom pilau, tarka dhal, sag aloo and pratha bread at a cost of £1500 ($A2942) for food that would normally cost about £140: "**We were shocked when we first got the order and thought someone was having laugh, but we then realised it was genuine**." But the plan was poo-pooed when Australian quarantine officials got wind of the scheme, declaring all of the food would be destroyed upon its arrival in the country.

● Former England captain Mike Gatting was selected as a curry judge in 2005 to coincide with Bangladesh's inaugural Test tour of the country. Gatting was on a panel of judges – which included one of Newcastle's most respected Bangladeshi restaurateurs – charged with choosing the best curry to be served at a special function for the touring cricketers: "**I'm a big curry fan. I fancy myself as a bit of a chef, but I am sure my talents will be put to shame by the local experts**."

"I've a penchant for cheese and pickle sandwiches and I'm very much a savoury man. The variety is wonderful … good fillings. I might have to go to the gym for an extra half-hour, but it's been worth it."

Mike Gatting judging a tea competition at the
Edgbaston cricket ground in 2003

● A brand of biscuits banking on Don Bradman was launched in India in 2005, the first time his name had been used on a food product. A portion of the sale proceeds from the Bradman chocolate-chip cookies was directed towards various charities across India, including under-privileged children.

● Marking the retirement of Gloucestershire's Jack Russell in 2004, Mike Atherton told of some of the quirky eating habits of his former England team-mate. Atherton spoke of the wicket-keeper's love of a cup of tea during matches – for which he was famous – drinking up to 20 cups a day: "**The tea bag that hung from his peg and that provided him with enough tea to last a five-day Test … his lunch of two Weet-Bix that had to be soaked for precisely eight**

minutes, so that their consistency was soft, but not mushy." He also reportedly spent every night during a Test match in Perth dining at a Chinese restaurant where he ordered the same meal – cashew chicken, without cashews.

● In 2004–05, a Victorian cricket team accused a rival side of providing marijuana-laced cupcakes for afternoon tea in a match in the Gippsland region. A number of players from the Nerrena club consumed the cakes during the tea break in the match against Inverloch, claiming the food must have been laced with marijuana or hash after their subsequent on-field performance had raised a few eyebrows.

One of the players, Tim Clark, ate five of the cupcakes: "**I thought, 'Gee, this is pretty good'. They usually feed us crap.**" While some players broke out in hysterical laughter soon after eating the cakes, it took another some 20 minutes to put on his pads. Nerrena ended up losing the match by 50 runs.

● Queensland batsman Martin Love's first-ever job was picking rock melons. Fast bowler Jason Gillespie's first job was delivering pizzas: "**I've heard these stories about horny women in negligees answering doors, and I was praying for it every time I knocked on a door, but it never happened to me.**"

● Having begun his working life in a bottle shop selling alcohol, Australian batsman Matthew Hayden later became the author of cookbooks. *The Matthew Hayden Cookbook*, published in 2004, showcased a variety of recipes from his grandmother's kitchen to ones collected on his many cricket tours around the world. The book, with a foreword from Sydney restaurateur Luke Mangan, proved to be a popular fare with a second helping published in 2006. Albeit a sponsor-dominated production, Hayden's team-mate Glenn McGrath followed suit in 2005 with a cookbook of his own, *Barbecue With The Master.*

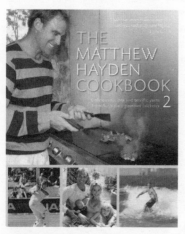

"I think I've had it [coffee] twice in my life and I was sick afterwards both times."

Glenn McGrath

● Alec Stewart and Shane Warne were two international players renowned for not being able to stomach curries while on tour of the sub-continent. During the World Cup of 1996, Stewart managed 43 consecutive days of eating the same meal of chicken breasts, mashed potato and broccoli: "**I don't do curry in England, so I'm not going to do it in India or Pakistan**."

In 2001, Warne signed a sponsorship deal with a major food company that enabled him to receive supplies of baked beans while on tour overseas.

Warne, who rates baked beans as one of his all-time favourite foods, announced the following year that as a way of preserving his playing career he was cutting out all junk food, including sausage rolls, chips and vanilla slices: **"The diet I have been on for most of my life has been pizzas and beer. With my diet, I've switched beer for wine and added a bit of lettuce in my sandwich which I used to soak with butter and cheese."**

"Nothing against Indian food and all that, but I get sick over here. Hopefully, I'm better prepared this time. I've got my protein shakes, a few tins of spaghetti, a few tins of beans. I've got some cereal. Some people don't like seafood, I just don't like curries."

Shane Warne on the eve of the 2004-05 Test series in India

● An England batsman was banned from drinking tea while on a tour of Sri Lanka in 2004-05. England A batsman Owais Shah was advised to abstain from the beverage after too many cups caused cramps and dehydration: **"I've learnt my lesson. I enjoy tea, but I've been told to put that on hold for a few days. All I've been doing all morning is drinking water and that's what I'll be doing from now on."**

THIS SPORTING LIFE

● During 2004, Lancashire fast bowler Sajid Mahmood made his one-day international debut for England, against New Zealand at Bristol, while his cousin Amir Khan won a medal in boxing at the Athens Olympics. Aged just 17, Amir won silver for Britain after losing 30-22 to Cuban Mario Kindelan in the lightweight final. Sajid had a knockout Test-match debut for England in 2006, taking 3 for 9 at the end of his first day, against Sri Lanka at Lord's.

● Two of Queensland's greatest-ever captains share the same birthday of 27 July. Allan Border, who captained Australia on a record 93 occasions, was born on 27 July in 1955, while rugby league's Gorden Tallis was born in the year 1973. The former Kangaroo counts Border as a close personal friend, along with Brisbane Broncos supporters Matthew Hayden and Ian Healy.

GORDEN TALLIS' ALL-TIME BEST TEST XI

Matthew Hayden (A)
Gordon Greenidge (WI)
Viv Richards (WI)
Steve Waugh (A)
*Allan Border * (A)*
Imran Khan (P)
Ian Healy † (A)
Shane Warne (A)
Malcolm Marshall (WI)
Jeff Thomson (A)
Dennis Lillee (A)

● A marketing ploy by Cricket New South Wales in 2006-07 saw rugby league international Andrew Johns trotted out to play Twenty20 cricket. Johns, who had played an occasional game of lower-grade cricket in Merewether, made his debut for New South Wales against South Australia at Newcastle, where he bowled a single over costing nine runs and with the bat, remained on zero not out.

His inclusion in the team was heavily criticised by some both before and after the game, with Blues captain Simon Katich forced to shield Johns from the bowling in the final over. Johns, the No. 11, joined Katich, but with 13 runs needed from the final six balls the skipper was unable to find the boundary and protected Johns by refusing to take any singles: **"I didn't want to get to the other end in the last over. I didn't want to get out and I didn't want to get hurt. Simon could have got the runs."**

On the same day that Johns made his ill-fated debut, former rugby league referee Bill Harrigan was also spotted on a cricket field. Playing in a charity cricket match in Sydney, Harrigan was joined by golfers Peter O'Malley and former US Open winner Michael Campbell.

"Bracks [Nathan Bracken] was bowling off about two or three steps and he was squealing when he was copping it in the thigh pad."

New South Wales batsman Ed Cowan on the Andrew Johns experiment

"I don't believe that Cricket NSW should sell itself short and start flirting with the integrity of what it should stand for. Andrew Johns should have been out there at the half-time interval, hitting sixes into the crowd, even being on a loudspeaker commentating on the game. But playing. I just don't get it."

Michael Slater

● Australia's most-capped rugby union player George Gregan enjoyed a brief flirtation with cricket in his younger days, playing against the ilk of Ricky Ponting, Adam Gilchrist, Stuart MacGill and Martin Love. Gregan, who overtook David Campese's record of 101 rugby Tests in 2004, played for the ACT against the AIS cricket team at Manuka Oval in Canberra in 1991-92: **"My cricketing days were very short. I played against Ricky Ponting and Adam Gilchrist. They can't remember me,** but I can remember them, as I was chasing leather all over the place. I learnt pretty quickly that cricket wasn't my go. I worked really hard at my cricket. But at an under-19s tournament in Perth I got a strong realisation that I wasn't at that level. I wasn't getting many runs and the blokes who were, are the guys you see now – Ricky Ponting, Martin Love and Jimmy Maher. Unlike me, they were scoring bundles of runs. Around the same time I was offered an AIS rugby scholarship, and I decided to devote my energies to that."

In 1990-91, Gregan enjoyed a meritorious debut season in club cricket in Canberra, scoring two centuries and three fifties in eight innings at an average of 69.86. With a top score of 157, Gregan was propelled into first grade the following season, earning a spot in the 1991-92 Australian Under-19 Championships in Perth.

George Gregan – the young cricketer and the seasoned footballer

● George Cakobau, who was Governor-General of Fiji between 1973 and 1983, represented his nation at both cricket and rugby union. He captained Fiji on its first rugby tour of New Zealand, in 1939, and is credited with introducing the so-called 'cibi' – a war-dance performed to this day by the Fiji rugby team before each Test match: "**We went to New Zealand and performed the cibi at every game. Of our eight matches, we won seven and drew one.**"

In 1947-48, Cakobau returned to New Zealand as vice-captain of Fiji's cricket squad and appeared in four first-class matches, with a highest score of 67 not out against Wellington. His best performance with the ball was a haul of 2 for 48 against Auckland.

● Harare-born left-arm fast bowler Scott Brant, who made his first-class debut for Queensland in 2001-02, represented Zimbabwe at junior level in a number of sports, including cricket, hockey, athletics and swimming. He competed in international swim meets in Europe and once won a gold medal at pole-vaulting in South Africa.

Team-mate Brendan Nash, who made a century and a first-ball duck in the match at Adelaide where Brant made his first-class debut, is the son of a former Olympic swimmer. Paul Nash represented Jamaica at the 1968 Mexico City Olympic Games and at the 1970 Commonwealth Games held in Edinburgh.

● The USA Amateur Tennis Champion of 1930 was a batsman of some standing, appearing in 96 first-class matches, in which he scored over 4000 runs with six centuries. Middlesex's Clarence Bruce – later Lord Aberdare – was also the British Isles amateur tennis champion in 1932 and 1938 and for two decades was a member of the International Olympic Executive, playing a major part in organising the 1948 London Games.

● Long before he became a champion all-rounder, Pakistan's Wasim Akram had wanted to be a professional table tennis player. Towards the end of his cricketing career, Wasim took up the sport of squash, after receiving a racquet from world-champion player Jahangir Khan.

"Believe it or not, I wanted to be a table tennis player from a young age. I was pretty good."

Wasim Akram

● Heath Streak's father, Denis Streak, who appeared in 14 first-class matches for various Zimbabwean teams, came close to reaching the semi-finals of the Champion of Champions bowls tournament in the West Australian capital Perth in 2003. Streak, who had only taken up the sport a few years previously, defeated one of the event favourites, Scotland's Darren Burnett.

"When you look at the Australian team, they're not the youngest now. Some of them are getting a bit long in the tooth. Someone told me that the Australian bowls team is a younger average age than the cricket team."

former Zimbabwe fast bowler Heath Streak on the Australians prior to the
2003-04 VB one-day international series

● South African batsman A.B. de Villiers, who made his Test debut in 2004–05, was a talented all-rounder in his youth, impressing at cricket, tennis and rugby football. His father was a union full-back and keen for his son to follow in his footsteps: **"When I was 18, I played for a provincial side, the Blue Bulls, and I got a couple of offers to sign for them and go to university. I considered it for a while, but it wasn't meant to be. I'd already decided I was set on cricket. The tennis happened when I was a bit younger. I was 13 when he had to decide whether I should go to Nick Bollettieri's academy in Florida, but in the end that didn't happen either. My parents didn't want me to go."**

● Amit Bhudia, who made his first-class debut for Kenya in 2004, had previously represented his country at tennis and table tennis. He was the youngest player in Kenya's 22-man World Cup squad in South Africa in 2003, but before turning to cricket had been a star performer with a racquet in his hand, dominating the local tennis scene winning countless titles: **"After all this excitement in lawn tennis and table tennis, I did not exactly see the reward and what the future held for me, thus the decision to quit and try my luck in cricket."**

● Australian rugby league international Arthur Clues, who played football and club cricket for Leeds in Yorkshire, is thought to be unique in scoring both a century and a try at Headingley. He played first-grade cricket in Sydney, where he also turned out for the Western Suburbs rugby league club, appearing in three Tests against England in Australia in 1946.

● Former Australian rugby league player Matt Adamson made his debut as a Test cricket commentator in 2004, appearing on Sky TV alongside the likes of David Gower, Ian Botham and Michael Holding. Adamson was a talented cricketer in his youth, opening the batting on a number of occasions with Adam Gilchrist for the New South Wales Under-17s: **"Gilly and I were good mates as young kids. At the time there were high expectations on Gilly to go on and do great things, and of course he has. I remember watching him back then ... he always had so much time as a cricketer. His footwork was great and he struck the ball as hard as he does now."**

Adamson, who also played first-grade cricket for the Western Suburbs club in Sydney with Greg Matthews, went on to play five Super League Tests for Australia before linking up with the Canberra Raiders in 2005. His coach at the ACT club was Matthew Elliott, who was also a handy cricketer in his youth, playing grade cricket in Sydney and representing a number of Queensland junior teams; which, on occasions, included former Australian wicket-keeper Ian Healy.

"As a young kid, my dream was always to play cricket for Australia, and there's always that little bit of 'Could I have?' or 'Would I have?', but I'm never going to complain because I've had a wonderful rugby league career that's taken me to all parts of the world representing my state and country."

Matt Adamson

RICKY STUART'S ALL-TIME BEST TEST XI

Mark Taylor (A)
Michael Slater (A)
*Ian Chappell * (A)*
Greg Chappell (A)
Ricky Ponting (A)
Doug Walters (A)
Gary Gilmour (A)
Rod Marsh † (A)
Shane Warne (A)
Dennis Lillee (A)
Glenn McGrath (A)

Former Canberra Raiders and Australian rugby league player Ricky Stuart

● New Zealand rugby legend Jeff Wilson completed a remarkable circle in 2004-05 when he was resurrected for a one-day international nearly 12 years after his last appearance. Wilson, who made his first-class cricket debut for Otago in 1991-92, gave the game away in 1996-97 to concentrate on rugby, which saw him post a record number of tries for the All Blacks. The double international made a return  to first-class cricket in 2002-03 after a rugby career that yielded him 60 Tests and 234 points: **"You know when your time is up. While I was still enjoying playing, I was really struggling to get to training. So I thought I'd give cricket another crack. Rugby only goes for 80 minutes, but cricket is a real thinking man's game. It's been a great challenge**."

Wilson made his one-day international debut against Australia at Dunedin in 1992-93 after a sensational double for Otago in a one-day match at Dannevirke Domain. Opening both the batting and bowling against Central Districts, Wilson scored a career-best 99 and bowling medium-pace, took 2 for 32.

Nearly 12 years elapsed between his fourth and fifth one-day internationals – against Australia at Christchurch in '04-05 – a world-record gap. The 271 ODIs played by New Zealand that he missed is also a world record.

One of the footballer's uncles – John Wilson – also played first-class cricket, appearing in 33 matches in which he secured 533 runs, average 13.66, and 90 wickets at 29.35. In his second first-class match for Otago, against Auckland at Dunedin in 1984-85, Wilson claimed what turned out to be his best innings-figures with both bat and ball, scoring 55 and taking 7 for 57.

● When James Packman received the call-up in 2004-05 to make his first-class debut for New South Wales, one of the first on hand to congratulate him was Wallabies flanker Phil Waugh. The rugby star stopped by at a practice session at the SCG nets on the first day of the NSW-Queensland match to offer support to his former school-mate.

Packman and Waugh had both played first-XI cricket together at Shore

Grammar in Sydney where, in Year 12, the footballer had captained his team to victory in the National Schools Championship. Packman also excelled at rugby, playing first-grade for the Gordon club as a halfback and five-eighth.

● Rugby union international Matt Dunning played cricket for North Sydney for a couple of seasons in the junior Green Shield competition, but decided his bulky frame might be better to suited to football. Dunning, who made his rugby Test debut in 2003, was a wicket-keeper in his youth: "**I had to give it away. I was 110 kilos at 16. I was never going to make it**."

● Former Brisbane Broncos player and rugby convert Berrick Barnes was a highly-rated wicket-keeper in his teens. He represented the Queensland under-15 and 17s sides.

● Freddie Brooks, who played rugby union for England, scored Zimbabwe's first-ever first-class fifty in the country's inaugural first-class match. No only did Brooks play cricket for Rhodesia, he also won the country's tennis championship and held national records in the high jump and sprint events.

On his first-class cricket debut, Brooks top-scored with 61 – batting at No. 3 – in the match against Transvaal at Johannesburg in the 1904-05 Currie Cup, and came up with another half-century (51) in his second, and final, first-class match, against H.D.G. Leveson-Gower's XI at Salisbury in 1909-10.

An outstanding rugby union three-quarter, the Indian-born Brooks played Currie Cup football, narrowly missing out on selection for a Springboks team that toured England. But he did manage to play *against* the Springboks, scoring England's only try in a 3-3 draw at Crystal Palace.

● Former England wicket-keeper Alec Stewart's father, Micky, who played in eight Test matches in the 1960s, appeared as an outside-right for the Charlton Athletic, Corinthian-Casuals and Wimbledon football clubs. His father's love of the game is one shared by Alec, who as a boy dreamt of being a professional footballer for his beloved Chelsea: "**I play on the right side of midfield in the David Beckham role. He says he plays in the Alec Stewart role. I played seriously until cricket took over. When I was a teenager, Dario Gradi was the youth team coach at Wimbledon. He gently told me he thought I would be better off going into cricket.**"

"Cricket ... it's rubbish. I simply don't like it. It's not a very emotive game. I don't think they look elegant in white, wearing trousers, long-sleeved shirts and jumpers when it's so hot."

Brazilian soccer star Juninho Pernambucano

"I'm probably the best Brazilian cricketer in the world because no one has actually heard anything in Brazil about cricket."

Adelaide United footballer Fernando Rech

● Norman Borrett, who played in one County Championship match, for Essex, in 1946, led England to a silver medal in hockey at the 1948 Olympic Games. Described by *The Times* newspaper as one of the country's greatest-ever amateur sportsmen, Borrett was highly proficient at tennis and golf and won the British Amateur Squash Championship on five consecutive occasions between 1946 and 1950.

Coincidentally, another first-class cricketer took out the squash title not too many years later. Alan Fairbairn, who uniquely struck centuries in his first two first-class matches for Middlesex, won the title in 1952, and successfully defended it the following year.

● Swiss tennis champion Roger Federer lists cricket as one of his favourite off-court pastimes, an interest he gained during his time with an Australian coach, Peter Carter. In 2005, Federer primed himself for the Wimbledon final with Andy Roddick by watching television coverage of the NatWest Series final between Australia and England at Lord's, before meeting several of the squad, including Adam Gilchrist, Glenn McGrath and Jason Gillespie, on match day. He was still talking to the cricketers five minutes before he went on court for his showdown with the second-seeded Roddick, which Federer won 6-2, 7-6, 6-4.

In Houston, Texas in 2004, Australia's Leyton Hewitt showed his prowess at cricket with an impromptu game using a tennis ball during a rain delay prior to his Masters Cup match with Federer.

"I really watch it just because it's relaxing, you know. I understand the rules. That's already something for a European. The other guys, all my friends, they don't understand the sport."

Roger Federer

"Why's that guy leaving? He can't just go. Is he fed up with it?"
American tennis champion Venus Williams watching a batsman after his dismissal in a club match in London in 2004

● An Australian Rules footballer who played baseball for Western Australia, Morgan Herbert came close to gaining Test selection in 1947-48 after taking 7 for 45 against the touring Indians in Perth. The slow-bowling Herbert was also a golfer of some note, achieving six holes-in-one.

● Jamaican speed merchant Asafa Powell was a fast bowler while at school, but later found fame in another arena. The sprint king won the 100 metres event at the 2006 Commonwealth Games in Melbourne after a drama-filled semi-final that featured a number of false starts and two disqualifications.

"It's a tough game, you know. But very slow."

Asafa Powell

● Keith Kildey, a competitor at the 1956 Olympic Games, once took the wicket of the great Len Hutton in first-class cricket. A right-arm medium-pace bowler born in New South Wales, his only first-class match was for Tasmania against the touring England side of 1946-47 at Launceston, where he claimed the wicket of Hutton for 51. Almost a decade later, Kildey was drafted into competing in the clay-pigeon shooting events at the Melbourne Olympics due to a lack of entrants, and came close to winning a bronze medal.

● Steve Waugh, who played soccer for Australia at schoolboy level, returned to the 'world game' after his retirement from Test cricket. Waugh turned out on a number of occasions for the Barden Ridge over-35s side in Sydney: **"I sort of lurk around the midfield."**

● The captain of the 1963 FA Cup-winning Manchester United appeared in a single first-class cricket match at Edinburgh in 1956. Representing Ireland, Noel Cantwell scored 31 and 17 not out against Scotland, but found greater fame as a soccer player, gaining 36 international caps and scoring 14 goals. A full-back, Cantwell made 248 appearances for West Ham United between 1952 and 1960, later switching to Manchester United.

● Coventry goalkeeper Steve Ogrizovic once lined up for a Minor Counties XI and bowled to champion West Indies batsman Viv Richards. A fast bowler, Ogrizovic came close to claiming the great man's wicket: **"I did bowl Viv Richards, but was no-balled. He was courteous enough to admit that he hadn't heard the call and not changed his shot. That was nice of him. Mind you, I think it upset him a bit and from then on he blazed away all over the ground."**
Ogrizovic appeared in 601 matches for the Coventry City club between 1984 and 2000, and played in the winning FA Cup team of 1987. In 1980, he opened the bowling for the Nottinghamshire second XI against Essex at Chigwell, taking 2 for 44 and 1 for 56.

● The father of swimming sensation Ian Thorpe was a cricketer of some standing in grade ranks in Sydney. Ken Thorpe played for Bankstown, opening for the club's first XI. Ken erected nets in the backyard for his then-eight-year-old son hoping to nurture a future cricketer, but soon realised that Ian's sporting prowess lay elsewhere: **"He was going to be a cricket player, but that didn't work out."**

● The year of 1877 not only saw the staging of the first cricket Test match, between Australia and England in Melbourne, but also the birth of the Wimbledon tennis tournament. Surrey batsman Spencer Gore, who was born at Wimbledon Common and appeared in five first-class matches, was the inaugural men's champion beating William Marshall 6-1, 6-2, 6-4. After losing the following year's final to Frank Hadow, 7-5, 6-1, 9-7, he then quit tennis, saying it was too boring.

● Champion batsman Mike Hussey almost chose another sport as a youngster, representing Western Australia at junior-level squash. He decided on cricket, preferring the team element of sport: **"The whole notion of winning together, losing together, celebrating together, and commiserating together. On the squash court there is just you and I battled with putting too much pressure on myself."**

● New Zealand's Don Cleverley, who played in two Test matches 14 years apart, was a national amateur boxing champion. His brother Alf boxed for New Zealand at the 1928 Olympic Games in Amsterdam.

● Victorian batsman and Aussie Rules footballer Roy Park headed the league's goal-kicking record in 1913 with 53, although his club, University, finished at the bottom of the ladder without a single victory the entire season. The full-forward possesses a Test batting average of 0.00 – he was bowled first-ball in his only innings during the second Test against England at Melbourne in 1920-21.

● Fiji batsman Nat Uluiviti, who played first-class cricket for his country and for Auckland in New Zealand's Plunket Shield, later starred as a rugby full-back. He scored 59 points on Fiji's tour of New Zealand in 1957, including a then-record six conversions in their 36-13 victory in the first Test against the Maori All-Blacks in Wellington.

● The 1.98-metre New Zealand all-rounder Jacob Oram, who made his Test debut in 2002-03, grew up in a region famous for its rugby, but pursued the sport of soccer as a youngster, reaching the New Zealand secondary schools team. He was, however, pursued year-in, year-out to take up the national game of rugby: **"When I was at school, every rugby pre-season coach would be in my ear trying to get me to play."**

● Two leading Australian cricketers had run-ins with prominent footballers during the year of 2006, with one coming to the aid of the other and defusing a potentially nasty incident in Cape Town. While touring South Africa with the Australian Test squad, Andrew Symonds had a difference of opinion with a Super 14 rugby player in a city nightclub, with both about to 'go outside' when Michael Clarke intervened: "**I was on my way out of the VIP area when Pup [Clarke] zoomed in to steer me away and calm things down. It was a sobering reminder that old-school ways where two men sort out their differences one-on-one are long gone.**"

A few months down the track it was Clarke's turn when Parramatta rugby league player Tim Smith was ejected from a hotel in Sydney after what was described as a 'minor misunderstanding' with the Australian batsman.

● Rugby league Test star, and occasional cricketer, Andrew Johns once recalled an encounter with Dennis Lillee when he, and team-mate Paul Harragon, spotted the former Australian bowler enjoying a beer at their local pub in Newcastle. After introducing themselves to the fast-bowling legend, the trio adjourned outside for a few hours of street cricket, using two bins for the stumps and a fence paling for the bat: "**It was gold, although I didn't want to face him. I was shitting myself, even though he was bowling with a tennis ball.**"

"I love cricket like you wouldn't believe. I'm always reading up on the players and checking out the stats. But it really blows me away when I look at the players now, and so many of them are absolute freaks. And then I realise that The Don was twice as good as them."

Andrew Johns

● Hayden Shaw, the leading goal-scorer for the New Zealand hockey team at the 2002 Commonwealth Games, later made the record books in cricket, achieving a match-winning haul of 5 for 14 in a limited-overs match for Canterbury. Regarded as one of the greatest drag-flick specialists in world hockey, Shaw made his first-class cricket debut in 1999–2000, and was a member of New Zealand's Olympic squad at Athens in 2004: "**I've had a huge amount of help with my cricket, and Canterbury Cricket has been exceptionally good to me. Hockey has become an all-year round sport and it means it's impossible to play both sports at the level I want. Looking further ahead, cricket certainly presents a challenge I want to take up. I would hate to finish my sports career wondering 'What if?'**"

● The New South Wales-born Test umpire Bill Alley, who remains the last batsman to have scored 3000 first-class runs in a season in England, was a middleweight boxer in his younger days, winning all 28 of his bouts. In a first-class career that began in 1945-46, Alley made 19,612 runs and claimed 768 wickets, mostly for New South Wales and Somerset.

"I had 28 fights and won the lot, but they were as much brawls as fights. I used to stare in the mirror the next morning surveying the damage and wondering what on earth my opponent must look like."

Bill Alley

● The brother of former Australian champion Test-match wicket-keeper Rod Marsh secured a 40,000-1 golfing feat in 2004, by achieving two aces on the same hole during the Senior British Open. The 60-year-old Graham Marsh secured two holes-in-one on the par-three 170-yard 11th at the Royal Portrush course in Northern Ireland, a feat unheralded in major tournament golf: "**This could just about take me out of professional golf. It's a freaky situation.**"

"I'd like to play on the seniors' tour one day. I've got a long way to go, but I reckon I could do it. I'm competitive at everything I do and golf is no exception."

Shane Warne

● Former Queensland team-mates Wade Seccombe and Clinton Perren are both BMX bike-racing champions. The wicket-keeping Seccombe won a title as a 13-year-old in Toowoomba, while Perren is a former national BMX champion in the side-cart class.

WOMEN AT THE WICKET

● Women's cricket created history in 2004 with England and New Zealand staging the first-ever Twenty20 international. The New Zealand women's team took the honours in the match at Hove, defeating England by nine runs. Back in 1973, the first women's World Cup was staged, preceding the inaugural men's event that was held in England in 1975.

Q. THE INAUGURAL MEN'S CRICKET WORLD CUP WAS PLAYED IN 1975. WHAT YEAR WAS THE WOMEN'S?

A. 1973

Female Cricketers. Eleven women of Lyndhurst and Minstead played other eleven of Poulner and Picket Post on Thursday, when the latter were victorious. The scene was a disgusting one and altogether discreditable to the district.

extract from a Hampshire newspaper, 1850

● During the 2003 Women's Cricket Council Trophy tournament in Holland, Japan marked its debut on the one-day international stage with an all-out total of 28, of which just eight runs came off the bat. After the openers Yuko Sasaki and Ema Kuribayashi both scored three, and Shizuka Kubota and Momoko Saito each contributed a single, the rest of the runs were delivered with the compliments of some wayward Pakistani bowling.

Although a standout statistic was the 12-year-old Sajjida Shah taking a career-best 7 for 4, Pakistan's attack conceded 17 wides, which represented 61.71 per cent of Japan's total, a world record. Pakistan's score of 181 was also boosted by a plethora of extras – 54, with 43 wides – but two days later Japan managed to double that effort with a staggering 104 extras – 67 wides – in 50 overs against The Netherlands (375-5) at Schiedam.

● Club cricketer Mark Barlow received an eight-week ban from playing in England's Bassetlaw League in 2004 after a disciplinary committee found him guilty of making sexist comments against a female player during a second-XI match. While Barlow and his Cutthorpe team-mates were celebrating a wicket in the game at Newark, he is alleged to have said:**"Come on, it's about time we got this woman out. She should be at home doing the washing up**."

The player in question, Kate Lowe, a former England representative, laid a complaint against Barlow which resulted in his banishment, and his team being docked six points:**"I cannot believe what has happened. Talk about a storm in a teacup. The comment I made was in a huddle with the players. There had been a bit of banter, but if you are a woman playing alongside men, you are going to get that. Neither umpire heard anything. It's PC gone bananas. What happens on the pitch should stay on the pitch. I apologised and shook her hand, but she got up on her high horse and got a bee in her bonnet. It is absurd and utterly ridiculous**."

● In 2004, a Chinese women's team, the Shanghai Pearls, hosted the country's first 'international' cricket match. Shanghai made 154 for 6 off 35 overs against the Hong Kong ladies national team, Michelle Richardson top-scoring with a match-winning unbeaten 52.

For Hong Kong, Sarah Eames claimed two wickets, with the opening combination of 14-year-old Betty Chan and Natasha Miles, 15, conceding just 35 runs between them from their 14 overs.

Shanghai, playing their first match outdoors, went on to claim victory by one run.

The victorious Shanghai Pearls women's team of 2004

● During the summer of 1974-75, a D. Rae and a J. Wilkinson came close to recording a 500-run partnership with an opening stand of 478 for Olympic against Melbourne. Their partnership was just a few runs shy of the best first-wicket stand by any openers in minor cricket anywhere in the world. In 1993-94, another two Victorian women – Jo Saliba and Bev Millichip – made the record books with a first-wicket partnership of 461 for Altona North against Essendon-Maribyronong in Melbourne. These two stands remain amongst the highest on record for any standard of women's cricket.

● Zoe Goss, who once famously took the wicket of West Indies batsman Brian Lara, posed naked – apart from some strategically-positioned cricket balls – for a sports magazine, *Total Sport*, during the summer of 1997-98. Regarded as a genuine all-rounder, Goss dismissed Lara for 23 in a celebrity-charity match – the Bradman XI v World XI – at the Sydney Cricket Ground in 1994-95.

The Goss dismissal of Lara mirrored a similar event involving Don Bradman himself in 1931. It was in a game at Newcastle between the Bradman Girls XI and McCabe's Girls XI that Eileen Thornton dismissed the great man for just 18.

● In 2004-05, Belinda Clark became the first female to appear in 100 one-day internationals when she captained Australia against India at Surat. During the 1997-98 World Cup, Clark plundered the highest-ever score by any player in a one-day international, with an unbeaten 229 against Denmark at Mumbai. Australia made 412 for 3 off its 50 overs and gained a massive 363-run victory, with Denmark dispatched for 49 in which no player reached double figures.

● Chasing a world-record total of 455 to win a one-day international at Christchurch in 1996-97, the Pakistan women's team was dismissed for just 47. The New Zealand total of 455 for 5 was the first total in excess of 400 in a women's one-day international, and their 408-run winning margin also established a new world record. This was not a good first-up overseas tour for the Pakistani women – they lost their inaugural one-day international by ten wickets after being rolled for 56 in 33.3 overs, suffered a loss to an under-17 team and failed to show up for a match against Canterbury. Things went from bad to worse when they continued their tour in Australia. In the first-ever one-day international between the two sides, in Melbourne, Australia made 397 for 4 off its 50 overs, then dismissed Pakistan – which could only field ten players – for a world-record low score of 23. Belinda Clark (131) and Lisa Keightley (156*) produced an opening stand of 219, while Pakistan's captain Shaiza Khan conceded 111 runs off her ten overs.

● Yorkshire's Kathryn Leng made history in 2001 when she became the first female cricketer to play in a university match in England, turning out for Leeds-Bradford. She hit the headlines again the following year when she was dropped, albeit temporarily, from the England one-day squad after taking an unauthorised holiday to Tenerife.

● Emma Liddell, a 15-year-old schoolgirl, took ten wickets in an innings, all bowled, without conceding a run for Metropolitan East in Sydney in 1995-96. In England in 1962, Rosemary White claimed all ten wickets in an innings, also for nought, for Wallington against Beaconsfield, emulating the feat of 15-year-old Rubina Humphries, who did the same for Dalton against the Woodfield Sports Club in 1931.

● When Australia and England met in a one-day international at Southampton in 1998, six members of the home team were run out. One of those to fall in such fashion was debutant Claire Taylor, who joined another similarly-named player in the side, Clare Taylor. Both players also represented their country in other sports – Clare appeared in World Cup cricket and football, while Claire played under-19 hockey for England.

● The first-ever Women's Test match, played between Australia and England at Brisbane in 1934-35, featured one bowler on each side taking seven wickets in an innings. England's Myrtle Maclagan marked her Test debut with 7 for 10 off 17 overs, while Australia's Anne Palmer countered with figures of 7 for 18 off 13.2 overs.

The scenario was repeated in 1957-58 when the two countries met in the second Test at Melbourne, with England captain Mary Duggan taking

The English women's cricket team in a reflective mood on their 1934-35 tour of Australia

7 for 6 and Australia's Betty Wilson 7 for 7, including a hat-trick. With a score of 100 in Australia's first innings, Wilson became the first cricketer – man or woman – to achieve the all-round feat of a century and ten wickets (11-16) in a Test match.

These four lots of seven-wicket hauls remained the best bowling performances in women's Test cricket until 1995-96, when India's Neetu David claimed eight in an innings. The left-arm spinner celebrated the 100th women's Test match with 8 for 53 against England at Jamshedpur.

● When Australia and England conducted the first-ever women's Test series, it featured the first set of twins to play Test-match cricket. The fast-bowling Fernie Blade (née Shevill), from New South Wales, appeared in her only Test match in the series-opener at Brisbane in 1934-35, while her twin sister Irene Shevill, a wicket-keeper, played in the remaining two Tests.

Their sister Essie Shevill, a spinner, also played in the series, winning caps for all three Tests. She, too, had a cricket-playing twin sister, Lily, who played for New South Wales.

● New South Wales twins Alex and Kate Blackwell emulated Steve and Mark Waugh in 2004-05 by becoming the second set of twins to play together for Australia. The sisters, from Wagga Wagga, played in the same match for the first time in the sixth one-day international against India at Vadodara – Kate, batting at No. 6, and Alex, at No. 7, scored 15 and 19 respectively.

The two made their first Test appearance together against England at Hove in 2005, with their first Test match together on home soil coming against India at Adelaide in 2005-06. Medium-pace bowler Jhulan Goswami dismissed both twins for a duck in the Adelaide Test, and in their following match – the first one-day international – dismissed Kate for another nought and Alex for one.

"The Blackwells are the future of not only women's cricket, but Australian cricket in general."

Steve Waugh

● In 1996, Charlotte Edwards became one of England's youngest Test cricketers when she was picked to make her debut at the tender age of 16. She opened the batting, scoring 34 and 31, against New Zealand at Guildford, having previously been the captain of the Huntingdonshire's under-16s boys' team: "**The things I had to put up with, playing in the boys team, weren't easy at all. I remember incidents where I would turn up and parents were going to pull their boys out of the game because they didn't want them to play against a girl. The opposition lads used to bowl beamers at me just to try and intimidate me, it was really quite hard. I'm not fazed by anything now after going through that. It makes you so much tougher**."

The day before her 18th birthday, Edwards scored 173 not out against Ireland at Poona in the 1997-98 World Cup, a record in one-day internationals until Australia's Belinda Clark made an unbeaten 229 against Denmark – at Mumbai – on the very same day.

● Slow bowler Holly Colvin was drafted into the England side for the first Test against Australia at Hove in 2005 after turning up to help out in the nets. Aged 15 years and 336 days, she became her country's youngest-ever Test player, taking three wickets on the opening day, and at one point was on a hat-trick. Her other claim to fame is appearing in the boys first-XI at Brighton College, emulating Clare Connor who went on to captain England.

"First, when you arrive at the ground, the whispers in the [male] opposition team go round. Then when I bowl at them they are nervous because they do not want to get out and they end up playing half shots. It is funny when they get out and you hear their mates taking the mickey."

Holly Colvin

● Clare Connor, who appeared in 16 Tests and 93 one-dayers for England, played alongside some legends of the game such as Sachin Tendulkar and

Aravinda de Silva in 2006, bowling her side to victory in two consecutive matches for the Lashings World XI. The first female player to represent the club, Connor took 5 for 36 against the Taunton School Invitational XI and then two days later snared 5 for 24 against the Sutton Valence School 1st XI.

In a previous match, one of Connor's former team-mates performed with great distinction *against* Lashings by scoring a half-century and taking two wickets. Charlotte Edwards – who succeeded Connor as England captain earlier in the year – scored 97 and claimed 2 for 37 for the Bunburys club in a match in Cambridgeshire, but Lashings still won, with Connor taking 2 for 9.

In 2005, and on the day of Don Bradman's birthday, Connor was captain of the England Test side when they defeated Australia at Worcester to take the 'Ashes' series 1-0, the first time they had won the event in four decades.

● The gloves came off when India toured England in 2006, with their captain Mithali Raj accusing her opponents of sledging and of being 'foul-mouthed'. Mithali also suggested that England's captain Charlotte Edwards was scared of the medium-pace bowler Jhulan Goswami: "**Jhulan was a nightmare for them, especially Edwards. They were so terrified of Jhulan that even if she bowled a full toss they never dared to hit that. Edwards was so scared after losing her wicket several times to Jhulan that she frequently changed her batting position. But I ensured that Jhulan greeted Edwards no matter when she came in.**"

● A 20-overs-a-side match at Chennai in India in the year 2000 provided the ultimate humiliation for the Cuddalore XI, with all of its members making ducks and the not-out batter also failing to disturb the scorer. The team was fortuitously able to escape the ignominy of a zero total, after the opposition – Chennai B – conceded six wides. One player did manage to hit the ball towards the boundary, but, just at that moment, developed cramp and was unable to run. In two previous matches, Cuddalore had managed totals of just 32 and 33, with 24 ducks in three outings.

● When the West Indies women's side took on Pakistan at Karachi in 2003-04, all of its players were making their Test debuts. Despite their lack of big-occasion experience, the tourists drew the match with wicket-keeper Nadine George becoming the first West Indian female to score a Test century (118). For Pakistan, its vice-captain Kiran Baluch opened the batting and matched George by scoring *her* country's first Test hundred, going on to make a double-century. Her mammoth 242 broke the record for the highest score by a woman in Test cricket, while Shaiza Khan, the captain, took the most wickets in a Test (7-59 & 6-167) and became only the second woman, after Australia's Betty Wilson in 1957-58, to take a hat-trick.

● Recognised as one of the highest-ever innings in the history of women's cricket, a 12-year-old girl hit an unbeaten 258 – with 16 sixes – in a 40-overs match played at her primary school in South Africa in 2002. Mignon du Preez performed the feat for Gauteng North's under-13s, having previously played for the under-19s and as an opener in boys' teams.

An indoor-cricket player of some note, Mignon once set a world record with Monique du Buys, posting a 114-run partnership in just four overs at the South African indoor championships. They twice broke the world record during the competition, with 102 against North West Province and then 114 the following day against KwaZulu-Natal.

● By scoring a match-winning 107 not out against India at Centurion in South Africa in 2004-05, Australia's Karen Rolton became the first player to hit a century in a women's World Cup final. The previous best was 91 by team-mate Belinda Clark against New Zealand at Lincoln in 2000-01.

"Nothing's changed. Life is back to normal. I've resumed my work at Australia Post where I work in the mail centre."

*Karen Rolton shortly after her match-winning century
in the 2005 Women's World Cup final*

● Former Sussex and Cambridge bowler Robin Marlar caused a stir upon his appointment to the MCC presidency in 2005 when he expressed indignation at the prospect of females playing cricket with men. His opposition was prompted by two schoolgirls, Holly Colvin and Sarah Taylor, named to play for the Brighton College XI: **"Girls? I think it's absolutely outrageous. The MCC's view is that mixed cricket at adult level doesn't happen. If there's an 18-year-old fast bowler who can bowl at 80 miles per hour and he's been brought up properly, then he shouldn't want to hurt a lady at any cost."**

"There is a terrific difference between social and competitive cricket. I do not see many men playing in women's league football."

Robin Marlar

"Robin is just being a gentleman. He just has some anxieties about a girl playing in a match which is reaching a tense conclusion and worrying if a male bowler will stick in a short ball."

former England captain Rachael Heyhoe-Flint

● Pakistan's Batool Fatima made four stumpings in a one-day international against the West Indies, at Karachi, in 2003-04, finishing the match with a record-equalling six dismissals. All four stumpings came off the same bowler, Urooj Mumtaz, who achieved a maiden five-wicket haul of 5 for 33.

The world record for most stumpings in a one-day international is five, by India's Venkatacher Kalpana, who gained six dismissals in all in the match, against Denmark in the 1993 World Cup. During the tournament, both Kalpana and New Zealand's Sarah Illingworth broke the world record for most dismissals in a match just 15 minutes apart. Kalpana only appeared in a total of eight one-day internationals for India, finishing with more stumpings (10) than catches (6).

● In 2006, Claire Taylor became the first female cricketer to pass 150 at Lord's, and only the second to score a century at the home of cricket. Taylor's unbeaten 156 in the first one-day international against India was higher than that of her opposition (153), whose cricketers were playing in their first-ever match at Lord's.

The first female to score a hundred at the ground was Australia's Lisa Keightley, who hit 113 not out against England in 1998. Coincidentally, Taylor's 156 not out matched Keightley's highest score at the same time (156★ v Pakistan at Melbourne in 1996-97).

● Cathryn Fitzpatrick, regarded as one of the fastest female bowlers in the world, was on hand to assist the Australian men's team in the one-day international series against a World XI in Melbourne in 2005-06. The 37-year-old's involvement in assisting the national coach John Buchanan caused some consternation among former fast bowlers, including Terry Alderman, and Geoff Lawson: "**It is bizarre. I don't know if Glenn McGrath or Brett Lee are going to pick up too much.**"

Fitzpatrick, who made her Test debut in 1990-91, became the first female to reach the milestone of 150 one-day international wickets, achieving the feat against Ireland at Dublin in 2005. The following year, she made history becoming the first female to play in a men's first-XI match in the Victorian Premier Cricket tournament. On her debut for Dandenong against Casey-South Melbourne in a Twenty20 match, she took 1 for 29 off four overs in a winning cause.

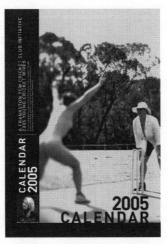

A calendar that formed part of a fund-raising initiative by the Frankston YCW Club in Victoria for the [Jane] McGrath Breast Cancer Foundation

TEAM SPIRIT

● After winning the toss and electing to field, Matabeleland lost its Logan Cup match against Mashonaland at Harare in 2000-01, falling for just 19 in 11.5 overs in its second innings. It was the lowest total in a first-class match in Zimbabwe and the lowest since Surrey made 14 against Essex in 1983. Bowling unchanged, Eddo Brandes' full analysis was 6-3-12-5, while Bryan Strang had figures of 5.5-3-6-5. But having recorded the lowest-ever total in first-class cricket in Zimbabwe, Matabeleland showed some pluck, making the highest provincial total in a first-class match in the country in their next innings. Batting against the CFX Academy at Bulawayo, Matabeleland amassed 508 for 9 declared, an innings that included centuries from Mluleki Nkala (168) and Heath Streak (119).

SHORTEST FIRST-CLASS TEAM INNINGS BY BALLS RECEIVED

Balls	Total			
53	15	Hampshire v Warwickshire	Birmingham	1922
57	26	Leicestershire v Kent	Leicester	1911
62	16	Warwickshire v Kent	Tonbridge	1913
67	26	England XI v Australians	Birmingham	1884
67	20	Derbyshire v Yorkshire	Sheffield	1939
69	12	Northamptonshire v Gloucestershire	Gloucester	1907
70	29	Sussex v Lancashire	Liverpool	1907
71	19	Matabeleland v Mashonaland	Harare	2000-01
72	16	MCC v Surrey	Lord's	1872
72	25	Gloucestershire v Somerset	Cheltenham	1891
73	15	Victoria v MCC	Melbourne	1903-04
75	30	South Africa v England	Birmingham	1924

● Chasing a humongous 612 runs for victory in a second-XI County Championship match at Taunton in 1997, Somerset came close to pulling it off, with one of its batsmen hitting more than half of the required runs.

Marcus Trescothick was the last batsman out, run out for 322, becoming the first player to score a triple-century in the competition's history. He struck 54 fours and three sixes, and with Michael Burns (68) – the only other batsman to pass fifty in the innings – took part in a third-wicket stand of 154. Earlier, Warwickshire's Mike Edmond clobbered an innings of 135, reaching 100 off just 48 balls, and achieved the most wickets in the match, taking 6 for 59 and 3 for 76, with his team snatching victory by just six runs.

● Two New South Wales imports played a major role in Scotland's history-making win over Northamptonshire in the 2006 C&G Trophy, one scoring a half-century, the other achieving a maiden five-wicket haul. Having triumphed over Worcestershire, Scotland won two matches in a row in a major competition for the first time, thanks to a 73 by Corey Richards and a 'Man-of-the-Match' 5 for 28 by Ian Moran. Batting first in a match reduced by rain, Scotland's total went past the 200-mark thanks to a massive six off the final ball by Queensland club cricketer Paul Hoffmann.

● When India played New Zealand in a one-day international at Bulawayo in 2005-06, only one batsman in the top four from either side was able to reach double figures. Indian opener Virender Sehwag made 15, while Jai P. Yadav and Irfan Pathan provided the first instance of a No. 9 and No.10 making fifties in the same innings of a one-day international. India's total of 164 became the lowest total to include a century partnership, with Yadav (69) and Pathan (50) putting on 118 for the ninth wicket. Yadav's 69 became the highest innings by a No. 9 batsman in one-day internationals, while Pathan's 50 was only the second half-century by a No.10.

● During the first Test against South Africa at Centurion in 2005-06, seven New Zealanders had a bowl in the second innings and each picked up at least one wicket. James Franklin took 2 for 60, Chris Martin 1 for 64, Kyle Mills 1 for 57, Jacob Oram 2 for 44, Daniel Vettori 2 for 42, Nathan Astle 1 for 15 and Scott Styris 1 for 3. This was only the fourth time that so many different bowlers had taken a wicket in a Test innings, and the first since Australia achieved the feat in 1966-67, also against South Africa, at Johannesburg.

● Despite losing its first three batsmen for a duck in the World Series Cup at Hobart in 1996-97, Pakistan went on to claim victory with Australia succumbing to its fourth consecutive loss in a one-day international. Openers Aamer Sohail and Zahoor Elahi, and the No. 3 Ijaz Ahmed, were each dismissed for nought as Pakistan spluttered to an all-out total of 149 which ended up being enough for a win, with Wasim Akram taking 3 for 13 and Shahid Afridi 2 for 1.

Australia was bowled out for 120 in 41.3 overs delivering Pakistan victory, despite conceding 28 extras – the 'top score' in the innings. Australia won just three of its matches in the tournament – which also featured the West Indies – failing to make the finals series for the first time since 1979-80.

● After Zimbabwe's Test stocks had been decimated in 2004 when most of the team withdrew their services in protest at selection policies, a second-string XI found itself in the record books after incurring two of the biggest Test floggings in history. Facing Sri Lanka in two Tests at home, Zimbabwe lost both matches by an innings margin – at the time, both defeats were amongst the worst twelve biggest Test losses by an innings margin of all time.

In the second Test, played at Bulawayo, Sri Lanka lost just three wickets in achieving its innings-and–254-run victory, with as many as six Zimbabwean bowlers conceding over 100 runs. The visitors piled on a record 713, thanks mainly to centuries from Marvan Atapattu (249), Kumar Sangakkara (270) and Mahela Jayawardene (100*). It signalled only the second occasion in Test history in which a country had achieved an innings-victory of over 200 runs after losing so few wickets. In the 2001-02 Asian Test Championship at Multan, Pakistan (546-3d) beat Bangladesh (134 & 148) by an innings and 264 runs inside three days, with a world-record-equalling number of batsmen (five) hitting centuries in the Pakistan innings – Saeed Anwar (101), Taufeeq Umar (104), Inzamam-ul-Haq (105 retired hurt), Yousuf Youhana (102*) and Abdul Razzaq (110*).

● When the West Indies went down to Australia at Bridgetown in 1990-91, they did so after all, but one, of its batsmen reached double figures. This was the first time in a one-day international that ten batsmen had gone past ten in the same innings. Jeff Dujon top-scored with 39, while the No.11 Courtney Walsh was the odd man out, scoring four.

● During the fourth Test against the West Indies at The Oval in 2004, every England batsman reached double figures in the first innings. The home-team made 470, with no batsman managing a century, the highest individual score being 72 by Andrew Flintoff, who went past 50 for the eighth Test running. It was the tenth occasion a side had finished an innings with all players passing ten, but the first time since Australia (471) did so against Sri Lanka at Colombo in 1992-93.

England's Oval performance also saw ten of its batsmen sharing in a 50-run partnership. Only Robert Key (10), who made the lowest score in the innings, missed out. It represented the first occasion in Test history of so many batsmen featuring in a half-century stand in the same innings, beating the record of nine, which had occurred on seven previous occasions.

● History was made on the second day of the second England-West Indies Test at Lord's in 2000 with wickets galore, one falling every 22 balls. For the first time in the history of the game, a part of all four innings took place on a single day. Dismissed on its overnight score of 267, the West Indies then bowled out England for 134 and replied with a measly 54, with the home-side none for none at stumps. The Test ended on the third day, with England limping home with two wickets to spare, after Curtly Ambrose had returned the extraordinary figures of 22-11-22-1.

● Both teams that contested the fourth Test at St John's in 2003-04 tied on the first innings. Australia was dismissed for 240, as was the West Indies. This was only the fifth occasion in history that a completed first innings in a Test match had been tied, but the first involving Australia – after England versus South Africa at Durban in 1909-10 (199), India against West Indies at Kanpur in 1958-59 (222), New Zealand versus Pakistan at Auckland in 1972-73 (402) and England against India at Birmingham in 1986 (390).

● During the 2004 County Championship, both Nottinghamshire and Warwickshire made the record books by posting totals in excess of 400 in six consecutive matches. Warwickshire went even further by stretching its record-run to ten successive matches. After scoring 546 against Surrey at Birmingham, they then made 600 for 6 declared against Sussex at Horsham, 405 against Worcestershire at Birmingham, 608 for 7 declared against Middlesex at Lord's, 524 against Northamptonshire at Birmingham, 499 versus Lancashire at Stratford-upon-Avon, 502 for 6 declared against Kent at Beckenham, 537 against Surrey at Guildford, 410 against Lancashire at Manchester and 457 versus Kent at Birmingham.

● Herschelle Gibbs established a world record against Pakistan at Sharjah in 1999-2000 by scoring a half-century in South Africa's all-out total of 101. While five of his team-mates made ducks, Gibbs carried his bat for 59, reaching his 50 off 62 balls with eight fours. The South African total became the lowest in the history of one-day international cricket to include a half-century, eclipsing the 123 made by Zimbabwe, also against Pakistan, at The Oval in the 1999 World Cup. Neil Johnson was the only batsman to shine hitting 54, as Saqlain Mushtaq chipped in with a match-winning hat-trick.

● Despite posting a record-breaking opening partnership in England's Northern Premier League in 2004, St Annes was sensationally beaten by Netherfield. Dismissed for just 35 in its previous match against Chorley, St Annes bounced back in spectacular style making 259 without loss, with former West Indies skipper Jimmy Adams making 142 not out and Danny Hagen an unbeaten 105. Netherfield, hunting its fifth crown in eight summers, knocked off the runs, reaching 260 for 3. Opening bowler Dale Benkenstein, who was dispatched for 95 runs, was at the crease with 29 runs beside his name when Netherfield reached its target.

● It was a slightly lop-sided affair in a match at Torquay in 1990, when Somerset meted out a 346-run thrashing of Devon in the NatWest Trophy one-day tournament. Somerset blasted a total of 413 for 4 off its 60 overs, which included a world-record 36-ball century to Graham Rose (110) and an unbeaten 162 by Chris Tavaré. In reply, Devon was skittled for just 67, with Dutchman Roland Lefebvre snaring 7 for 15.

● As many as six batsmen were dismissed for the score of two in the third Test between India and Australia at Nagpur in 2004-05. Three of the dismissals came consecutively in India's second innings from the much-vaunted middle-order trio of Rahul Dravid, Sachin Tendulkar and V.V.S. Laxman.

The triumvirate, which had haunted Australia in their previous two contests, failed to fire throughout the entire series, except for a brief spurt in the very final innings, in the fourth Test at Mumbai, where India's top-scorers were Laxman with 69, Tendulkar 55 and Dravid 27. All three ended the series with just a single half-century each, and none was able to establish an average of 30.00, with Dravid the best at 27.83.

Batsman & Series	Scores	T	100s	50s	Runs	Avge
Rahul Dravid						
India 2000-01	9, 39, 25, 180, 81, 4	3	1	1	338	56.33
Australia 2003-04	1, 43*, 233, 72*, 49, 92, 38, 91*	4	1	3	619	123.80
India 2004-05	0, 60, 26, 21, 2, 31*, 27	4	-	1	167	27.83
V.V.S. Laxman						
India 2000-01	20, 12, 59, 281, 65, 66	3	1	3	503	83.83
Australia 2003-04	75, 24*, 148, 32, 19, 18, 178	4	2	1	494	82.33
India 2004-05	31, 3, 4, 13, 2, 1, 69	4	-	1	123	17.57
Sachin Tendulkar						
India 2000-01	76, 65, 10, 10, 126, 17	3	1	2	304	50.66
Australia 2003-04	0, 1, 37, 0, 44, 241*, 60*	4	1	1	383	76.60
India 2004-05	8, 2, 5, 55	2	-	1	70	17.50

● Despite scoring a formidable 527 against Northamptonshire in 1995, Nottinghamshire went on to lose the County Championship match by an innings. Tim Robinson hit a double-century (209) opening the batting, while Graeme Archer made 158 at No. 3.

Northamptonshire responded with a whopping 781, its highest-ever first-class total, before declaring with seven wickets down, the innings studded with four centuries – 130 by Alan Fordham, 115 from Allan Lamb, 154 by Russell Warren and 114 not out by David Capel. Batting a second time, Nottinghamshire was bundled out for just 157 – with Anil Kumble taking 5 for 43 – to lose the match by an innings and 97 runs.

● At Georgetown in 1997-98, the fourth West Indies-England Test match ended without a single batsman being bowled. This was the first occasion in Test history where all 40 wickets fell without a batsman bowled – there were 29 catches, ten lbw's and one run out. In 2000-01, the third Test between Pakistan and Australia at Chennai saw a total of 38 wickets taken without a batsman bowled. Twenty-eight wickets fell to catches, seven to lbw decisions, while one batsman was run out, one was stumped and another dismissed 'handled the ball'.

● In the opening match of New Zealand's inaugural tour of Bangladesh, in 2004-05, as many 18 players were called on to have a bowl. The match against the Bangladesh Cricket Board XI at Savar featured ten of the local team bowling in the New Zealanders' second innings. The first-class record for most players bowling in a match is all 22 in the game between A.E.R. Gilligan's XI and the touring Australians at Hastings in 1964, while 21 players bowled in the match between the Maharashtra Chief Minister's XI and a Governor's XI at Pune in 1963-64.

● Venugopal Rao, with a total of 286 runs undefeated, was one of three batsmen to hit centuries for South Zone as they beat the touring England A side at Gurgaon in 2003-04, after being set what was presumed to have been an impossible target of 501 runs for victory. The England captain James Tredwell declared his second innings closed once the lead had reached 500, but the Indian batsmen made it home with ease, winning by six wickets, thanks to centuries from Rao (228★), Sridharan Sriram (117) and Subramaniam Badrinath (100★). South Zone broke the world record in losing the least number of wickets in reaching a 500-run target to win a first-class match.

● At Dhaka in 2000-01, Bangladesh captain Naimur Rahman celebrated his country's inaugural Test by claiming 6 for 132 in the first innings against India. His haul included the sought-after wickets of Rahul Dravid (28), Sachin Tendulkar (18) and Sourav Ganguly (84), recording the best bowling figures in a country's first Test match since Tom Kendall took 7 for 55 in the second innings against England at Melbourne in 1876-77. Earlier in the match, Aminul Islam made 145 in Bangladesh's first-innings total of 400 – the highest debut-century in a country's inaugural Test since Kendall's team-mate Charles Bannerman made 165 (retired hurt) at Melbourne in 1876-77.

● Victoria bounced back in sensational style against Queensland at the 'Gabba in 2004-05 to achieve the biggest comeback-win by a team in Australian domestic first-class cricket. After the home-side made 371 and dismissed the Bushrangers for 188, Jimmy Maher enforced the follow-on, only to see Jason Arnberger hit 152, Cameron White a maiden first-class century of 119 and Ian Harvey an unbeaten 90 batting at No. 8. White declared the innings closed at a mammoth 508 for 8 and witnessed history as Queensland crumbled to be all out for 169 in 59 overs: **"When you're dead and buried in the first innings and your back's against the wall, it's always great to have a really good victory like that."**

Victoria won the match by 156 runs, only the fourth occasion in the 112-year history of Australia's domestic first-class competition that a team has triumphed after being forced to follow-on. The Bushrangers did it again the following season, beating Tasmania after following on in a Pura Cup match at Bellerive Oval.

● Quick bowler Mark Ilott almost single-handedly demolished the Northamptonshire line-up at Luton in 1995, taking a record-breaking 9 for 19, including a rare all-lbw hat-trick. Ilott dismissed five batsmen leg-before for a duck, with Northamptonshire all out for just 46, their lowest total since 1946. Thirty wickets perished on the opening day of the match – the most in a day in the County Championship since 1960 – with Northamptonshire losing its last six batsmen for just one run.

Ilott backed up his nine-wicket haul with 5 for 86 in the second innings, yet ended up on the losing side, in a match in which neither side reached 200 – Essex 127 and 107, Northamptonshire 46 and 192 for 8.

● Faisalabad achieved victory in unexpected circumstances against Karachi during the 2004-05 Quaid-e-Azam Trophy, after their opponents refused to complete the match, claiming conditions were unsafe. After Shahid Nazir – who appeared in eight Tests for Pakistan in the 1990s

– claimed the top four in the order – all lbw – the opposing captain Rashid Latif declared the innings closed at 33 for 4.

Karachi conceded the match, with Rashid receiving a six-month ban and a $325 fine as a result: "**I didn't want any serious injury to take place. The pitch was not fit for a first-class match, and the batsmen were getting bat on ball with difficulty due to the unusual movement and variable bounce**."

● Set a target of 218 in 25 overs in a Ranji Trophy match in 1991-92, Madhya Pradesh went on the proverbial rampage, securing victory with 15 balls to spare. Having made 476 in its first innings against Vidarbha (190 & 503), MP reached its victory-target with a scoring rate of 161 per 100 balls faced. They were particularly savage on the opening bowlers, with Harvinder Singh – in his only first-class match – taking 2 for 79 off eight overs, and Prashant Vaidya, none for 35 off three.

In 1998, Leicestershire set off on an even more remarkable run chase, pursuing a target of 204 off 20 overs in the County Championship match against Northamptonshire at Leicester. Malcolm Devon was removed from the attack after just six balls, his first over costing 16 runs, while his opening partner, the Jamaican-born Franklyn Rose (9.1-0-93-3) went for more than ten runs per over, as did the only other bowler used, Paul Taylor (9-0-91-1).

Opener Vince Wells got Leicestershire off to a flying start, mauling Devon's opening spray reaching 50 in 25 balls, while Chris Lewis smashed an unbeaten 71 off just 33 balls, with four sixes and five fours: "**You could try that a thousand times and pull it off only once. We had nothing to lose, and the closer we got the more we started to believe that it was possible. The fact that we won, shows that the only limitations on this side are those that we place on ourselves**." Leicestershire crossed the line in 19.1 overs, a scoring rate of 177.

● After his opening partner Matthew Hayden made a duck against New Zealand at Auckland in 1999-2000, Damien Martyn carried his bat for a century, his first three-figure score in a one-day international. While passing the milestone of 1000 ODI runs, Martyn hit 116 not out with Australia falling for 191. Hayden, already humbled by a three-ball duck, was given the chance to bowl for the first time in his one-day international career and was creamed for 18 runs off his one over.

● Australia celebrated its inaugural Test match against the West Indies, in 1930-31, with a ten-wicket victory at the Adelaide Oval. Openers Bill Ponsford (92★) and Archie Jackson (70★) knocked off the 170 runs required for victory, establishing a Test record for the highest score to win a Test by ten wickets. In one-day internationals, the West Indies secured a ten-wicket victory over Pakistan at the MCG during the 1992 World Cup, having been set a target of 221. After Brian Lara retired hurt on 88, his opening partner Desmond Haynes, with an unbeaten 93, and Richie Richardson, 20 not out, guided their team home with three overs to spare.

● The only Test match of the 1887-88 season, played at the SCG, was the result of two English touring parties, one led by George Vernon, the other by Arthur Shrewsbury, combining to take on Australia. The fixture – which saw Australia dismissed for under 100 (42 & 82) twice in the same match for the first time – required the services of only seven bowlers, the fewest needed to take all 40 wickets in a Test match. Australia used four bowlers to dispose of England (113 & 137) – Charlie Turner (5-44 & 7-43), J.J. Ferris (4-60 & 2-43), Tom Garrett (0-5) and George McShane (1-39), while England needed just three – George Lohmann (5-17 & 4-35), Bobby Peel (5-18 & 5-40) and William Attewell (1-4).

● During the 2004-05 Pura Cup, South Australia became the first state in history to record a total of under 30 on three occasions in first-class cricket. Facing New South Wales at the SCG, South Australia was dismissed before lunch on the opening day for just 29 – its lowest total in a first-class match in nearly 50 years. No batsman reached double figures as Blues left-arm quick Nathan Bracken returned the stunning figures of 7 for 4 off seven overs, dismissing five South Australians for a duck.

The red-faced Redbacks total was the second-lowest in the history of the Sheffield Shield/Pura Cup, two runs off the record held by the same state, when it was consigned to the scrap-heap by the same opposition at the same venue in 1955-56, a match in which another fast bowler – Keith Miller – claimed seven wickets (7-12).

The Blues needed just 80 minutes and 89 balls to account for South Australia, the least number of deliveries required in a first-class match in Australia in a hundred years, Bracken claiming his seven wickets in 40.

After losing its opening Pura Cup match of the season, New South Wales went on to flog the South Australians by an innings and 133 runs, securing their third consecutive victory by an innings margin. The hat-trick of wins – against Western Australia, Victoria and South Australia – was only the second such achieved in Australian domestic first-class cricket, after Victoria did so in 1946-47.

● A team of Indian schoolboys climbed new heights in 2004 scaling the 1000-mark in a Harris Shield match, a record total which included a 500-run partnership. The Anjuman-I-Islam School registered the highest-known total in any class of cricket, finishing on 1121 for 6 declared – a score boosted by 132 penalty runs – against Thane Baptist School (46 & 145), which lost the match by an innings and 930 runs. Fifteen-year-old Shishir Tiwari, with 318, and Sufiyan Shaikh, 202 not out, put on a world-record fifth-wicket stand of 531 in less than five hours, while opening batsman Salim Ansari chipped in with a handy 287.

● When Australia hosted Pakistan in 1999-2000, two Test matches featured two batsmen from each side who had scored a century on their Test debuts. Mark Waugh and Greg Blewett had done so for Australia, Mohammad Wasim and Azhar Mahmood for the visitors. In the first Test at Brisbane, Waugh scored a neat 100 off 200 balls, while the two Pakistanis marked the occasion by each making a duck in the second innings.

● Every cricket team's worst nightmare became a reality for an English village club in 2006 when each member of Goldsborough was dismissed for a duck by Dishforth in a Nidderdale League match in North Yorkshire. Luckily the Goldsborough second-XI was spared further humiliation when the opposition let through five extras, and even they made hard work of the six-run victory-target, with both of its openers also making a duck.

For the winners, opening bowler Gavin Hardisty took 7 for 0 under the captaincy of Steve Wilson: "**I wouldn't have thought it possible if I hadn't seen it happen. It was really tough for them. Everything they hit just went wrong. Each of their batsmen was caught and there were chances for them to run now and again, but they didn't take them. The five runs they notched were byes and they left the field looking a bit dejected afterwards to say the least.**"

● New Zealand went into the first Test against Zimbabwe at Hamilton in 1995-96 with one of its most inexperienced bowling attacks, a line-up that included three debutants. Joining Chris Cairns and Dipak Patel were newcomers Greg Loveridge, Geoff Allott and Robert Kennedy. Loveridge, a leg-spinner, broke his thumb while batting in the first innings – retiring hurt on four – and never bowled a ball in what turned out to be his only Test match.

● In one of Test cricket's most one-sided contests, Zimbabwe was comprehensively thumped by South Africa at Cape Town in 2004-05, falling for its lowest-ever total of 54. In response, the South Africans stormed to 340 for 3 off 50 overs, setting up the biggest-ever lead (286) on the first day of a Test match, beating the record of 233 by England over Australia at Lord's in 1896. South Africa scored its runs at a record rate of 6.80 per over, feasting on the Zimbabwean attack after the tea break scoring 249 in 33 overs.

The Test was over in a flash with Zimbabwe incurring an innings defeat, and the match completed within two days. The only bright spot for the tourists came with the return to the fold of Andy Blignaut. In the second innings, the all-rounder smacked a 58-ball 61 batting at No. 9 – the lowest individual score in a Test match to include six sixes, beating Chris Cairns' innings of 69 against Australia at Wellington in 1999-2000.

● Pakistan was sent packing after four day's play at the WACA in Perth in 2004-05, with Australia gaining its biggest victory by a runs margin since it beat England by 562 at The Oval in 1934. The 491-run triumph over Pakistan came when the tourists were routed for 72, which followed a double dose of sub-100 totals – 59 & 53 – in the previous encounter between the two sides, at Sharjah in 2002-03. Pakistan earned another dubious distinction, becoming the first country to record two totals of under 100 in Tests in Perth, after a score of 62 in 1981-82.

With Australia's victory came another record for spinner Shane Warne. At the end of the match, his wicket-tally stood at 555, becoming the first bowler in Test history to accrue 400 wickets in a winning cause – a little over 72 per cent of his wickets had come in Tests won by Australia.

Australia's follow-up victory over Pakistan, in the Boxing Day Test match at Melbourne, saw it become the first country to record 300 Test wins. The second Test at the MCG was Australia's 661st overall, and at game's end, there were 300 victories since the inaugural Test in 1876-77, two tied results, 176 losses and 183 drawn matches. The nine-wicket MCG victory also gave Australia its fifth Test series of the calendar year – a first for any country in the history of the game (v Sri Lanka, away and at home, v India, away, and v New Zealand and Pakistan at home).

● The first three Pakistan wickets to fall in the second innings against Bangladesh at Multan in 2003 fell to catches by a substitute fielder. Each catch was taken by the same sub, fast bowler Mashrafe Mortaza.

● When England whipped Bangladesh in the two-Test series in 2005, the home-team included players from ten different counties. The first Test XI chosen for the Lord's match – which England won by an innings and 261 runs – comprised Marcus Trescothick from Somerset, Andrew Strauss from Middlesex, Yorkshire's Michael Vaughan and Matthew Hoggard, Warwickshire's Ian Bell, Surrey's Graham Thorpe, Lancashire's Andrew Flintoff, Kent's Geraint Jones, Worcestershire's Gareth Batty, Durham's Steve Harmison and Glamorgan's Simon Jones. The second Test at Chester-le-Street, where England triumphed by an innings and 27 runs, featured the same 11 players. England has on two occasions gone into a Test match with all players from a different county – the third Test against South Africa at Durban in 1930-31 and the third Test against the West Indies at Nottingham in 1950.

● When the West Indies took on South Africa at St John's in 2004-05, eight batsmen – four from each side – scored a century, a record number for a single Test match. Chris Gayle led the way with a triple-century

(317), becoming just the fourth West Indies batsman – after Garry Sobers, Lawrence Rowe and Brian Lara – to score a Test-match 300 and the first to do so against South Africa, beating Don Bradman's old mark of 299 not out at Adelaide in 1931-32. And while Gayle registered the 20th instance of a Test-match triple-century, his partner Wavell Hinds scored nought – the first instance of a 300 and a duck by an opening pair in a Test.

Ramnaresh Sarwan, Shivnarine Chanderpaul and Dwayne Bravo also reached three figures in the West Indies' mighty total of 747, which saw the South Africans providing only the fourth instance in Test annals of all 11 players bowling. Both Mark Boucher and Herschelle Gibbs were given their first-ever chance at the bowling crease in a Test match, with Boucher becoming just the ninth wicket-keeper to claim a Test wicket. Boucher had to wait 84 Tests and Gibbs 70 to bowl their first ball, breaking the previous mark of 68 Tests by Indian wicket-keeper Syed Kirmani. A total of 19 bowlers were used in the match, one off the Test record of 20 in the South Africa-England Test at Cape Town in 1964-65.

Earlier in the match, the Proteas skipper Graeme Smith and A.B. de Villiers became the first pair to each score a century at the top of the order in two consecutive Test innings. In the third Test at Bridgetown, Smith made 104 and de Villiers 178, coming back at St John's with innings of 126 and 114, respectively. The pair improved their best opening stand each time they batted in the series with 15 and 46 at Georgetown, 70 and 117 at Port-of-Spain, 191 at Bridgetown and 245 at St John's, with Smith scoring centuries in three successive innings.

● Bangladesh's two-Test series in England in 2005 was one of the most lop-sided meetings of all time, with the home-team needing just 380. 1 overs to wrap up the contest two-nil. England won both Tests by an innings margin, with Bangladesh dismissing the fewest number of batsmen ever in a two-Test series. They managed to take only six England wickets – Marcus Trescothick, twice, Andrew Strauss, twice and Michael Vaughan, twice.

● When Australia beat New Zealand in the first-ever Twenty20 international, at Auckland in 2004-05, they added the victory to its initial triumphs in the Test and one-day international arena. Australia had also played in and won the first-ever Test match, against England in 1876-77, and the first one-day international, also against England, in 1970-71.

"I don't even bother with it. It's rubbish."

Fred Trueman on Twenty20 cricket

"Youngsters need to learn good techniques ... they cannot do that by watching rubbish. There is nothing good about Twenty20 cricket. People who disagree don't know what they are talking about."

former West Indies speedster Michael Holding

"If one-day cricket was pyjama cricket, then Twenty20 is underwear cricket."

former Indian batsman Navjot Sidhu

● When Surrey took on Gloucestershire at Bristol in 2005, its first-innings total of 603 included seven batsmen who passed 50 but none who went on to make a century. Three made it into the eighties, including Pakistan import Azhar Mahmood with 89 at No. 7 and India's Harbhajan Singh, who struck 84, batting at No. 9. The total became the highest in County Championship cricket in England not to include an individual century, just behind the 605 made by Madhya Pradesh against Haryana at Rajnandgaon in 1998-99, in which the highest individual score was 90 by opener Jai P. Yadav.

● Australia staged an impressive comeback to claim victory over New Zealand at Christchurch in 2004-05, after Ricky Ponting had sent the opposition in to bat, for the first time in his captaincy career. On the back of Shane Warne taking five wickets in the second innings and a blistering Adam Gilchrist century, Australia triumphed for only the seventh time in its history after the opposition had scored 400 batting first.

Seven New Zealanders were dismissed lbw in their second innings of 131, equalling the Test record established by England against Zimbabwe at Chester-le-Street in 2003. With four batsmen given out leg-before in the first innings, the total of 11 broke the world record for the highest number of lbw dismissals by one team in a Test match. The previous mark of ten was also held by the Kiwis – against Pakistan at Lahore in 1996-97 – with New Zealand becoming the first country to twice finish a Test match with ten or more lbw's.

● When New South Wales declared its first innings against Tasmania at Hobart in 2003-04, it did so with the assistance of just one extra from the opposition. The Blues total of 453 for 5 included a record-breaking third-wicket partnership of 270 between Simon Katich (171) and Steve Waugh (157) and one leg-bye. In 2005-06, Queensland made 342 against South Australia at Adelaide – the second-highest innings total in Australian first-class cricket to include just one extra. The record belongs to Victoria, which made 287 – without the help of any extras – against Queensland at Brisbane in 1953-54, having made 285, against the same opposition and at the same venue, in 1951-52, again without the aid of a sundry.

● During the drawn second Test match at Christchurch in 1998-99, South Africa's lowest individual scorer made more runs than New Zealand's highest scorer. In South Africa's only innings of 442 for 1 declared, the lowest score was 65 by Gary Kirsten, whereas New Zealand's top score for the match was 56 by Matthew Horne.

● After just two days' play of the Pakistan-India Test at Lahore in 2005-06, four batsmen had scored a century, while four bowlers also had a century listed beside their name. Pakistan's first-innings total of 679 for 7 declared included hundreds from Younis Khan (199), Mohammad Yousuf (173), Shahid Afridi (103) and Kamran Akmal (102★), with India's bowlers suffering as a result – Irfan Pathan taking 1 for 133, Ajit Agarkar 2 for 122, Harbhajan Singh 0 for 176 and Anil Kumble 2 for 178.

Seeking to score back-to-back double-centuries against India, after an innings of 267 at Bangalore in 2004-05, Younis Khan became the first batsman in Test history to be run out for 199, while the always-flamboyant Shahid Afridi blasted a 78-ball century, which included a Pakistan-record 27 runs off a single over. Facing Harbhajan Singh, Afridi smacked four consecutive sixes, hankering to match Garry Sobers and Ravi Shastri in achieving six sixes in a first-class over: **"I thought the fifth ball will spin a bit, but it didn't because it had got wet after the fourth six.**

I didn't get hold of it and ended up getting a big leading edge."
Two runs shy of beating the Test record of 28 runs off an over, Afridi
became the first batsman in Test cricket to hit four sixes off the first four
balls of an over. All in all, Afridi collected seven sixes and seven fours off
80 balls.

With constant weather interruptions, India faced just 77.2 overs in
reply, but still managed over 400 runs in its only innings. Virender Sehwag
(254) became the third batsman of the match to reach triple figures in
less than 100 balls (93), registering the second-fastest 200 on record (182).
Rahul Dravid, in the unaccustomed role of opener, hit 128 not out and
with Sehwag built a stand of 410, four runs shy of breaking the the then
first-wicket partnership record of 413 between Pankaj Roy (173) and
'Vinoo' Mankad (231) against New Zealand at Chennai in 1955-56. With
Younis Khan and Mohammad Yousuf putting on 319 for Pakistan's third
wicket, the Sehwag-Dravid stand provided the first instance of two triple-
century partnerships in the same Test.

"No. I don't know anything about them. I haven't heard about them."
Virender Sehwag – when asked about the Indian Test-record opening
partnership held by Pankaj Roy and 'Vinoo' Mankad

"That Sehwag doesn't know who Pankaj Roy and 'Vinoo' Mankad are is nothing
short of shocking. It shows the growing lack of knowledge and awareness
about Indian cricketing history and tradition. We knew of them since our teens.
It was told to us by our coaches. It was the Mumbai tradition."
former captain Dilip Vengsarkar

The second Test at Faisalabad was another high-scoring affair, with
Pakistan's match-aggregate of 1078 runs (588 & 490) the highest in a
five-day Test match, while the combined total of 1702, the fourth highest
in Test history. By being dismissed for 588, Pakistan narrowly missed out
on becoming the first country to score 600-plus in three consecutive Test
innings, after totals of 636 for 8 declared against England at Lahore in
2005-06, and 679 for 7 declared at Lahore.

The match produced a bucketful of boundaries, with exactly 200
fours and a record 27 sixes, beating the 23 by New Zealand and England

at Christchurch in 2001-02. Six individual centuries were scored at Faisalabad – matching the six scored in the first Test at Lahore – with nine instances of a bowler conceding 100 runs in an innings, another world-first.

After starting the third Test at Karachi in absolute tatters, Pakistan went on to achieve one of its biggest-ever Test victories. Irfan Pathan began proceedings by becoming the first bowler to claim a hat-trick in the first over of a Test match, dismissing Salman Butt, Younis Khan and Mohammad Yousuf with his fourth, fifth and sixth deliveries. In a matter of moments, Pakistan was 0 for 3 – one of the worst-ever starts to an innings in Test history – and then 39 for 6.

With an eventual first-innings total of 245, Pakistan stormed back in the second with 599 for 7 declared, their third total in excess of 500 in five innings of the series. For the first time in a Test match, the top seven batsmen in the line-up all scored a half-century – Salman Butt with 53, Imran Farhat 57, Younis Khan 77, Mohammad Yousuf 97, Faisal Iqbal 139, Shahid Afridi 60 and Abdul Razzaq 90. Set an improbable 607 for victory, India was all out for 265 with Pakistan gaining victory by 341 runs and taking the series 1-0.

Three individual centuries were scored at Karachi, taking the three-Test series' total to a record-equalling 15, with Pakistan's ten a new record for any one side in a three-match series. A total of 49 sixes was struck, eclipsing the previous record of 40 in a three-match contest, between New Zealand and England in 2001-02.

Pakistan's top seven players all posted a batting average of over 50.00 in the series – Younis Khan 110.60, Kamran Akmal 97.67, Mohammad Yousuf 92.20, Faisal Iqbal 72.00, Shahid Afridi 66.00, Inzamam-ul-Haq 60.00 and Abdul Razzaq 51.00 – a world first.

● When New Zealand took on the West Indies at Auckland in 2005-06, just 12 runs separated all four completed innings. The home-side claimed its tightest-ever margin of victory in a Test match after scoring 275 and 272 and disposing of the visitors for 257 and 263. The win came on the 50th anniversary of their country's first-ever Test victory, against the same opposition, and at the same venue. On the very same day half-a-century before, New Zealand (255 & 157-9d) had defeated the West Indies (145

& 77) at Eden Park to secure their first win at Test-match level after a record 45 attempts and 26 years.

● The Nondescripts Cricket Club belied its name in a Twenty20 match in Colombo in 2005-06, smashing a domestic-record 245 runs against the Sri Lanka Air Force Sports Club. Test wicket-keeper Kumar Sangakkara belted 93 off 49 balls, while Kosela Kulasekara whacked 98, also off 49 deliveries. Their match-winning total of 245 for 4, scored at a rate of 12.25 runs per over, included 12 sixes, with eight coming off the bat of Kulasekara.

In the same season, Victoria was crowned the inaugural Australian Twenty20 winners with a double-figure run rate in the final against New South Wales at North Sydney Oval. Led by a 54-ball century from Brad Hodge (106), Victoria piled on 233 for 7 at 11.65 runs per over, with the Blues all out for 140 in reply.

Hodge's Victorian team-mate Cameron White (116*) and WA's Justin Langer (90) launched an astonishing assault on English county side Gloucestershire a few months later, guiding Somerset to a record-high total of 250 for 3 in the Twenty20 Cup at Taunton. The first time 250 had been achieved in any Twenty20 match in the world, White reached his hundred off 48 balls in 54 minutes, hitting nine sixes and seven fours off a total of 53 deliveries while sharing in a 186-run second-wicket partnership with Langer.

"I've never played a Twenty20 game before. I've watched it a few times on telly and if they can be all that much fun, I might play until I'm 50."

Justin Langer – after scoring 90 on his Twenty20 debut

● A rampant Waqar Younis was in full swing in the 1989-90 Austral-Asia Cup first semi-final at Sharjah, taking 5 for 20 and consigning New Zealand to an all-out of just 74. Andrew Jones, the last batsman dismissed, shone with a defiant 47, while the rest of the team surrendered with scores of 5, 1, 4, 0, 4, 4, 0, 1, 0 and 0 not out.

● On its way to a four-wicket victory over Gujranwala in Pakistan's Quaid-e-Azam Trophy in 1997-98, Lahore City's first-innings total of

502 for 8 declared was ably assisted by a world-record-number of extras. Gujranwala conceded a hefty 99 sundries in the innings, with 64 no balls, 16 wides, ten leg-byes and nine byes.

Essex came close to matching the record in 1999, with 98 extras (48 no-balls, 17 byes, 17 leg-byes, 16 wides) in the first innings of the County Championship match against Northamptonshire (579) at Northampton. The home-team went on to gain an innings victory over Essex, despite six of the first seven batsmen in its line-up failing to reach double figures. Of the recognised batsmen, only David Sales (303*) went past ten, becoming the youngest Englishman, at 21 years and 240 days, to score a first-class triple-century.

● A team of up-and-comers from around the states toured Africa in 2006 and returned home a happy bunch, with six wins from six games. In the first of three limited-overs matches against Kenya, the Australian Academy XI gained a ten-wicket win thanks to openers Tim Paine (66) and Shaun Marsh (70), with the second game another one-sided affair. The Academy made 404 for 3, which included an unbeaten 207 from Marsh, who clobbered 12 sixes and 17 fours, in a second-wicket stand of 274 with Tasmania's George Bailey (152).

The second match against a Zimbabwean Board XI in Harare saw victory in the bag by a margin of 201 runs after Bailey hit 116. In the third match, Bailey then hit a scorching 136 off just 65 balls, with ten sixes and 14 fours. A former national under-19 representative, Bailey is related to the Sri Lankan-born George Bailey, who was part of the Australian squad that toured England in 1878.

● Kenya opened the President's Cup one-day international series in 1997-98 with a 150-run victory over Bangladesh at Nairobi, thanks to both of its openers scoring a century and its captain achieving a five-wicket haul. Dipak Chudasama, with 122, and Kennedy Obuya 144, combined for a then world-record opening partnership of 225, while Aasif Karim bowled his side to victory with 5 for 33. The first bowler to take five wickets for Kenya in a one-day international, he also became the first, and to date only, player to get a 'five-for' in his first match as captain.

● The opening match of the 1997–98 Wisden Trophy came to an abrupt end on the opening morning when play was abandoned after 90 minutes. After England's batsmen had been hit seven times in the first ten overs of the match at Sabina Park in Kingston, play was called off after 56 minutes to assess the pitch with the visitors teetering at 17 for 3. The shortest Test match in history, it lasted just 61 deliveries, before the umpires called off proceedings.

● The tiny island-state of Singapore took a big step in 2002 when its national cricket team amassed a record total of 440 for 2 off 50 overs in the Asian Cricket Council Trophy tournament. The hosts bludgeoned their opponents Thailand, with openers Zubin Shroff (159) and Kapila Mendis (191) both scoring centuries in a gargantuan first-wicket stand of 334. Singapore claimed victory by 325 runs, after bowling out the Thais for just 115.

The Singapore Cricket Club playing fields dwarfed by the city's skyscrapers

● After beating Zimbabwe by an innings in its two Tests of 2005–06, New Zealand went on to amass, what was at the time, the highest-ever total in a one-day international involving Test-playing countries. In the opening match of the Videocon Triangular Series, played at Bulawayo – which means 'place of slaughter' – the Black Caps raced to 397 for 5 off just 44 overs, based on a New Zealand-record opening stand of 204 between Lou Vincent (172) and Stephen Fleming (93). It was Vincent's maiden century in a one-day international, obliterating by more than a hundred runs his previous best, an innings of 60 not out against the West Indies at Gros Islet in 2002. He also established a new record high for a New Zealand batsman, beating Glenn Turner's unbeaten 171 against East Africa at Birmingham in the 1975 World Cup. The NZ total came at the high-voltage rate of 9.02 runs per over and contained 16 sixes.

Three weeks previously New Zealand (452-9d) had posted its biggest-ever win in Test cricket after its massacre of the Zimbabweans by an innings and 294 runs – within two days – in the first match at Harare. The home-team was dismissed for totals of 59 and 99, becoming only the second country to be bowled out twice in a day, following India's 58 and 82 against England at Manchester in 1952.

"Most teams, you know, only the next player to bat puts pads on. With Zimbabwe, everyone puts pads on."

a Zimbabwe supporter after his country's massive Test losses to
New Zealand in 2005-06

● After the first 2348 one-day internationals no side had ever reached 400 in an innings. But that all changed, and dramatically so, in 2005-06, when two countries – both wearing green-and-gold – broke the barrier in the same match. Meeting in a series-decider (2-2) at Johannesburg, South Africa posted an audacious 438 for 9 to overtake Australia's 434 for 4 and take the match by one wicket with one ball to spare.

The Johannesburg thriller saw a total of 872 runs scored, beating the previous high in a one-day international of 693, when India (349-7) defeated Pakistan (344-8) by five runs at Karachi in 2003-04. It was also the highest-scoring aggregate in any limited-overs match, beating the 867 runs scored by Surrey (438-5) and Glamorgan (429) at The Oval in 2002.

After winning the toss and batting, Australia became the first country to reach 400 in a ODI, with the top four batsmen in the order all passing fifty – Adam Gilchrist made 55 (off 44 balls), Simon Katich 79 (90), Ricky

Ponting 164 (105) and Mike Hussey 81 (51). By the tenth over, Australia was none for 66. It was only nine days previously that they had struggled to make just seven runs in the first ten overs of the second match at Cape Town – the worst start by any country in more than 1000 previous one-day internationals.

Facing what was presumed an impossible victory-target of 435, the Proteas made the highest total batting second and winning a one-day international, erasing the recently-set record established by New Zealand (332-8) against Australia (331-7) at Wellington earlier in the summer. Herschelle Gibbs struck a match-winning 175 off just 111 balls, with a record 126 runs in boundaries – 21 fours and seven sixes – and getting his hundred off 79 balls. His 150 was reached in 100 balls, one delivery more than Ponting, who earlier had brought up his 100 off 71 deliveries. Gibbs' 175 and Ponting's 164 represented the first occasion that one batsman from each side had both scored 150 in a one-day international.

For the first time in ODI history, over 500 runs in boundaries were scored in a match, with a record number of fours (87) and sixes (26). The total of boundary-runs was a massive 504, smashing the previous match aggregate of 386 (65 fours & 21 sixes) shared by New Zealand and Australia at Christchurch three months previously.

Of the six bowlers employed by Australia, only Michael Clarke – with 1 for 49 off seven overs – avoided conceding 50 runs, with Mick Lewis (10-0-113-0) becoming the first bowler to shed 100 runs in a 50-overs one-day international: **"It's not like I bowled a heap of pies. I actually bowled quite well. It was just one of those freaky games. I wouldn't have bowled ten overs if I was bowling a heap of crap. I'm not a selector, but they're in the job for a reason, they're smart and I'm sure they don't just look at one game and say 'He's not up to it'."**

With a one-wicket victory gained by Australia in the previous match at Durban, South Africa's win in Johannesburg provided the first instance of two successive one-day internationals with such a slender margin of victory.

● A record four batsmen scored 150-plus in a first-class innings in 2005-06, when Queensland plundered a massive 900 for 6 declared against Victoria in the final of the Pura Cup at the 'Gabba in Brisbane. Sealing its sixth domestic title, after its first in 1994-95, the Bulls registered the highest total in first-class cricket in Australia since Victoria reached the 1000-mark against New South Wales in 1926-27.

Captain Jimmy Maher made 223, Martin Love 169, Shane Watson retired hurt with cramp on 201 and Clinton Perren struck 173, while a record-equalling number of bowlers (5) – Mick Lewis (1-156), Dirk Nannes (3-150), Shane Harwood (0-152), Jon Moss (0-108) and Cameron White (0-139) – conceded over 100 runs with the ball.

After being outclassed in the previous competition final – bowled out for 102 in the first innings by New South Wales – the Bulls commanded a 556-run first-innings lead over Victoria, powering its way into the top-dozen highest totals in all first-class cricket. This was the eighth time in a row Queensland had made the final of the Sheffield Shield/Pura Cup, and avenged the last occasion the two sides met in the decider, when Victoria posted a match-winning 710 against the Bulls at the MCG in 2003-04. Maher was captain in that match as well, one in which he made a second-innings duck: **"We'll never forget that day in Melbourne. We copped it left, right and centre. We were cooked. That day in Melbourne, I said I knew what it felt like to be a real bull because all we did was look at grass. They ran into a Queensland side** [this time] **that was hungrier than you've ever seen. The last side that was this hungry was in 1994-95 and we'd never won it then."**

With the dismissal of Andy Bichel for just three, the Bulls total stood at 878, the highest score at the fall of the fourth wicket in first-class history. Queensland went on to win the match by an innings and 354 runs, Victoria's biggest-ever defeat in Sheffield Shield/Pura Cup cricket.

HIGHEST SCORE AT THE FALL OF EACH WICKET IN A FIRST-CLASS MATCH				
1	561	Karachi Whites (561-1d) v Quetta	Karachi	1976-77
2	618	Delhi (637-3d) v Himachal Pradesh	Delhi	1994-95
3	778	Maharashtra (826-4d) v Kathiawar	Pune	1948-49
4	878	Queensland (900-6d) v Victoria	Brisbane	2005-06
5	921	Sri Lanka (952-6d) v India	Colombo	1997
6	941	Hyderabad (944-6d) v Andhra	Secunderabad	1993-94
7	956	Victoria (1059) v Tasmania	Melbourne	1922-23
8	1043	Victoria (1107) v New South Wales	Melbourne	1926-27
9	1046	Victoria (1107) v New South Wales	Melbourne	1926-27
10	1107	Victoria (1107) v New South Wales	Melbourne	1926-27

● In the fifth Test at Kingston in 2000–01, all eleven South Africans featured in the dismissals of the West Indies in their second innings. Allan Donald, Shaun Pollock, Jacques Kallis, Paul Adams, Justin Kemp and Lance Klusener each took at least one wicket, while Mark Boucher, Daryll Cullinan, Neil McKenzie, Herschelle Gibbs and Gary Kirsten all took catches. This was the first occasion in Test history where all players from one side rate a mention on the same scorecard.

● When the West Indies took on Pakistan in the third final of the 2000 C&W One-Day International Series at Port-of-Spain, the visitors limped to the victory-target of 115 in an excruciatingly-patient 45.1 overs. Inzamam-ul-Haq's 39 not out off 98 balls was the highest individual score on either side, with the Pakistani run rate of 2.57 the lowest for a team securing a one-day international victory.

The lowest run rate in any one-day international occurred in 1979 when Canada made 45 off 40.3 overs – a run rate of 1.11 – against England at Manchester. In Test-match cricket, the lowest is 0.70, when Australia made 27 for 5 off 38.1 overs in the fourth innings of the drawn fifth Test against England at The Oval in 1956.

SLOWEST TEAM RUN RATES IN A TEST INNINGS
Qualification: 10 overs

RR	Total	Overs				Result
0.70	27-5	38.1	Australia v England	The Oval	1956	D
0.76	69-6	90	New Zealand v Pakistan	Dhaka	1955-56	D
0.96	26	27	New Zealand v England	Auckland	1954-55	L
1.00	17-1	27	New Zealand v West Indies	Auckland	1951-52	D
1.00	48-8	48	New Zealand v England	Christchurch	1965-66	D
1.00	187	185.3	India v West Indies	Bridgetown	1961-62	L

● A 45-overs match played in California in 2006 made the record books with a 600-run team total, an individual triple-century and a hat-trick. Shabir Mohammed, representing the United Cricket Club, smashed a record score of 353 not out in a total of 630 for 5 against Bay Area. After ten overs, United had scored 130 runs without loss, by 20 overs the scoreboard read 259 for 1, they had 378 runs in the bank by 30 overs and 529 runs after 40. In reply, the Bay Area XI went kaput, all out for 181, with United opening bowler Ashok Kumar starring with a hat-trick.

● During a one-day international against India at Napier in 1998-99, three consecutive New Zealand wickets fell to run outs. A total of five Kiwis were run out in their total of 213, and with three Indians also succumbing to this mode of dismissal, the total of eight run outs constituted a world-record number in a one-day international.

Australia suffered a similar fate during the VB Series finals against Sri Lanka in 2005-06, losing five of its batsmen to run outs in the match in Adelaide, with a record four credited to Tillakaratne Dilshan.

● Chasing a fairly insignificant total of 134 for victory against South Australia at Adelaide in the 2006-07 Pura Cup, New South Wales lost its first four wickets with just one run on the board, with all four out for a duck. A total of six batsmen failed to get off the mark as the Blues scraped home thanks to Stuart Clark, who scored a maiden first-class fifty. After taking 6 for 39 in South Australia's second innings, Clark ripped his way to 62, scored off just 37 balls with three fours and four sixes.

● When England took on Sri Lanka at home in 2006, a trio of left-handers occupied the top of both batting orders in each of the three Tests. This was a first in Test-match cricket, with England's Marcus Trescothick, Andrew Strauss and Alastair Cook and Sri Lanka's Jehan Mubarak, Michael Vandort, Upul Tharanga and Kumar Sangakkara the batsmen concerned.

● After being routed for 192 by England at Lord's in 2006, Sri Lanka bounced back scoring 537 for 9 following on and drawing the match. After four of the Sri Lankans made ducks in the first innings, seven scored fifties in the second, matching the record set by Australia at Old Trafford in 1934 and equalled by Pakistan against India at Karachi in 2005-06. All the Sri Lankans scored better in the second innings than they did in the first, providing only the third instance of such a feat in Test cricket, after the South Africans (30 & 390) did so against England at Edgbaston in 1924, and when England (75 & 475) came back stronger in the second innings against Australia at Melbourne in 1894-95.

It was Sri Lanka's highest second-innings total in Test cricket and provided just the tenth instance of a team scoring more than 500 after following on. Coincidentally, the previous occasion occurred when the two sides had met at the same venue in 2002 – Sri Lanka making 555 for 8 declared and 42 for 1; England 275 and 529 for 5 declared.

After winning the third Test at Nottingham, and taking the inaugural Twenty20 match between the two countries, Sri Lanka then blitzed England 5-0 in the ODI series to end the tour with seven international wins in a row. In the final match, at Leeds, the Sri Lankans successfully hunted down England's victory-target of 322, with their openers setting a new high for the biggest opening stand in a one-day international. Upul Tharanga, with 109, and Sanath Jayasuriya, an imperious 152, wrecked England with a first-wicket partnership of 286 that beat the previous high of 258 by India's Sourav Ganguly (111) and Sachin Tendulkar (146) against Kenya at Paarl in 2001-02.

Both of the Sri Lankans got to their hundred in fewer than a hundred balls, with Jayasuriya doing so in 72 and Tharanga 82. Having reached his 50 off just 26 balls, which included nine fours and a six, Jayasuriya – on the day after he celebrated his 37th birthday – swept his way to the 150-mark off a mere 95.

By the end of the second over the two left-handers had already stamped their authority on proceedings with 28 runs on the board. They brought up the 100 in eight overs; after ten overs were 94 ahead of England at the same stage, and reached the 250-run milestone in 26.1 overs. Steve Harmison was picked on, becoming the first England bowler to concede 90 runs in a one-day international innings, his none for 97 off ten overs the worst since Derek Pringle's none for 83 against the West Indies at Gujranwala in the 1987 World Cup.

Sri Lanka reached the target of 322 with just the two wickets down and had more than 12 overs up its sleeve as England recorded its first 5-0 drubbing in a head-to-head one-day international series. And, for good measure, Sri Lanka then thumped The Netherlands in a one-day international a few days later at Amstelveen piling on 443 for 9 off its 50 overs. Jayasuriya became the first batsman to score back-to-back 150s in one-day internationals belting 157 off the Dutch side to follow his 152 three days previously at Leeds.

Jayasuriya's hundred at Headingley included 104 runs in boundaries – 20 fours and four sixes – while his hundred in Holland also contained a century in boundaries, with 24 fours and a six. To add to his ever-burgeoning list of achievements, Jayasuriya ventured past the milestone of 11,000 one-day international runs in what was his 363rd match, which, at the time, represented a world-record number of ODI appearances.

● Sri Lanka kicked off the 2006 Test series against South Africa with a bang, batting through an entire day's play, scoring 300 runs and not losing a single wicket. After collecting a rather sedate 128 runs for two on the opening day of the opening Test at Colombo, Sri Lanka let loose on the second, matching the West Indies' 1957-58 record against Pakistan of 357 runs at Kingston. The stars of the day were Sri Lanka's captain Mahela Jayawardene, and Kumar Sangakkara who went on to become the first pair in first-class history to stack on 600 runs in partnership, with the tourists reaching 756 for 5 declared.

After hogging 157 overs between them, their third-wicket stand ended at a monumental 624, with Sangakarra scoring 276 and his skipper 374, breaking the 340-run record of team-mate Sanath Jayasuriya. It was also the highest Test score by a right-handed batsman, beating the 68-year-old record of England's Len Hutton, who hit 364 against Australia at The Oval in 1938.

Having come to the crease with Sri Lanka wobbling at 14 for 2, Sangakkara and Jayawardene went on to break the long-standing first-class record of Baroda's Vijay Hazare (288) and Gul Mahomed (319), who put on 577 for the fourth wicket against Holkar in 1946-47. For the South African bowlers, one to suffer in particular was Nicky Boje, who became the first spinner to concede 200 runs in a Test innings without taking a wicket. He sent down 65 overs, with five maidens, and conceded 221 runs: **"I've bowled worse in my life and taken five wickets. I actually felt that I bowled quite nicely here and there's been no reward for it. It's hard if you bowl 65 overs and you don't take a wicket. But you can't take it away from Sangakkara and Jayawardene. They played awesome cricket. They just kept scoring runs all the time."**

● When Tasmania hosted Queensland at Hobart in the 1995-96 Sheffield Shield, only four wickets fell on the first three days while over 900 runs were scored. Dene Hills scored an unbeaten 220 at the top of the order for Tasmania – his maiden first-class double-century – while

Matthew Hayden (152*) and Martin Love (185*) put together a record second-wicket stand of 368 for Queensland. Ricky Ponting hit two unbeaten centuries (118* & 100*) in the match, his second coming off 97 balls, while Stuart Law (107*) also scored a hundred for the visitors.

An extraordinary six not-out centuries came in the match, with 1385 runs scored in total for just 11 wickets – the average of 125.91 runs per wicket setting a new record in Australian first-class cricket. The world record remains 189.14 runs, when Cambridge University (594-4d) took on the touring West Indians (730-3) at Fenner's in 1950. Five batsmen scored centuries in the three-day match with an aggregate of 1324 runs and just seven wickets, Everton Weekes contributing an unbeaten 304.

● After falling for a meagre total of 180 in the first Test at Perth in 1981-82, Australia struck back in devastating style, blowing away Pakistan for just 62 in 21.2 overs. Thanks to Dennis Lillee, who took 5 for 18, and Terry Alderman, 4 for 36, Australia was able to achieve the highest first-innings lead (118) ever seen in a Test match for a side scoring 200 or less. Alderman came up trumps with his very first delivery in a Test match in Australia by dismissing Rizwan-uz-Zaman for a duck, while Lillee became the first Australian fast bowler to achieve five wickets in an innings 20 times.

In 2006, India (200) concocted a first-innings lead of 97 over the West Indies (103) in the fourth Test at Kingston, with Harbhajan Singh taking 5 for 13 in a 27-ball spell at the crease. The 97-run lead was second on the list behind Australia, with Singh's strike rate of 5.40 one of the best efforts for a bowler taking five wickets in a Test-match innings. His spinning team-mate Anil Kumble finished off the Windies in the second innings, taking 6 for 78, having become only the second player, after Shane Warne, to reach the Test double of 500 wickets and 2000 runs.

● Kenya won the third match of the Associates Tri-Series in 2006-07 when Canada failed to field an eleven. For the first time in Test or one-day international cricket history, a match was forfeited because one side couldn't get a team together. At least five of the Canadian squad reported in sick, with what was later diagnosed as a viral stomach condition.

● South Africa twice scaled the 400-mark in one-day internationals during the calendar year of 2006, achieving the unique feat in the space of just four matches. Having taken 438 for 9 off Australia at Johannesburg in March, the South Africans then chiselled 418 for 5 off Zimbabwe's bowlers at Potchefstroom in September, with the top four in the batting order all passing fifty.

Loots Bosman (88) and Alviro Petersen (80) came into the match with just three appearances between them and got proceedings off to a flier, securing an opening partnership of 165. Both batsmen scored their maiden half-centuries and both reached their fifties with a six.

Jacques Kallis followed with 50, while Mark Boucher, appearing in his 220th one-day international scored a maiden century, one that was reached in break-neck speed. He got to the 50-mark in 26 balls, and made it to 100 in a South African-record 44, finishing on 147 not out. Boucher occupied the crease for just 90 minutes during his onslaught, faced 68 balls, smashed just eight fours, but ten sixes, and finished with a strike rate of 216.17.

● Two gifted young schoolboys tore apart the record books in 2006 when both scored unbeaten triple-centuries in an opening stand worth an unprecedented 721 runs in a 40-overs match in India. Mohammed Shaibaaz Tumbi and close friend, class-mate, B. Manoj Kumar – batting for St Peter's High School – hit 320 and 324 respectively, in the under-13 school tournament of the Hyderabad Cricket Association.

Although not a single six was scored, Shaibaaz struck 57 fours and Manoj 46 fours in their humiliation of the boys from St Phillip's High School who capitulated to be all out for just 21 in response. Their stand shattered the previous world-best of 664 runs – for the third wicket – between Sachin Tendulkar and Vinod Kambli in a schools match in 1987-88; it was the first time two triple-centuries had been scored in the same limited-overs innings, while their team total and margin of victory also set a new standard in any form of limited-overs cricket.

● Stepping up to the plate to try and win back a treasured trophy lost two years previously, Australia launched its 2006-07 Ashes campaign with a match-winning 600-run total, the first time such a scoreline had been achieved in the series in 60 years. Riding on an innings of 196 from skipper Ricky Ponting, Australia made 602 for 9 declared in the opening innings at the 'Gabba in Brisbane, the best start to an Ashes series since Australia made 645, at the same ground, in 1946–47.

After skittling England for just 157, Ponting decided against enforcing the follow-on and batted again to set the tourists an intimidating victory-target of 648. The 445-run first-innings lead was the biggest in a Test match on Australian soil since Don Bradman's debut Test, at Brisbane, in 1928–29, when the home-side commanded 399-run lead.

BIGGEST FIRST-INNINGS LEAD IN A TEST MATCH
WITHOUT ENFORCING THE FOLLOW-ON

Lead				Result
563	England (849 & 272-9d) v West Indies (286 & 408-5)	Kingston	1929-30	D
445	Australia (602-9d & 202-1d) v England (157 & 370)	Brisbane	2006-07	W
399	England (521 & 342-8d) v Australia (122 & 66)	Brisbane	1928-29	W
380	Australia (701 & 327) v England (321 & 145)	The Oval	1934	W
340	Australia (619 & 394-8d) v West Indies (279 & 352)	Sydney	1968-69	W

● All but one of the Australian team that took on England in 2006–07 was aged over 30, and more than half was over the age of 35. Michael Clarke was the pup of the group, aged 25 years and 235 days on the first day of the first Test at Brisbane, while Shane Warne was the oldest at 37 years and 71 days.

Justin Langer and Glenn McGrath were both aged 36, while Matthew Hayden, Damien Martyn and Adam Gilchrist were 35. The other over-30s in the XI were Ricky Ponting (31), Mike Hussey (31), Stuart Clark (31), Andrew Symonds (31) and Brett Lee (30). In less than a month, Martyn, Warne, McGrath and Langer all announced their retirement from Test cricket during the series that Australia won 5–0, the first such Ashes whitewash perpetrated upon the Poms since 1920–21.

● When England went down by an innings in the fourth Ashes Test at Melbourne in 2006–07, Australia became the first country to play ten Tests in a calendar year and win them all. The year of 2006 saw Australia overtake England's record of most Tests in year without a loss. In 2004, England had played in 13 Tests, winning 11 and drawing two, for an 85 per cent success rate.

England surrender the Ashes at the WACA in 2006-07 – England's hold of the Ashes title it gained in 2005 lasted a mere 462 days. It was the shortest tenure of the Ashes urn on record, with Australia regaining the trophy in emphatic style after the third Test at Perth

---

"It took 16 years to lose them and 15 days to win them back."

Adam Gilchrist after Australia won the third Test at Perth in 2006-07
to win back the Ashes

"I feel so bad about mine I'm going to tie it round my cat. It's a joke."

Geoff Boycott on MBEs awarded to the England players
after their 2005 Ashes win

● Having successfully retrieved the Ashes from England in 2006-07, Australia went on to lose two consecutive one-day international series, and in the process surrender its No. 1 crown. After conceding the prestigious triangular series at home to a reinvigorated England, Australia travelled across the Tasman to contest the Chappell-Hadlee Trophy, but without its star attractions Ricky Ponting, Adam Gilchrist and the injured Andrew Symonds. The first match at Wellington was a bleak one for Australia, suffering its first-ever ten-wicket flogging in 646 one-day internationals played over 36 years. All out for just 148 in the 49th over, Lou Vincent (73★) and Stephen Fleming (70★) polished off the required runs in just 27 overs for the highest opening partnership by New Zealand against Australia.

The second match at Auckland saw the Black Caps overhaul a massive total of 336, with Australia losing its first series to New Zealand and the top position in the game to South Africa. Two days later, in the third and final match at Hamilton, Australia cranked it up reaching 346 for 5 with opener Matthew Hayden breaking his toe and the record for the highest individual score by an Australian in a one-day international. His unbeaten 181 included ten sixes and saw him gain the unwanted record of highest score in a losing cause, with New Zealand eclipsing its performance at Auckland by successfully hunting down another huge total. At the end of the match, Australia had been on the receiving end of the world's four largest successful ODI run-chases in the space of a little over a year.

● During the 1984 Texaco Trophy, the West Indies' Viv Richards savaged England at Manchester, securing the highest undefeated innings in a one-day international. But while Richards dominated proceedings smashing 189 off 170 balls, all those around him failed. No other recognised batsman in the Windies line-up – Gordon Greenidge (9), Desmond Haynes (1), Richie Richardson (6), Larry Gomes (4), Clive Lloyd (8) and Jeff Dujon (0) – managed to reach double figures.

During the 1983 World Cup, India's Kapil Dev played a similar red-hot innings, thrashing the Zimbabweans at Tunbridge Wells to the tune of 175 runs after the openers Sunil Gavaskar and Kris Srikkanth both made ducks, and the other top three in the line-up had also failed to reach double figures. The next highest score in the innings came from the No.10, Syed Kirmani, who made an unbeaten 24.

● South Africa opened its 2007 World Cup campaign with aplomb, posting 353 for 3 off just 40 overs in a rain-affected match against The Netherlands at St Kitts. After opener A.B. de Villiers made a duck, the next four batsmen all swaggered past 50, with three century partnerships in the innings, a first in one-day international cricket. Graeme Smith (67) and Jacques Kallis (128★) put on 114 for the second wicket, Kallis and Herschelle Gibbs (72) added 105 for the third, while Kallis and Mark Boucher (75★) shared a fourth-wicket stand of 134.

Two instances of 30 runs off a single over were also witnessed, another first in one-day international cricket. Gibbs hit the jackpot blasting six sixes off a Daan van Bunge over, demolishing Sanath Jayasuriya's individual 30-run record, something the Sri Lankan achieved twice in one-day internationals.

The aftermath of Herschelle Gibbs' six sixes in an over against The Netherlands at St Kitts in the 2007 World Cup – a smashed commentary box window

Gibbs won a million US dollars for charity after a tournament sponsor had pledged the money for any batsman to become the first to achieve the feat of six sixes in an over in a one-day international: "**If the ball presents itself, I'll try everything. I was lucky the straight boundaries were quite small … but the six sixes was a bonus.**"

Boucher was also in devastating form, slamming 75 off 31 balls, reaching his fifty off just 21. Luuk van Troost was another bowler to suffer, with Boucher (4, 1) and Kallis (2, W, 5, 6, 6, 6) combining to record another 30-run blitzkrieg.

Another world-first involving South Africa occurred later in the tournament, when Sri Lanka's Lasith Malinga took four wickets in four balls at Guyana. After securing the fifth instance of a World Cup hat-trick, Malinga went on to take four in four, the first bowler to achieve the feat in international cricket.

● Surrey came within a boundary of becoming the first team to crack 500 in a 50-overs match when it slaughtered Gloucestershire at The Oval in 2007. Batting first, the home team romped to a record 496 for 4 off its allocated overs, with openers James Benning (152) and Alistair Brown (176) putting on an England-record first-wicket stand of 294. Brown was almost unstoppable, reaching his hundred off just 50 balls, and made 176 off 97, with 20 fours and eight sixes. A total of 22 sixes and 47 fours was struck by Surrey, which triumphed by a massive margin of 257 runs.

CRICKET & SHOWBIZ

● Salil Ankola, who made history in 1988-89 by taking a hat-trick on his first-class debut, later found fame and fortune as an actor. Appearing for Maharashtra in a Ranji Trophy match against Gujarat at Pune, Ankola took six wickets in the first innings, including a hat-trick and then scored 43 with the bat. After one Test match for India and 20 one-day internationals, the fast bowler pursued an acting career in both television and film: "**I feel it was destined for me to be in showbiz.**"

Ankola starred in a cricketing movie *Silence Please ... The Dressing Room,* which tells the story of a goodwill cricket match between India and Pakistan. Set against the backdrop of a terrorist threat to bomb the cricket ground stadium, most of the film takes place in the players' dressing rooms, with Ankola playing the part of the Indian captain.

● Australian actress Ruth McDonald, who starred in the TV drama *Blue Heelers*, appeared in a London play *Long Gone Lonesome Cowgirls* in 2004, the same year that her husband, England's Andrew Strauss, made his debut on the Test-match stage. Set in a remote town in Queensland, the play explores the friendship between two women who share a love of country music.

● The first *Australian Idol* winner Guy Sebastian fulfilled a childhood dream in 2003 when he paid a visit to the Lord's cricket ground. Sebastian, and Heinz Winkler, South Africa's winner of the competition – both in London to compete in *World Idol* – had a bat and a bowl on the hallowed turf after a tour of the ground's facilities with the MCC's Head of Coaching, the former Australian Test all-rounder Tony Dodemaide: "**It was great to see a fellow countryman enjoying the thrill of**

Singers Guy Sebastian and Heinz Winkler at Lord's in 2003

**playing on the famous turf here at Lord's, though I don't think
that Glenn McGrath has too much to worry about just yet.**"

Earlier in the year, Heinz Winkler had been part of a star-studded line-
up that performed at the opening ceremony of the 2003 World Cup at
Newlands. He sang the West Indies cricket anthem, drawing high praise
from the capacity crowd and players alike: "**It was quite daunting, but
it was an awesome experience. When I got back to my seat, some
guys from the Windies management told me that I had done
them proud. It was a big compliment to get that sort of response
from people who hadn't heard me sing before.**"

● Ted Lewis, the founder of one of the biggest record companies in Britain, was a life-long supporter of cricket, who played occasionally for the Trinity College XI at Cambridge. Sir Edward presided over the Decca label, which in its heyday had The Rolling Stones on board, and was a vice-president at the Surrey Cricket Club, and a member of the MCC.

● When Australian singer Kamahl contacted Don Bradman in 1987 seeking permission to use his name in a song, it started a stream of correspondence between the two that led to several personal meetings. The song was written for the 1988 Bicentennial celebrations and included a line which referred to Australian icons Joan Sutherland, Robert de Castella and Bradman: **"I was conscious of the fact he's a private man, and that I had used his name in one of the songs without his permission. And I was concerned that if he should refuse it, what should I do, you know? But instead, he was very kind, very generous in his remarks. And, of course, I replied, and he replied, and I replied. And then an invitation came for me to visit him at his home – Melbourne Cup Day, 1988. And that I'll never ever forget. I don't think I will ever have a friendship quite like the friendship with Sir Donald. It's one of a kind, and I feel very lucky. I'm one of many singers, but there was only one Bradman."**

● Australian comedian Steve Abbott, who hosted a cricketing show on the SBS television network in 2005, once played third-grade cricket in Wollongong. Famed for his quirky character 'The Sandman', Abbott lists one of his greatest achievements the day he passed his cricket-umpiring test in 2004.

● India's Shanthakumaran Sreesanth, the first bowler to take a Ranji Trophy hat-trick for Kerala, is recognised as a talented dancer. The fast bowler, who made his Test debut in 2005-06, once took out a national break-dance competition when a youngster: **"When I was on stage, I used to do all silly things to be in the limelight. I love dancing."** The fast bowler admits he's always yearned for the spotlight with a sister a big name in acting in India, and a singing brother-in-law: **"I wanted it** [fame] **badly because this recognition is priceless."**

During the first Test against South Africa at Johannesburg in 2006-07, Sreesanth starred with the ball taking eight wickets and then entertained all with an impromptu dance routine mid-pitch in the second innings. His unscheduled hip-shaking, bat-twirling performance came after he'd smashed Andre Nel for a six, who had taunted him the previous ball after beating his bat.

● Soprano Charlotte Church, who, at the age of 12 years and nine months, made history by becoming the youngest artist to hold the No. 1 spot on the classical album charts, hit a batsman in the groin when she bowled the opening over in a charity cricket match. In 2004, Charlotte (pictured) turned out for a Welsh celebrity-XI, which also included former *Coronation Street* star Charles Dale, at the Sophia Gardens ground in Cardiff. One onlooker remarked that: **"Charlotte had a lovely bowling action for a beginner. One ball beat the batsman and got him right in the privates. But he saw the funny side of it, and they had a laugh about it."**

● Celebrated British television producer Harry Thompson, who never smoked a cigarette in his life but died of lung cancer in 2005, famously ran his own cricket team for 25 years. He appeared in all 640 games the Captain Scott Invitational XI had played since its inception, pulling out only when he received his diagnosis. The co-founder of the team, Thompson launched numerous top-rating TV comedies in Britain, including *Have I Got News For You*, *They Think It's All Over* and Sacha Baron Cohen's *Da Ali G Show*.

Borat: *Every Englishman must have a hobby. Some like to collect the stamp. Some like to make the jam. But the most fun is to kill a little animal with a shotgun or rip him up with a wild dog. This is why I come to the countryside to find out about English hobbies. You are English policeman?*

Policeman: *Yes*

Borat: *Hello. Do you believe in the hunt?*

Policeman: *I have to remain impartial with my views.*

Borat: *Because you are English policeman. The greatest police in the force!*

Policeman: *And they say "Everything is cricket" in England, don't they?*

Borat: *Everything is cricket? This is cricket?*

Policeman: *No, no, no. It's just a saying, just a saying.*

Borat: *They play?*

Policeman: *Cricket?*

Borat: *Yes, cricket.*

Policeman: *Cricket is a gentleman's sport and everyone has the right to be gentlemen in England, as such.*

Borat: *And they play cricket today?*

Policeman: *No, no, no. I am confusing you now. Forget the cricket side of things. It's just a saying anyway.*

Borat: *And people, they protest against the cricket?*

Policeman: *Forget the cricket! It's just a saying. I just said "Cricket". It has nothing to do with the hunting.*

Borat: *So why did you say it?*

Sacha Baron Cohen's Kazakhstani character Borat

● Fast bowler Brett Lee, who was a member of the Australian squad in India in 2004-05 but didn't play in any of the Tests, did perform with some distinction on another stage while on tour. Lee, who plays bass guitar for the band Six & Out, was invited to jam with an Indian rock group Aqua Flow in Mumbai: "**The band has great voices, and they**

are great players. For these guys to let me up there and play some instruments with them, it's an awesome thing."

Lee launched his music career internationally in India in 2007, topping the charts with 'You're The One For Me', a duet he recorded with a 73-year-old singer, the legendary Asha Bhosle.

"I have been an avid cricket fan, so naturally I know almost all cricket players. Brett Lee could sing and strum. He's young, good-looking, intelligent, and a singer."

Asha Bhosle

"She is the Aretha Franklin of India. It was amazing to work with her."

Brett Lee

● During the innings break of the third and final match of the 2005 Chappell-Hadlee one-day international series at Wellington, a special version of the Green Day hit 'Time of Your Life' was played over the ground's loudspeakers. The vocals on the track were actually provided by Brett Lee, and guitar by Mark McLeod, internationally renowned for arranging music at major sporting events. New Zealand really did have the time of its life after the break, successfully chasing a then world-record target of 332, defeating Australia with an over to spare.

● Actor Ian Lavender, who joined the cast of the British TV drama *EastEnders* in 2001, once revealed he had at least three television sets positioned around his home so he would never miss the cricket. Lavender was also a much-loved cast member of *Dad's Army*, the long-running TV comedy that once featured an on-camera role for England fast bowler Fred Trueman. In a 1970 episode entitled 'The Test', Trueman was brought in as a secret weapon for a cricket match between the wardens and Captain Mainwaring's platoon.

Bill Pertwee, who played the part of Chief Warden William Hodges in the show, has a cricketing connection in his past. In 1946, he was a baggage boy for the Indian cricket team on their tour of England.

● Robert Powell, who played the lead role in the 1977 British TV mini-series *Jesus of Nazareth* and appeared in films such as *Mahler*, *The Thirty-Nine Steps* and *Tommy*, was president of the Lord's Taverners Club in 2001–02. In 1999, Powell turned out for a Taverners XI against the Los Angeles Social Cricket Alliance XI, a team that featured a number of British expatriates, including Patrick Stewart, from *Star Trek*, John Rhys-Davies, of *Lord of The Rings* fame, and Michael York. Other celebrities including Monty Python's Eric Idle, John Taylor from the pop group Duran Duran and John Lydon, formerly of The Sex Pistols, supported the charity event played at the Woodley Cricket Field at Van Nuys in southern California.

● The award-winning Australian rock group Powderfinger named one of their albums *Vulture Street*, the thoroughfare in Brisbane that houses the 'Gabba cricket ground. All members of the band are big fans of the game, fielding its own team – the Webfinger XI – in a local cricket competition in Brisbane.

"I'm a cricket nut ... always have been."

Powderfinger vocalist Bernard Fanning

"I've got a small computer set up at home and I work on music all the time – when I'm not surfing or watching the cricket."

Powderfinger drummer Jon Coghill

● British rock band The Kinks, which had a string of Top 40 hits, including 'Waterloo Sunset', 'You Really Got Me' and 'Lola', scored with a quirky cricketing song in the early 1970s. The track, simply called 'Cricket', first appeared on their album *Preservation Act 1*, released in 1973.

Some people say that life is a game, well if this is so
I'd like to know the rules on which this game of life is based
I know of no game more fitting than the age-old game of cricket
It has honour, it has character and it's British

● When The Rolling Stones toured Australia in 2003, they travelled under the aliases of former England Test cricketers. Mick Jagger was W.G. Grace – the others were Trevor Bailey, Len Hutton, Peter May and Fred Trueman.

"Cricket is the channel we need most of all."

Mick Jagger nominating his band's top priority as a TV with cricket in a list of demands for the Rolling Stones' 2006 tour of the United States

● Former Rolling Stones bass player Bill Wyman attained an unusual personal milestone in 2003 after batting in a charity cricket match in Surrey. While scoring 41 not out for the Alec Stewart Bunbury XI against Eric Clapton's XI, he went without a cigarette the entire time while at the crease, some 90 minutes. Famous for smoking at least 40 fags a game, Wyman once caught former England batsman Brian Close one-handed, while still holding onto his cigarette.

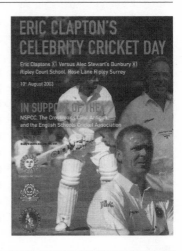

"I bat slow and keep one end up. I let the other guy do the jogging around. And because I'm a smoker, I used to get run around quite a lot. I kept wicket once that was quite embarrassing because I'm quite short. I had to do it, because there was no one else, just like I had to play bass because no one else wanted to ... I fill a vacant spot."

Bill Wyman

● The talents of star Indian batsman Sachin Tendulkar inspired a musical that premiered in Mumbai in 2004, described by its producer as a show 'that will add value to people's lives'. *Main Sachin Tendulkar (I Am Sachin Tendulkar)* used the cricketer's career-milestones as its backdrop in promoting symbols of success and excellence for others to aspire to.

● Tara Palmer-Tomkinson, a part-time London actress, pianist and well-known socialite, won £32,000 for a charity on a celebrity edition of Britain's *Who Wants To Be A Millionaire?* in 2003 after her 'Phone-a-Friend' successfully answered a question on cricket. Ms Palmer-Tomkinson was stumped when the compere Chris Tarrant asked her to name the decade in which England had last won the Ashes. Using a 'lifeline', she turned to former England footballer Gary Lineker, whose correct response saw the Leukaemia Research Fund considerably better off: **"I was a little bit nervous because so much money for the charity was riding on the question, but fortunately I got it right."**

● Shane Warne came within a whisker of scooping the grand prize on Australia's *Who Wants To Be A Millionaire?* in 2005, coming unstuck on a question relating to sixties pop music. In a celebrity-charity edition of the show, Warne – and partner Trevor Sauer, a former big-winning contestant – failed to name the first No. 1 hit for The Supremes. Warne's 'Phone-a-Friend', the actor-writer Rob Sitch, was unable to come up with the answer in the required 30 seconds, so the Australian bowler decided to leave the show, walking away with a $500,000 cheque payable to the Shane Warne Foundation.

"I notice when you get a celebrity up there, particularly sportsmen and sportswomen, they are actually so used to the pressure they zone in, rather than zone out. He [Warne] put himself on the chopping block. He's prepared to have a go, and the thing you notice is he plays along and has a sense of humour. He was pumped, as you would imagine."

Eddie McGuire – host of Who Wants To Be A Millionaire?*, 2005*

● Australian radio and TV hosts Adam Spencer and Wil Anderson staged an impromptu game of cricket at the 2002 Livid Music Festival. A makeshift cricket pitch was set up in the mosh-pit area in front of the main stage the night before the event got underway.

Some of the players included guitarist Joe Hansen and singer Phil Jamieson from Grinspoon, and Pinky Beecroft from Machine Gun Fellatio. Spencer's team won the game, 62-61, after his cousin, Scott, hit the last ball for six.

ADAM SPENCER'S ALL-TIME BEST TEST XI

   Matthew Hayden (A)
   Arthur Morris (A)
   Don Bradman (A)
   Sachin Tendulkar (I)
   Allan Border (A)
   Garry Sobers (WI)
   Adam Gilchrist † (A)
   *Adam Spencer * (ABC)*
   Stuart MacGill (A)
   Dennis Lillee (A)
   Glenn McGrath (A)

ABC presenter Adam Spencer: "Spencer chosen as much for his ability as a leader of men as his cricketing class."

● Chloe Traicos, the daughter of former South African and Zimbabwean Test cricketer John Traicos, made a name for herself in Australia as a documentary filmmaker, playwright and actress. Born and raised in Zimbabwe, Chloe and her family moved to Perth in 1997, where she appeared in numerous theatre productions.

In 2005, she won the New York Film Festival award for best director with her critically-acclaimed documentary *A Stranger In My Homeland*. Filmed in Western Australia, the documentary features interviews with four Zimbabwean refugees.

● The Paul Kelly song 'Bradman', which appears on the 1987 album *Under The Sun*, runs for seven minutes and 32 seconds, or 452 seconds – 452 (not out) being Don Bradman's highest score in first-class cricket. The Australian songwriter penned another cricketing song called 'Behind the Bowler's Arm', the B-side to a single released in 1996: **"It's all about going to the traditional Boxing Day cricket Test at the Melbourne Cricket Ground. Let's say it's become a bit of a ritual for me. It's a great game. What can I say?"**

● A 'Test match' between England and Australia takes place in an early series of *Doctor Who*, with the Doctor's TARDIS landing on the cricket ground during a tense period of play. Episode eight of 'The Daleks' Master Plan', first aired on the BBC in England in 1966, sees two cricket commentators, Trevor and Scott, calling the action when the game is brought to a halt with the arrival of the Doctor's time-machine.

Trevor: *Well, the English batsmen are really fighting against the clock now, Scott.*

Scott: *My word, yes. Seventy-eight runs in forty-five minutes to win.*

Trevor: *It really has been an exciting game, hasn't it, Scott?*

Scott: *Very exciting.*

Trevor: *Well, let's have a look at the scoreboard, shall we?*

[the TARDIS appears on the outfield]

Trevor: *Now, you'll see ... Goodness me, take a look at that, Scott.*

Scott: *Take a look at what, Trev?*

Trevor: *There's a police telephone box on the pitch.*

Scott: *My word, yes.*

Trevor: *Well this really is extraordinary. You don't remember anything like this happening before, do you, Scott?*

Scott: *No. No.*

Trevor: *Well, anyway, Ross is looking through the record books and if there has been anything like it before, I'm sure he'll find it for us.*

● British actor Colin Baker put it down to his love of cricket for helping him secure the lead role in *Doctor Who* in 1984, following the retirement of Peter Davison. Baker – whose TV credits include *The Bill*, *Blakes 7* and *Casualty* – attended a meeting with the show's producer and BBC-1 controller, David Reid, who was watching a Test match on television in his office. After asking how the game was going, Baker said the two chatted about cricket for 20 minutes or so: "**After that we talked about the role of the Doctor for a minute or two, and David Reid said, 'Well, I think that's great, excellent.' Apparently, the fact I liked cricket did it for me**!"

"It's got everything. It requires the mind, the physical side, and of course, it's an unbeatable social occasion. I've seen different sports all over the galaxy and nothing beats cricket."

Colin Baker

● Award-winning British actress Emma Thompson is a regular visitor to a cricket ground in England so she can keep fit and burn off unwanted calories. Ms Thompson, of *Stranger Than Fiction* and *Howards End* fame, works out on a cricket field that adjoins her English property: "**I do it eight times almost every day. It's the only way I can manage it, because I want to drink wine and eat what I want. The tops of my legs are a bit of a worry.**"

● The debut album from British rock band Lowgold, released in 2001, was titled *Just Backward of Square*. The opening act for Chris Martin's Coldplay in a national UK tour in 2000, many a game of backstage cricket was played, with Lowgold frontman Darren Ford admitting "… **playing cricket with Chris was plain scary. He is a lethal bowler, super quick.**"

In 2003, Martin took a break from his world tour with Coldplay to play in a game of cricket with his father Anthony's team at Exeter in southwest England. Martin – who developed his cricketing skills at public school in Dorset – played for the Countess Wear Cricket Club, but suffered a big defeat in front of a crowd that reportedly included his wife, the Oscar-winning actress Gwyneth Paltrow.

"Do I get cricket? Sort of. Better than I used to. I understand the point of it now. I can't keep score or anything like that, but I can follow what's going on … sort of."

Gwyneth Paltrow

"A few years ago, I was chatting up a girl in a lift and she was not having any of it. She thought I was too tall and geeky and all that, and I needed a wingman. In walked Shane Warne and he was the best wingman."

Chris Martin

"We bumped into each other in a lift in England during the 2001 Ashes series and became very good friends. I went over to his house for dinner in London. We spoke all the time on the phone and hung out a few times. He's a really good guy."

Shane Warne

● Oscar-winning actor Russell Crowe dedicated parts of a private cricket oval on his property near Coffs Harbour in New South Wales to members of his famous cricketing family. The ground itself was named after his uncle Dave Crowe – father of his NZ Test-playing cousins, Jeff and Martin – while the pavilion bears the name of Jeff Crowe, who appeared in 39 Test matches between 1982-83 and 1989-90.

"I might have more than 5000 Test runs, but he makes 40 million bucks a movie."

former New Zealand batsman Martin Crowe on his cousin Russell Crowe

● New South Wales batsman Jim de Courcy, who played in three Test matches, all against England in 1953, was the inspiration for a character in the Tim Rice musical *Chess*. One of the main characters is Walter DeCourcey, the personal manager of American chess player Freddie Trumper, who shares the surname of one of Australia's greatest-ever batsmen, Victor Trumper.

"Keep a straight bat in cricket as in life."

Tim Rice

● Two British television newsreaders appeared in a charity cricket match in 2004, with one delivering the opening over, the other claiming figures of 2 for 22. Trevor McDonald – voted the most popular newscaster at the 1996 National Television Awards – captained his own XI against the David English-Bunbury XI at Esher in Surrey in aid of the Missing Person Helpline. The first over of the 35-overs match was sent down by ITV's evening

news presenter Katie Derham, with Sir Trevor claiming the prized wicket of former Essex batsman Paul Prichard (136), together with *EastEnders* star Rudolph Walker.

The Bee Gees' Barry Gibb (left) with David English at a charity cricket match in 2004

David English – who once managed Eric Clapton and The Bee Gees – matched Sir Trevor as captain by claiming two wickets, while former England Test batsman Mike Gatting scored 106. The Sir Trevor McDonald XI defeated the Bunbury XI by seven wickets in the 29th over.

"For all their necessary and admirable professionalism this was an England side that knew that cricket is not a sport but a game. A game that cannot be won by a fighting unit alone, no matter how tough, but can be won, and won gloriously by a team."

British actor and cricket fan Stephen Fry on the Bunbury charity cricket team

---

● Jason Krejza, who made his first-class debut for New South Wales in 2004-05 and moved to Tasmania two seasons later, is a big music fan who once contemplated auditioning for *Australian Idol*. Krejza is also on record saying the one song he never wanted to hear again was 'Drive' by *Idol*'s Shannon Noll: **"My mates were always pushing me to have a go. So, when I was in Brisbane for a short time I thought about attending auditions there. I don't know why, but I opted out in the end."**

● A cricket bat used in the Indian Oscar-nominated film *Lagaan* sold at auction in 2004 for six million rupees. Bollywood actor Aamir Khan, who struck a match-winning six with the bat in the movie, donated the souvenir item for a fund-raising dinner in aid of a cancer hospital run by former Pakistan captain Imran Khan.

● Pop superstar Elton John once scored a useful 24 in a charity cricket match at Lord's, but upset some present at the ground when he turned up in green hair. Sir Elton, who dressed up in cricket whites – and pink boots – for the cover of his *Greatest Hits Volume II* album, later recalled his hair style didn't go down too well: **"The looks I got … it was the longest walk out to the crease that I can**

ever remember and I thought, 'Please let it end'." The following week, he played in a match at Barnes, and was dismissed first ball by former England bowler Robin Jackman.

"I used to love hanging around cricketers. We had a lot of fun and got up to a lot of mischief together. When we won at Melbourne in 1986 it was one of the greatest – and most drunken – nights I can remember."

Elton John

● Darren Gough strutted his stuff on BBC television in 2005 winning *Strictly Come Dancing*, the British equivalent of Channel Seven's *Dancing With The Stars*. The following year, a former Test team-mate of Gough's was crowned champion.

The player of 58 Test matches for England, Gough's partner on the floor was Lilia Kopylova, a Latin-American dance champion. More than three million viewers voted for him on the final night: "**I learnt how committed dancers are. I'm a blokes' bloke and I thought it would be a laugh. I'll try anything, me. I've always liked having to prove things. Suddenly, I thought, I like this. Every man would love to dance but they wouldn't have the guts to do it. Everyone should be able to waltz. At school it should be compulsory to learn the waltz.**"

So impressed was Gough's county captain Ronnie Irani, he announced that dancing should became a part of Essex's training regime: "**Darren got himself so fit during the 11-week programme that we'll definitely be incorporating dance into our pre-season fitness routine. Goughie lost a stone in weight and built-up so much leg-strength because of the dancing. I think it could benefit us all greatly. It should also improve our poise and balance.**"

Mark Ramprakash, who topped 2000 first-class runs in England in 2006, emulated Gough by taking out the follow-up series. The Surrey batsman, like Gough, was teamed up with a Latin-American dance champion, Karen Hardy: "**When I was initially asked to do the show, I said 'no' – it's so far from anything I've ever done before. But then you look at Darren Gough and you realise that you might be up to the challenge.**"

"I won a prize for rock'n'roll dancing at a youth club when I was 16 ... but only three people entered."

"I can't dance like a nancy on national TV."

>*Darren Gough prior to making his debut on the BBC's*
>Strictly Come Dancing *in 2005*

"I'm a massive Mark Ramprakash fan. I'm like 'Mark is going to win it!' And he's so gorgeous."

>*former Spice Girls member Emma Bunton on Mark Ramprakash,*
>*who won the 2006 edition of* Strictly Come Dancing

● Former Australian batsman Michael Bevan made his singing debut in 2006 when he appeared live on national television in a duet with Jade MacRae. The two formed part of Channel Seven's *It Takes Two*, a show that teamed a professional singer with someone famous in a field other than singing.

With a panel of judges reviewing the performances and the public determining their fate week by week, MacRae and Bevan came equal-fifth on the opening night singing the Frank Sinatra classic 'I've Got You Under My Skin'. They lasted another four weeks before getting the heave-ho.

The following year, former England Test cricketer Mark Butcher appeared on *Just The Two Of Us* – the British version of the show: "**It's not a blood sport. This is music. It's not about hurting people ... it's about making you feel good**."

● Vinod Kambli, who appeared in 17 Tests for India during the 1990s, was chosen to star in a TV show in 2004, playing the part of a fashion photographer. His small-screen debut in *Miss India* followed an appearance in a Bollywood action movie *Annarth*, released in 2002. According to the TV show's producer Rupesh Goel, Kambli immediately accepted the offer to play one of the lead characters: "**I had seen *Annarth* and I had found Vinod to be a cool guy with a lot of style and a great personality. That's what I wanted for the character in the serial**."

● During the filming of *The Dish*, which tells the story of Australia's involvement in the first landing on the Moon, some of the actors, including Sam Neill, played cricket between takes. The New Zealand-born actor revealed that at a reunion of staff from the 1969 mission, some admitted they had played cricket on the giant dish of the radio telescope at Parkes in New South Wales – an event portrayed in the film – something they say they probably would have denied at the time.

"The most pleasurable experience to me was actually playing cricket on the dish. I'm not sure if this is something that happens very often ... people playing cricket in the middle of a radio telescope."

Sam Neill

● Singer Phil Burton, a member of the group Human Nature, was crowned the winner of Channel Ten's *Australia's Brainiest Musician* show in 2006, having selected 'Australian 1980s Cricket' as his specialist subject. Although Burton was only able to correctly answer two of his five cricket questions, he managed to sneak across the line and claim victory over his two rivals, fellow band member Toby Allen and singer-songwriter Dave Graney.

In a following edition of the same Channel Ten series, former Australian all-rounder, and current umpire, Paul Reiffel came out on top in the show *Australia's Brainiest Cricketer*. After the elimination of former Test players Greg Blewett, Ray Bright, Damien Fleming, Rodney Hogg, Kim Hughes and Greg Matthews, the final three consisted of Geoff Lawson, Colin Miller, and Reiffel.

● Sam Mendes, who directed the Kevin Spacey film *American Beauty*, was a handy all-round cricketer, coming second in both the batting and bowling averages at Oxford's Magdalen College in 1981. With the bat, he scored 601 runs at 40.06 – with a highest score of 114 not out – and took 46 wickets at 15.19.

Mendes later taught cricket at the Summer Fields School in Oxford and is said to have incorporated some of the ideas of former England captain Mike Brearley in his directing, providing a foreword for the 2001 edition of Brearley's book *The Art of Captaincy*, which was first published in 1985.

"I wasn't a very bright schoolkid. But, I was good at sports, specifically cricket. Hitting a small ball with a big stick is one of my talents."

Sam Mendes

● 'Jerusalem', the song that became England's unofficial crowd anthem throughout the 2005 Ashes campaign, featured on a number of commercial CDs that year, with one version reaching the UK Top 40. The William Blake hymn was recorded by the England team with classical singer Keedie, who had originally performed the song at the Professional Cricketers'  Association awards night at London's Royal Albert Hall. So positive was the reaction to her performance, it was later recorded with the England players, with proceeds going to a relief fund for a massive earthquake that had devastated areas of Pakistan and India. The song peaked at number 19 on the official British Top 40.

"I feel honoured and privileged to sing with the team on an anthem like 'Jerusalem'. The guys were all great, really down to earth and I had a lot of fun recording it."

British classical singer Keedie

● A movie with a cricketing storyline served as the opening-night attraction at the Israeli Film Festival in New York in 2004. A visit by the England cricket team to the Negev Desert in *Turn Left at The End of The World* sees local groups putting aside their differences to assemble a team good enough to take them on. The movie starred several local Israeli cricketers.

● Queensland cricket authorities were forced to issue an apology during the opening Test of the 2006-07 Ashes series for a song considered derogatory of English cricket fans. Performed by Greg Champion during tea breaks at the 'Gabba, members of the Barmy Army had complained of lyrics they considered to be offensive in a parody of the hit song 'The Lion Sleeps Tonight'.

"We'll definitely be targeting him [Ricky Ponting] ... he's the key guy. We think he's a weak link, a weak captain. There's the song 'I can't drink, I can't fight, my name's Ricky Ponting and I chatted up that transvestite'. How can Australia have a captain who chats up transvestites? There's lots of stuff we can get him with."

Barmy Army co-founder Dave Peacock
in the lead-up to the 2006-07 Ashes series

"I'm a professional musician who plays the trumpet for a living, not some drunk trying to play 'The Last Post' on a didgeridoo."

Barmy Army, and occasional London Philharmonic Orchestra, trumpeter
Billy Cooper after being evicted from the 'Gabba by Brisbane police during
the opening Ashes Test match in 2006-07

● For the fifth Test against the West Indies at Adelaide in 1988-89, the Australian bowling attack was opened by two players who would later appear in top-rating television shows. Merv Hughes – who made his highest Test score (72★) in the match – starred in an episode of *The Flying Doctors* on Channel Nine in 1991 and in the ABC comedy *Frontline* in 1995, while Mike Whitney – who claimed his first-ever five-wicket haul (7-89) – had a cameo role in *Neighbours* in 1994.

Hughes made his debut on the silver screen in 2003, in the film *Fat Pizza*, playing the part of a crazed axe-wielding serial killer, while Whitney later went on to appear in, or host, a number of TV shows, including *Who Dares Wins*, *Gladiators*, *Sydney Weekenders* and *Mike Whitney's Walkabout*. In 1998, Whitney and Tania Zaetta – co-host of *Who Dares Wins* – took up their own dare on national television singing Aqua's novelty hit 'Barbie Girl'.

"When I was playing cricket, being out in the middle of the ground was basically performing for a crowd and that's largely how I feel about television."

Mike Whitney

"In cricket, the worst that can happen is you get a grass stain on your pants. And there's so much standing around you feel like you're at a funeral. If they had cricket with chicks in bikinis, then I'd be on the hill, mate. And maybe between each run they could have a car do a burnout on the pitch. That would be a sport – I'd be the captain of that team."

Paul Fenech – star of the 2003 Australian film Fat Pizza

Australian fast bowler Merv Hughes, with Paul Kelman and Christopher Stollery, in a 1991 episode of the Channel Nine drama The Flying Doctors, *and (right) Channel Seven's intrepid Mike Whitney on location in New Zealand, from a three-episode 2005 special of* Mike Whitney's Walkabout

● Cricket gets a run in the third and final season of the Emmy award-winning American TV comedy *Arrested Development*. The episode 'The Ocean Walker', first broadcast in 2005, includes scenes that feature a cricket bat and a cricket magazine.

● American actor-director Ron Howard, best known as Richie Cunningham in the 1970s TV sitcom *Happy Days*, was spotted at The Oval in London in 2005, watching the fifth England–Australia Ashes Test match. The narrator of *Arrested Development*, Howard had only recently learnt the finer points of the game from Australian cricket team physiotherapist Errol Alcott. On the recommendation of Shane Warne, Alcott helped Russell Crowe with an injured shoulder during the filming of *Cinderella Man*, the $115m boxing movie directed by Howard.

"I sat and watched it and they said it was 244 for four and I thought that sounds like devastation to me. In baseball terms that's a shutdown."

American actress Renee Zellweger on the 2005 Ashes

"I was on tour when we won by two runs at Edgbaston. I was in the south of France and on the phone to Michael Caine, who is a big cricket fan. I was saying 'For God's sake' and he was saying 'I can't look'."

Elton John

"Defeating the Australians is the finest thing I know ... ever since I lost the part of Maximus to Russell Crowe."

British comedian Ronnie Corbett

⬤ Tim Brunero, a runner-up on the Australian version of *Big Brother*, had a run-in with SCG officials in 2005-06 when he turned up for a day's play of the Australia-South Africa Sydney Test match. He was refused entry at the members' gate, because he was not wearing a collared shirt.

Other entertainment heavyweights seen at the SCG over the five days included *Cinderella Man*'s Russell Crowe, *Brokeback Mountain* star Heath Ledger, British TV personality Michael Parkinson and Hugh Cornwell, who fronted the UK rock band The Stranglers in the 1980s.

"My school had a cadet regiment that taught 14-year-old kids how to fire semi-automatic weapons and throw hand grenades. I wanted out of that. I did everything I could — community service, reading bingo numbers and playing cricket for the school team — so I didn't have to be part of the military corps."

Hollywood actor Heath Ledger

"It's great fun. I'm not much good, but I get to do things like stand in the slips with my heroes like Graham Gooch."

musician and occasional cricketer Hugh Cornwell

⬤ The 2006 England cricket season got underway in toe-tapping fashion with two of the country's top all-rounders thrust into the limelight as virtual pop stars. Fresh from winning the BBC dancing competition *Strictly Come Dancing*, Darren Gough sang the line "ner, ner, ner, ner" in British punk band Koopa's 2006 World Cup football song 'Stand Up 4 England'. According to the official Koopa website: "**Darren dazzled with his silky football skills and really got in to the spirit of the song. Darren said 'As a keen football fan, it's exciting to be doing my bit for the World Cup cause'.**"

Andrew Flintoff then appeared live on stage in a duet with Elton John singing the chorus of the 1972 hit 'Rocket Man' as part of a benefit function held at London's Battersea Park: "**It's my great pleasure to bring to the stage one of the greatest vocalists currently singing in Britain. I mean, I've sung with Aretha Franklin, Ray Charles, George Michael ... but I've never sung with anybody like this. Ladies and gentlemen, please give a really big warm welcome to my guest performer, Andrew Flintoff.**"

"I joined in for the chorus of 'Rocket Man', but luckily he drowned me out."

Andrew Flintoff

"The evening was only slightly spoilt when some people got up and started dancing while Elton was still singing, obscuring the view for the rest of us. One of them was Stephen Gateley, who used to be in the pop group Boyzone, so I'm told. I had to get up, tap him on the shoulder and say: 'Excuse me, we've come here to watch Elton singing, not you dancing. Would you kindly sit down?'"

England fast bowler Matthew Hoggard

"Andrew puts bums on seats, makes the game as exciting as it can be. And he plays the game in a sporting manner, the manner in which all sports should be played."

Elton John

● *Kal Ho Naa Ho*, which won eight awards at the 2004 India International Film Awards including best film, stars Saif Ali Khan, the son of former Indian cricket star Mansur Ali Khan, the Nawab of Pataudi. Mansur Ali Khan's wife, Sharmila Tagore, is a legend in Indian film, having appeared in well over 70 movies, while their daughter, Soha Ali Khan, is also an actor: "**Mere name cannot ensure success. Like the other newcomers, I, too, will have to struggle to become successful. My mom is** like my friend. When I was thinking of joining Bollywood, I discussed it with my mother who talked about the ins and outs of the industry and the nuances of acting."

● Kapil Dev, the champion Indian all-rounder, made his 'fully-fledged' cinematic debut in 2005, with the launch of the film *Iqbal*, the story of an aspiring young handicapped cricketer who dreamed of playing for his country. The award-winning movie was not Kapil's first, having played himself in others, including *Stumped* in 2003, and *Mujhse Shaadi Karogi* from 2004 that also showcases the thespian talents of other leading cricketers Navjot Sidhu, Harbhajan Singh, Irfan Pathan, Mohammad Kaif, Ashish Nehra, Parthiv Patel and Javagal Srinath.

● Silverchair drummer Ben Gillies turned out for a celebrity cricket match in Newcastle in 2005, a game held to aid the victims of a series of bomb attacks at the Indonesian resort of Bali. A fast bowler in his younger days, Gillies used to play local club cricket in Newcastle with the band's lead singer Daniel Johns.

● A celebrity cricket team from Britain, featuring London radio announcer Chris Evans, hip-hop star Jay Sean and drummer Harry Judd embarked on a tour of India in 2006 to play a series of matches against the stars of Bollywood to raise money for charity. The Red Socks team was captained by celebrity-TV star Phil Tufnell ... who also appeared in 42 Test matches for England. In 2003, Tufnell had retired from first-class cricket to pursue a career in TV, becoming the unlikely winner of a reality show, *I'm A Celebrity, Get Me Out Of Here!*

Harry Judd – musician and cricketer

"We cobbled together a team and embarked on a training programme that saw us improve no end. We actually thought we weren't bad – until we got to India and found out we were crap!"

"The best player on tour from the celebs was without doubt Harry Judd from McFly. He was an awesome batsman, he could bowl really quickly and he kept wicket like one of the best goalies you have ever seen. He was amazing ... an amazing, amazing cricketer and apparently he could have played for England school boys."

London radio DJ Chris Evans

● Shane Warne has likened his own life to a soap opera, and in 2006 he fittingly became a part of Australia's longest-running TV soap *Neighbours* when he made his acting debut. Warne played himself in two back-to-back episodes 'Ain't That a Shane' and 'The Warne Identity', ostensibly to promote his charitable foundation.

Mishka: *Harold, where you keep the ashtrays?*

Harold: *Ah, now if there's to be any smoking, it can happen outside, preferably in the street.*

Mishka: *But, we cannot ask Warnie to step outside.*

Harold: *I'm sorry, but that's my last word on it. It's a vile habit. I won't have it under my roof.*

Mishka: *We cannot treat Shane Warne like this.*

Janelle: *Hi Shanie.*

Shane: *Hello.*

Janelle: *Janelle Timmins. I, ah, half wrote a book called* The Bogan's Tipped Hair.

Shane: *OK.*

Janelle: *Anyway, enough about me. I was wondering, that, uh, if you're free afterwards, maybe you'd like to head out for a shandy.*

GRAEME BELL'S ALL-TIME BEST TEST XI
Matthew Hayden (A)
Bill Ponsford (A)
*Don Bradman * (A)*
Sachin Tendulkar (I)
V.V.S. Laxman (I)
Ian Botham (E)
Alan Knott † (E)
Jim Laker (E)
Bill O'Reilly (A)
Dennis Lillee (A)
Curtly Ambrose (WI)

*Australian jazz legend
Graeme Bell*

● Celebrated cricket commentator John Arlott lent his voice to a 1984 British TV movie *P'tang, Yang, Kipperbang*. The film tells the story of a love-struck young schoolboy, set to a background cricket commentary provided by Arlott.

● Steve Waugh's love of the baggy green inspired him and New South Wales team-mate Gavin Robertson to write a poem in its honour which was included on a John Williamson album, *Anthems – A Celebration of Australia*. Featuring the voices of Waugh and Robertson, as well as boys from the Bankstown District Cricket Association, 'The Baggy Green' is sung to the tune of 'Click Go The Shears' and followed another cricketing track on the CD, 'Sir Don', a tribute to Don Bradman.

● Ron Haddrick, an Australian actor with a long list of television shows to his credit, played Sheffield Shield cricket in the 1950s, and also opened the batting against the touring South Africans. Haddrick – who has appeared in TV shows such as *Home and Away*, *Water Rats*, *Mother and Son* and *Homicide* – made his highest first-class score of 27 on his debut for South Australia against Queensland at Brisbane in 1951-52, with an appearance against the South Africans on his home ground the following summer completing his three-match first-class career.

RON HADDRICK'S ALL-TIME BEST TEST XI
Len Hutton (E)
Arthur Morris (A)
*Don Bradman * (A)*
Everton Weekes (WI)
Garry Sobers (WI)
Keith Miller (A)
Don Tallon † (A)
Shane Warne (A)
Michael Holding (WI)
Dennis Lillee (A)
Curtly Ambrose (WI)

● Hollywood actor Keanu Reeves spoke glowingly of cricket during an appearance on *The Tonight Show With Jay Leno* in 2003 upon his return from a filming assignment in Australia. When asked by the host **"Doesn't it go for days and days**?", Reeves put up a strong defence, declaring **"Cricket's cool. In five days you have time to … like, get into it."**

● When American rock'n'roll idol Buddy Holly toured England with his band The Crickets in 1958 he took part in a publicity photo shoot, where he was 'taught' the basics of the game of cricket by England Test players Denis Compton and Godfrey Evans. A cover-band called Buddy Holly & The Cricketers became a big hit when formed in the early 1990s, with its members making several appearances at charity cricket matches around the country.

● When Sunil Gavaskar made his Test debut at Port-of-Spain in 1970-71, the Indian XI included two players who would later appear on the silver screen. India's No. 3 batsman Salim Durani starred in a 1973 drama called *Charitra*, while Gavaskar later appeared in two films released at the zenith of his cricketing career, *Savli Premachi* and *Zakhol*. He also had a cameo appearance in *Maalamaal*, which premiered in 1988.

Another two of Gavaskar's team-mates, Sandeep Patil and Syed Kirmani, also appeared in film. All three played together in the same Test for the final time at Delhi in 1984–85, against England, with both Patil and Kirmani appearing in *Kabhi Ajnabi*, a romance flick that hit the screens in India a few months later.

Gavaskar's extraordinary feats with the bat in his debut Test series in the West Indies in '70–71 – he scored 774 runs at 154.80 – prompted Lord Relator, born Willard Harris, to write 'Gavaskar', a tune that was once rated No.68 in a poll to find the best calypso tune of the 20th century: "It was Gavaskar. The real master. Just like a wall. We couldn't out Gavaskar at all. Not at all. You know the West Indies couldn't out Gavaskar at all."

● British opera singer and cricket fan Seán Ruane was a star performer of the 2005 Ashes series where he sang at a number of Test venues around the country and at victory celebrations in London's Trafalgar Square. So popular did he become during the series, he ended up taking the sponsor's Ashes trophy to his hometown in Lancashire as part of an NPower promotion: **"It was strange really. I travelled back on Friday night with the NPower trophy in the boot of my car. Then on Saturday we put in on the mantelpiece. It was hard to believe that the trophy which England and Australia had been battling for all summer was at my home in Rawtenstall."**

Known as 'The Operatic Voice of Sport', he was back in the spotlight for the return Ashes series of '06–07, singing 'God Save The Queen' at the commencement of the fifth Test in Sydney, and then the Sarah Brightman–Andrea Bocelli hit 'Time To Say Goodbye' as a special tribute to the retiring trio of Shane Warne, Glenn McGrath and Justin Langer.

"When I did the Old Trafford sound test, Shane Warne said 'You sounded pretty good to me, mate.' When I sang the next day as he came out, he gave me the old thumbs up. It was a euphoric feeling chatting to [Andrew] Flintoff, Michael Vaughan, Simon Jones at Trafalgar Square. Even though they'd had a few, they said 'God, this guy can sing.'"

Seán Ruane

"He [Andrew Flintoff] said he would trade it all in to do what I do. He's very passionate about singing. A big karaoke man and he loves crooning."

British opera singer Jon Christos

SEÁN RUANE'S ALL-TIME BEST TEST XI

Michael Bevan (Rawtenstall)

Michael Clarke (Ramsbottom)

Steve Waugh (Nelson)

Allan Border * (East Lancashire)

Tony Mann (Bacup)

Peter Sleep † (Rishton)

Shane Warne (Accrington)

Jason Gillespie (Rishton)

Dennis Lillee (Haslingden)

Neil Hawke (East Lancashire)

Ray Lindwall (Nelson)

Seán Ruane, who chose an XI based on Australian cricketers who have played in his local area, which hosts the Lancashire League

● British rock band Half Man Half Biscuit recorded a number of songs with references to cricket, with two appearing on their 1991 album *McIntyre, Treadmore and Davitt*. Side two kicks off with 'Hedley Verityesque', while 'Christian Rock Concert' makes mention of Wendy Wimbush, the former long-serving and high-profile scorer for BBC Radio's *Test Match Special*.

Their first album, *Back In The DHSS*, released in 1985, features the track "F**kin' 'Ell It's Fred Titmus", while "Them's The Vagaries" – from *Cammell Laird Social Club* – includes the line "And what I call pressure, you might call pain, I'm talking five-day Tests."

"One of my fantasies was to have a load of folk shouting something ridiculous like 'F**king hell, it's Fred Titmus!' back at the stage as a counterblast to all those rock acts whose audience would hold their lighters aloft during some Godforsaken dross concerning 'a girl no longer with us due to flagrant disregard of the speed limit by persons unknown.' Much more fun thought I to have 'em shouting the name of a Middlesex spin bowler ... certainly more believable anyway."

Half Man Half Biscuit lead singer Nigel Blackwell

● Members of the Kent cricket team played pop stars for a day in 2006 when they recorded a CD of their official club song. 'This is Our Time' written and performed by the New Zealand-born Ryan Edwards also features the voices of various Kent players.

● The co-host of a British gardening TV show and a part-time actress combined resources in 2006 to produce a special video, one that showcased the off-field talents of Shane Warne. In an exposé published by *News Of The World*, the newspaper revealed that the two maidens who 'bowled Warne over' were Coralie Eichholtz, a pop music-video model, who played the part of a prostitute in the 2001 film *Moulin Rouge*, and an Australian-born actress Emma Kearney, star of TV shows such as *Nice House – Shame About The Garden* and *Coronation Street*.

The newspaper printed, in somewhat lurid detail, claims how Warne had arranged the threesome after sending a series of text messages, the story accompanied by photographs captured by a hidden camera set up in Kearney's flat: **"Shane's a stallion and was up for anything."** The day after his night-time romp, Warne was in fine form on the cricket pitch, snapping up 7 for 99, while captaining Hampshire to a ten-wicket win over Middlesex in the English County Championship.

"If I'm honest, I'm tired out."

Shane Warne on returning figures of 7 for 99 for Hampshire against Middlesex in 2006, the day after he had 'two for dirty-sex' in a London flat according to the British tabloid newspaper News Of The World

---

● Dave Stewart, one half of the British pop outfit The Eurythmics, produced and sang the official 1999 World Cup theme song, a CD that was released the day after England was bundled out of the tournament. 'All Over the World', written by Stewart and latino musician Chucho Merchán, sank just like the England cricket team, failing to reach the UK Top 40.

For the 2007 tournament staged in the West Indies, the Jamaican-born hit-maker Shaggy was teamed up with two other Caribbean stars for the official Cup theme 'The Game of Love and Unity'.

"I don't think nothing can worth we doing anything to jeopardise the children's education. Mi nuh say we nuh need the spin-offs of the cricket World Cup and the extra revenue, but nothing fi come inna di way of education. If you can find alternatives, if you can keep the thing and facilitate the children going to school, then that would be good 'cause when the cricket done and gone, the youth dem still a goh dey yah."

Jamaican reggae singer Coco Tea on whether schools should be closed in Kingston, Jamaica during the 2007 World Cup

● Former Australian batsman Mark Waugh captained a colourful team of characters in India in 2005, losing a match to a side led by a 12-year-old. In front a crowd of some 45,000 at Mumbai to promote a television cartoon network, Waugh's team, Mark's Maniac's, was defeated by the Super Smashers, skippered by Devin Bhatia. Waugh's side featured players such as Popeye, Olive Oyl and Noddy, which was up against an opposition with players including Scooby Doo, Johnny Bravo and Bob the Builder.

● Former Australian Test batsman Michael Slater tried his hand at prime-time reality TV in 2006, coming a cropper during rehearsals for an ice-skating show. While training for Channel Nine's *Dancing On Ice* extravaganza, Slater took a heavy fall, with his partner Anya D'Jamirze's blade running over his left hand: **"It was the biggest flesh wound I've ever seen on my body. I was spurting blood all over the ice."**

"It's like *Dumb and Dumber* when the girl says 'You've got one in a million chance of sleeping with me', and Jim Carrey says 'So you're saying I've got a chance.' I live by that."

Michael Slater in 2003, on his chances of playing for Australia again

● The American TV series *The Simpsons* has made mention of cricket, most notably in the episode 'Missionary: Impossible' first aired in the year 2000. Homer and Bart are seen watching a British TV show where cricket bats are used as weapons. And the cricketing term 'sticky wicket' pops up in 'A Tale of Two Springfields' – the series' 250th episode – that features the British rock band The Who, which came to town to perform a concert.

Cricket also features in the award-winning US TV comedy *Frasier* that starred Kelsey Grammer. In a 1996 episode, one of the central characters, Niles Crane, talks of a cricket bat in 'The Two Mrs Cranes', an episode about a former boyfriend of Daphne, the Manchester-born health-care worker, who pays her a visit.

A reference to cricket is also found in 'Where Every Bloke Knows Your Name', a season- five episode of *Frasier* set in an English pub. It's that same scene-set – an English pub – that sees the US cartoon *Family Guy* paying homage to the sport, in an episode first broadcast in 2001.

Daphne: *Oh sod off! You'd think with all your dozens and dozens of men, you'd at least leave one for me.*

Roz: *Dozens?* **[to Frasier]** *Did you tell her that?*

Frasier: *Well forgive me for keeping track.*

Niles: *Why are you fighting over that man anyway? He's got all the charm of a cricket bat!*

Roz: *You're right. You know what, Daphne you can have him.*

> *from 'The Two Mrs Cranes' episode of* Frasier, *1996*

Peter [watching cricket on British TV]: *What the hell is he talking about?*

Englishman: *Oh, it's cricket. Marvellous game, really. You see, the bowler hurls the ball toward the batter who tries to play away a fine leg. He endeavours to score by dashing between the creases, provided the wicket-keeper hasn't whipped his bails off, of course.*

Peter: *Anybody get that?*

Cleveland: *The only British idiom I know is that 'fag' means 'cigarette'.*

Peter: *Well, someone tell this 'cigarette' to shut up.*

> *from the 'One If By Clam, Two If By Sea' episode of* Family Guy, *2001*

● Not long after England had taken the Ashes from Australia in 2005, Kevin Pietersen, who topped the batting charts with 473 runs, was spotted hobnobbing with actors Mickey Rourke and Paris Hilton at a swish Hollywood party. According to an article on the *People* website, Pietersen – who had just split from his TV-host girlfriend Natalie Pinkham – was seen in the company of the blonde model at LA's Mondrian Hotel:"**Kevin sidled over to Paris and delivered a few of his best chat-up lines. He soon had her giggling and they were flirting all night.**"

"It would take a lot for the England cricket team to make a movie. Footballers are great actors – all you have to do is touch them on the ankle and they roll over screaming for a penalty."

Kevin Pietersen after viewing the 2005 football film Goal

● While watching a game of cricket on TV, music industry heavyweight Ian 'Dicko' Dickson had an epiphany that convinced him to become an Australian citizen. One of the original judges on *Australian Idol*, the British-born 'Dicko' received his papers at a ceremony in Canberra in 2007 having lived in the country since 2001: **"I was watching Australia play India and Matthew Hayden scored a century. I jumped up and punched the air and spilled my beer. I couldn't work out which I was more upset by, the fact that I was cheering on Australia or that I had spilt my beer, and I thought either way, that sort of makes me an Aussie."**

● A short film about cricket was voted the winner of a major film festival in Canada in 2006. *Cricket and The Meaning of Life* was filmed in Toronto, Trinidad and India, exploring Sanjay Talreja's move from India to Canada, and how a thriving Asian and West Indian cricketing community rekindles his love for the game in his new country.

Cricket plays a major part in a Canadian feature film that took out an award at the Sundance Film Festival in 2004. *Seducing Doctor Lewis* tells the story of a run-down Canadian island that needs a resident doctor to survive. A young, urbane, cricket-loving MD, named Chris Lewis, is enticed to the island on the promise of it being a thriving, exciting – and cricket-crazy – community. No one on the island has even heard of the game. Nominated for a string of awards internationally, the film was a huge hit in France where it topped blockbusters such as *Pirates of The Caribbean* and *The Lord of The Rings*.

A cricket scene from the 2003 French-Canadian film Seducing Doctor Lewis

● Rock star Eric Clapton, cajoled into playing the occasional game of cricket for the Bunbury XI, once broke a finger while fielding in the slips and as he left the field had his other hand stung by a bee. After a visit to hospital, he later returned to the ground with both hands bandaged just in time for tea.

● Veteran US comedian and actor Billy Crystal paid a visit to the Sydney Cricket Ground in 2007, but left no wiser in understanding the finer points of the game. In Australia to present his award-winning autobiographical stage show *700 Sundays*, Crystal went to the SCG for a net session with Australian spinner Stuart MacGill: "**I'll try to get the balls before they get me. It's a rough game, I'm not sure I understand it. You can hit the ball any place, and apparently the game goes on forever.**"

● Henry Olonga, the Zimbabwean Test cricketer-turned professional singer, released a debut album in 2006. *Aurelia*, containing ten tracks, was produced by Robbie Bronnimann – he's also worked with the  likes of the Sugarbabes and Howard Jones – and was made available for purchase only by download from Olonga's personal website.

It turned out to be a big year for the fast bowler who reigned supreme on Britain's *All Star Talent Show*. Singing Puccini's 'Nessun Dorma' on finals night, the studio audience 'clapped' him to a 94 per cent vote, but it was the television viewers that saw him acquire half of the SMS text messages and phone calls to clinch the title.

● England's Ashley Giles was sent off to the rehabilitation unit of the Birmingham Royal Ballet in 2006. The slow bowler was in the throes of overcoming a groin injury leading up to the defence of the Ashes in Australia.

"I've never been a huge fan of Kylie's music, although I've always had a soft spot for her. We are within spitting distance of the stage, and I'm sure she looked at me a couple of times."

Ashley Giles after seeing a Kylie Minogue concert during the
2006-07 Ashes tour of Australia

● Don Bradman's love of music made a mark on his granddaughter Greta who became a professional ensemble singer, performing with outfits such as the Adelaide Symphony Orchestra and the Adelaide Chamber Singers. After gaining a university degree in music in 2002, she teamed up with the Eve Vocal Trio, releasing their first CD *Evesong* in 2004.

The Eve Vocal Trio – (from left) Greta Bradman, Emma Horwood and Christie Anderson

Her grandfather also featured on record, with the Don, on piano, playing 'Old-Fashioned Locket' and 'Our Bungalow of Dreams' on a 78-rpm disc released in 1930.

● Australian stage and screen actor Hugh Jackman branched out into television production in 2006, with his first venture a five-part cricket documentary on the Barmy Army. *An Aussie Goes Barmy* featured Gus Worland, one of Jackman's friends since childhood, who travelled with the support group as they followed England around the country during the 2006-07 Ashes series: "**I thought I would have earned some respect from Jacko after 32 years, but he put me up to this! We both love cricket and this is his brainchild. We played together as kids.**"

Jackman, who began attending Tests in Australia from the age of eight, was working on a movie in England in 2005 when Australia lost the Ashes: "**I was making X-Men: The Last Stand with Patrick Stewart, who's a mad cricket guy like me. I went on set after England finally won, and he had gone into my tent and inside placed a**

Union Jack and a cricket bat. He even put an urn with ashes in it sitting on my chair."

Prior to the disappointment of the series loss, Jackman had been on a high having met up with some of his cricketing heroes in London. While driving through Knightsbridge, Jackman, while stopped at a set of red lights, spotted Ricky Ponting walking with his wife, a chance meeting that resulted in the actor and Worland both spending time with a number of the Australian squad: "**He** [Ponting] **looked at me funny. I said, 'Mate, mate'. I started to gush because I am a huge sports fan. I'm like, 'What you guys have done'. I said I was going to the game on Saturday and he said, 'Come back and see the boys and have a beer after the game'.**" Matthew Hayden later presented Jackman with a cricket bat: "**He signed it and gave it to me. I went outside and stood there with Gus, who was in shock.**"

"The boys say I am a nutter ... a cricket head."

Hugh Jackman

● Former *Big Brother* contestant Gaelan Walker appeared in a charity cricket match in Melbourne in 2007, admitting his form with the bat was 'pretty atrocious' after being dismissed seven times in four overs. His multiple dismissals gave rise to some light-hearted scorn from his teammates, including actor Rhys Muldoon: "**Gaelen's 15 minutes of fame have been bumped down to eight. He has alienated most of the industry.**"

Big Brother *contestant Gaelan Walker at a charity cricket match in Melbourne in 2007*

Others who took part in the celebrity fundraiser for St Kilda's Sacred Heart Mission included actors Gary Sweet, John Jarrett, Joel Edgerton and Stephen Curry, and comedians Dave Hughes and Peter Helliar.

IT'S A RELIGION

● One of the earliest references to adults playing cricket surfaced in 1611 in Sussex when two men were prosecuted in the village of Sidlesham, south of Chichester, for playing cricket instead of going to church. Eleven years later in the village of Boxgrove – north of Chichester – six men got intro trouble when caught playing cricket in a churchyard on a Sunday.

● During a first-class match in India in 1915-16, a record 14 ducks were recorded by the Muslims when they played the Europeans at Poona. Five of the Muslim batsmen made pairs in their totals of 21 and 39.

● So upset was Sourav Ganguly's mother at the dumping of her son from the Indian team in 2006, she brought in a priest to try to reverse his misfortune. Kartik Chatterjee performed a special ceremony – at a cemetery in Lucknow – which he claimed would see Ganguly back in national colours within six months: "**Sourav will be back in action anytime between July 15 and October 15**." His 'powers' proved to be unsuccessful, although Ganguly was back in the Test side in December.

● Cardinal Henry Manning, a leader of the Roman Catholic Church in England, attended school at Harrow, where it was noted that he gained no major distinction apart from playing cricket. He appeared in the first-ever match between the Harrow and Winchester schools at Lord's in 1825.

● Mary Doyle, one of the oldest Sisters of Mercy in the world, died in New Zealand in 1996 at the age of 109. Sister Mary attributed her longevity to her faith in God and her love of cricket.

● The sometimes eccentric New Zealand umpire Billy Bowden, the son of a retired Baptist minister, believes that God already knows the decisions he's going to make in his next cricket series. Bowden says he came close to forgoing his beliefs when he was struck down with arthritis just at the time he was on the verge of breaking into the Auckland cricket team: **"It really hit me for a six. I lost a lot of faith. I was angry and frustrated. I thought, 'I'm a good man, I've done everything for the good of others' and I just couldn't understand why I got this disease. It taught me a lesson that you can't control everything you do, that sometimes God has other plans for us. It taught me that every day you're alive is a blessing. You have to take each day as it comes, because you never know when you're going to be called to heaven."**

"God is my best friend. He's always been my third umpire. He's there behind me, beside me, in front of me."

NZ umpire Billy Bowden

● Off-spinner Mark Beban made his first-class debut for Wellington in 1969-70 shortly after he'd been ordained as a Catholic priest. In the last of his four first-class matches, he took five wickets against Auckland, where one of the umpires was the Reverend David Bindon.

● The Reverend Robert Gwynn was a member of a prominent Irish cricket family and played for the Gentleman of Ireland XI. In one match in Dublin, he had the distinction of taking the wicket of W.G. Grace first-ball.

● The Anglican Archbishop of Sydney Peter Jensen possesses an unbridled passion for the game, having played Green Shield cricket for the Waverley and Paddington clubs. He only ever competed in one or two church cricket matches, but fondly recalled one game where a team-mate scored a double-century: **"We played a team of portly Baptists if I remember, and one man scored 250 against them and they were very angry that he was playing out of his league. If you can imagine portly Baptists, in their fifties. That was good fun."**

"It's surely the greatest game of all. Cricket and Christianity both require to be taken with utter seriousness. There's no point playing either if you're not utterly serious."

Sydney Anglican Archbishop Peter Jensen

⬤ In the midst of the match-fixing crisis that engulfed cricket in 2000, a group of supporters performed a religious ceremony in the Indian city of Rajkot to purify the game. Kartavya Vyas, with the help of a Hindu priest, soaked a cricket bat, ball and stumps in water and cow's milk against a background of chanting, and then presented the items to the secretary of the Indian Cricket Board.

Cricket-playing monks from the Namdroling Monastery in India, and (right) disciples take a break in between their religious studies at Karnataka's Horanaadu Temple

⬤ In the summer of 2005-06, Barbados skipper Ryan Hinds became the first batsman to top 150 in each innings of a provincial first-class match in the West Indies, later dedicating his feat to God. Hinds hit 150 and 168 against Leeward Islands at St Thomas: **"It is a great achievement. I told myself just hang in there and get another hundred. I didn't know I would get 150. Praises to God for guiding me. I'm very grateful."**

⬤ Canada's first tour of England, in 1880, was plunged into disarray after the fifth match when its captain was arrested on charges of deserting the army. After being trotted off to prison, the Reverend Thomas Phillips was summoned from Canada as his replacement.

● Anil Dalpat, who made his Test debut against England in 1983-84, was the first Hindu to play Test cricket for Pakistan. The second to do so was his cousin Danish Kaneria, who also made his Test debut against England, in 2000-01.

● An inter-faith cricket match was staged in England in 2006 to commemorate the fifth anniversary of the September 11 terrorist attacks in the United States. Local Christian clergy and Muslim imams from Leicestershire played a 20-overs match at Grace Road that included a Jewish and a Hindu umpire.

"The work of the Muslim-Christian dialogue is seen as a model of how to break down negative stereotypes and adds to community cohesion."

The Right Reverend Tim Stevens, Bishop of Leicester

● Pakistani spinner Sheikh Fazal-ur-Rehman, who appeared in a single Test match, against the West Indies at Georgetown in 1957-58, later gained a masters degree in Islamic studies, becoming a highly-respected religious scholar. A devout Muslim, he took 96 wickets in just 29 first-class matches and also scored one century.

● In 2006, the Pakistan Cricket Board issued a plea to its players to restrict displaying their religious beliefs in public. The call by its chairman Nasim Ashraf came as the national team was seen more and more to pray in public places, including cricket venues and hotels: "**There is no doubt their religious faith is a motivating factor in the team. It binds them together. But there should be balance between religion and cricket.**"

He also appealed to the captain not to force Islam upon the squad, with claims that players who didn't participate in prayer might find their place in the team in jeopardy. It was an accusation rejected out-of-hand by Inzamam-ul-Haq: "**I have never forced anyone to offer prayers in the team. I've never linked team selection to offering prayers and reports suggesting otherwise are all wrong.**"

HUNDREDS & THOUSANDS

● Sachin Tendulkar, the first batsman to score 30 and 40 centuries in one-day internationals, had to wait an agonising five years for his first. The maiden hundred (110) came in his 78th match, against Australia at Colombo in 1994. Quite inexplicably, he then made a duck in his following three one-day internationals – one against Sri Lanka and two against the West Indies.

● During the international season of 1999-2000, Steve Waugh twice scored a Test century for Australia as captain, both of which were identical innings of 151 not out. The first came in Australia's all-out total of 422 against Zimbabwe in Harare, while the second was contained in Australia's all-out 419 against New Zealand at Wellington some six months later.

● When Ricky Ponting made a century against Bangladesh in 2003, he became the first batsman to complete a full set of hundreds in one-day internationals against all other nine Test-playing nations. The Australian captain's 101 in the third one-day international at Darwin saw him move ahead of a number of batsmen – Sourav Ganguly, Herschelle Gibbs, Brian Lara, Sachin Tendulkar and Mark Waugh – who, at the time, had all scored centuries against eight different Test countries.

During the 2003 World Cup, Tendulkar (152) and Ganguly (112*) both scored hundreds against Namibia at Pietermaritzburg, sharing in a match-winning double-century partnership. When Tendulkar reached three figures, he became the first batsman to score a one-day international century against ten different teams, a feat that was equalled by Ganguly later in the innings.

● In the course of hitting 160 against Bangladesh at Chittagong in 2004-05, India's Rahul Dravid became the fourth batsman, after Steve Waugh, Gary Kirsten and Sachin Tendulkar, to score a century against all Test-playing nations. He also became the first player to score a century in all ten Test-playing regions of the world – India, England, New Zealand, Australia, South Africa, West Indies, Pakistan, Sri Lanka, Zimbabwe and Bangladesh. Although Waugh was unable to score a century in Sri Lanka, and did not appear in a Test match in Bangladesh, his tally is boosted by the inclusion of a century scored at the neutral venue of Sharjah in 2002-03 (103★ v Pakistan).

● Cambridge University student Stuart Moffat celebrated his first-class debut in 2002 by scoring a century. Appearing in his only first-class innings – against Oxford at The Parks – Moffat produced a knock of 169, spiced with 17 fours and five sixes. He left the first-class arena with an average of 169.00, one of the highest in the history of the game.

● During the fourth Test at The Oval in 2004, the West Indies' Chris Gayle smashed a 79-ball century, the second-fastest Test ton in England, just behind Gilbert Jessop in 1902. On his way to 105, Gayle hit Matthew Hoggard for six consecutive fours in an over, the first time this had been achieved in a Test match. Only two batsmen before him had hit every ball of an over to the boundary in a Test match – New Zealand's Craig McMillan hit five fours and a six (4-4-4-4-6-4) off Pakistan's Younis Khan at Hamilton in 2000-01 and Brian Lara, who achieved four fours and two sixes (4-6-6-4-4-4) off South Africa's Robin Peterson at Johannesburg in 2003-04.

By reaching his Oval hundred in 79 deliveries, Gayle became the first batsman in Test history to twice reach 100 in fewer than 80 balls, after a 79-ball effort against South Africa at Cape Town earlier in the year.

● In the century-rich third Test at Cape Town in 2003-04, two batsmen hit a hundred runs in a session. The Test match produced seven centuries – four for South Africa and three for the West Indies – with Chris Gayle (116) and team-mate Dwayne Smith (105★) scoring a hundred runs in the tea-to-stumps session. Gayle's century came up in 99 minutes off a mere 79 balls, with 19 fours and a six, between tea and stumps on day two, while Smith, on his Test debut, powered his way to 100 in 103 minutes off just 93 balls on the final day.

● Brian Lara finished the four-match Test series against England in 2003-04 with exactly 500 runs. His tally was assisted by his colossal world-record knock of 400 not out in the fourth Test at St John's, while he accumulated just 100 runs in his other six innings (23, 0, 0, 8, 36 & 33). It was the seventh occasion Lara had scored 500 runs in a Test series, breaking Garry Sobers' West Indian record.

En route to his 400 at Antigua, Lara became just the sixth batsman to feature in two double-century partnerships in the same Test innings. The West Indies skipper put on 232 runs for the third wicket with Ramnaresh Sarwan (90) and 282, unbroken, for the sixth wicket with Ridley Jacobs (107★).

● Rahul Dravid emulated the great Don Bradman in 2003-04 when he scored 270 against Pakistan at Rawalpindi, his third double-hundred in as many Test series. Dravid's innings spanned 740 minutes – the longest knock by an Indian batsman in Test cricket – and followed double-centuries against New Zealand and Australia earlier in the season. Only Bradman, before him, had scored a double-century in three consecutive Test series, posting as many as six 200s in contests against England, the West Indies and South Africa in the early 1930s.

Dravid's 270 was his third consecutive score of over 100 which exceeded 200. A sequence of nine Tests in 2003-04 revealed innings of 222, 73, 13, 5 (v New Zealand), 1, 43 not out, 233, 72 not out, 49, 92, 38, 91 not out (v Australia), 6, 33, 0 and 270 (v Pakistan).

On two occasions Bradman registered sequences that included four centuries in excess of 200 – 254, 1, 334, 14, 232 versus England in 1930 and 4, 25, 223 against West Indies in 1930-31; and then 304, 244, 77 versus England in 1934 and 38, 0, 0, 82, 13, 270, 26, 212 against England in 1936-37.

● After scoring a maiden first-class triple-century and a near double-hundred in his next match, Surrey's Mark Ramprakash reached the relatively rare milestone of 2000 first-class runs in a season in 2006.

Playing against Worcestershire at New Road, Ramprakash became the first English batsman to pass the milestone since he did it back in 1995, before falling for 196 to the last ball of the second day's play. He got to the 2000-mark in just 20 innings, eclipsing the record of Don Bradman, who reached the target in 21 innings in 1938, and Graham Gooch, in 1990. In his previous match, Ramprakash had become a member of the 300-club, reaching 301 not out against Northamptonshire at The Oval. His nine-hour innings was the first triple-hundred for the county in the County Championship since Jack Hobbs hit an unbeaten 316 against Middlesex at Lord's in 1926.

At the age of 37, Ramprakash scored first-class 2278 runs – with eight hundreds and nine fifties – in 15 matches during the summer at 103.54. With 2211 runs in the Championship, he became only the third cricketer to achieve a triple-figure average (105.28). He reached double figures in all 24 first-class innings during the season, a new record, and made a score of 150 in five consecutive matches, incinerating Vijay Merchant's world record set in 1941-42. He also passed 2000 runs at a century average the following season.

● India's Kris Srikkanth, who played in 43 Tests and in 146 one-day internationals, finished his career with an identical highest score in both forms of the game. In Test cricket, he made two hundreds, the highest of which was 123 against Pakistan at Chennai in 1986-87. The highest of his four one-day international centuries was also 123, also against Pakistan, at Calcutta in the same season. Srikkanth also had an average of 29 in both Tests and one-day internationals.

● Playing against the West Indies in 1957, Peter May (285*) and Colin Cowdrey (154) celebrated the first Test match held at Birmingham in 28 years by recording England's highest-ever partnership. Their stand of 411 remained the Test record for the fourth wicket until 2008-09. When Cowdrey was dismissed, May declared England's innings closed, depriving himself the opportunity of scoring a triple-century and it turned out to be his highest-ever score in Test cricket.

In the fourth Test against India at Hyderabad in 1982-83, Javed Miandad (280*) made his highest score at Test level, but was also denied the chance to make 300 when his captain, Imran Khan, made a declaration. After a record third-wicket partnership of 451 between Javed and Mudassar Nazar (231), Imran's strategy paid off, with Pakistan securing an emphatic victory, by a margin of an innings and 119 runs.

● Bermuda hosted and appeared in the final of the inaugural '20-20 World Cricket Classic' tournament for the over-35s in 2006, in which South Africa's openers both scored hundreds. Off its 20 overs, the South Africans reached a winning total of 266 for 5, after Gary Kirsten hit 103 and Steven Jack, a former Transvaal fast bowler, 109. Both reached their centuries in under 50 balls in a first-wicket partnership of 180.

● Middlesex batsman Andrew Strauss secured a heavenly double in 2004 when he made a century on his first appearance in both Test and one-day international cricket at Lord's. The first leg of the double came on his Test debut, when he starred with 112 against New Zealand, and then made a neat 100 against the West Indies in his 11th one-day international, but his first at the home of cricket, performing the feat in front of his home crowd.

On his Test debut overseas, at Port Elizabeth in 2004-05, Strauss made 126, and 94 not out, against South Africa, becoming just the second England batsman to record a hundred in his debut Test at home and abroad. He also became the first batsman to score a century in his maiden Test against three different countries, having made 123 against the West Indies at Lord's a few months beforehand.

With 112 and 83 on his Test debut, at Lord's, and his double at Port Elizabeth, Strauss established another precedent, becoming the first batsman to score a century and a half-century in his first Test at home and first Test away. With 136 in the second Test at Durban, he then struck another century (147) in the fourth Test at Johannesburg, reaching the milestone of 1200 runs in the first

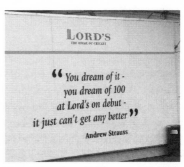

LORD'S
THE HOME OF CRICKET

❝ You dream of it -
you dream of 100
at Lord's on debut -
it just can't get any better ❞
Andrew Strauss

11 Tests of his career. After the first four Tests of the series, the opening combination of Strauss and Marcus Trescothick had breezed past 1000 runs in tandem. Strauss had 612 runs from eight innings in the bank, and Trescothick 421, with a total of five hundreds between them.

"He's so calm and composed."

Marcus Trescothick after a 273-run stand made in concert with his opening partner Andrew Strauss at Durban in 2004-05

In 2006, Strauss assumed the role of England captain – in place of an injured Andrew Flintoff, who, himself, was filling the void vacated by an injured Michael Vaughan – and scored a century in his first match in charge, making 128 against Pakistan at Lord's. Coupled with his 112 on debut in 2004, Strauss became the first player to score a century on his Test debut and a century on his debut as captain where both instances occurred at the home of cricket. He was also only the second player to achieve the double anywhere, following Australia's Greg Chappell, who hit 108 on debut, against England at Perth in 1970-71, and then celebrated his first match as captain by scoring 123 and 109 not out against the West Indies at Brisbane in 1975-76.

● Chris Broad scored a total of seven centuries for England, but never made one at home. He scored six in Test matches and another in a one-day international, with a highest score in England of 99 against Pakistan at The Oval in the 1987 Texaco Trophy, and of 86 in a Test, against Sri Lanka at Lord's in 1984. His broad bat produced hundreds in three consecutive Tests in Australia in 1986-87 – 162 at Perth, 116 at Adelaide and 112 at Melbourne.

● During the calendar year of 1997, Sri Lanka's Aravinda de Silva scored seven Test centuries, with two lots of three hundreds coming in consecutive innings, all six made in the same city. He began his unique purple patch with 168 against Pakistan at Colombo's R. Premadasa International Cricket Stadium and then became the first batsman to complete a Test match with two unbeaten hundreds, scoring 138 and 103 against the Pakistanis at the Sinhalese Sports Club ground.

After a two-match Test series in the West Indies where he scored a duck, 47, 35 and 78, de Silva returned home and thumped three hundreds on the trot against India – 126 at Premadasa, where the Sri Lankans made Test cricket's highest-ever total of 952 for 6 declared, and then 146 and 120 in the following Test at the SSC ground.

● After a lean trot of 51 consecutive County Championship innings without a hundred, John Crawley made up for it in a big way by posting his maiden first-class triple-century. At Trent Bridge in 2004, the former England batsman hit an unbeaten 301 for Hampshire against Nottinghamshire, sharing a double-century partnership with Australian import Michael Clarke (140) who hit his first hundred for the club, and finished the match with another (103). Three hundreds were also scored for Nottinghamshire in its only innings of 612 – 103 by Darren Bicknell, 113 not out by Mark Ealham and 170 by Australian import David Hussey.

Crawley struck another unbeaten triple-century the following summer, taking the prize for the highest first-class innings in England in 2005. Crawley, with an obvious penchant for the Notts attack, hit 311 not out at Southampton, posting an unbeaten 254-run stand for the sixth wicket with Dimitri Mascarenhas (103*) as Hampshire built a match-winning total of 714 for 5 declared.

● A precocious talent, Vinod Kambli made it to the milestone of 1000 Test runs in a record 14 innings for India, yet his career was all over by the age of 24 after 21 innings and another 84 runs. He only appeared in 17 Test matches in which he scored four centuries – with two doubles in successive innings – and had an average of over 54.00.

Kambli was a big-occasion player in the first innings of Test matches, averaging 69.13, but averaged just 9.40 in the second, a record difference of 59.73.

● Sanath Jayasuriya came within twelve runs of a double-century against Pakistan at Kandy in the year 2000, while his opening partner Marvan Atapattu made an unbeaten 207 sharing a record first-wicket stand of 335. Had Jayasuriya pieced together just another dozen runs, he and Atapattu would have become only the second set of opening batsmen to both score double-centuries in the same Test innings. In 1964-65, Australia's Bill Lawry (210) and Bob Simpson (201) both hit 200s in a record opening stand of 382 against the West Indies at Bridgetown.

● Of the first six centuries made by Australia's Bob Simpson in Test cricket, only one was under 150. His maiden century was a mammoth 311 – against England at Manchester in 1964 – while his next five hundreds were 153, 115, 201, 225 and 153.

Other batsmen whose first three Test centuries were innings of 150-plus include the Sri Lankan Mahela Jayawardene (167, 242, 167), Pakistan's Javed Miandad (163, 206, 154*), the New Zealand pair of Andrew Jones (150, 170*, 186) and Mathew Sinclair (214, 150, 204*), and Brian Lara, who twice exceeded 250 (277, 167, 375).

● During the third Test against India Bangalore in 2004-05, Pakistan's Inzamam-ul-Haq became the first batsman to celebrate his 100th Test match with an innings of over 150, making 184, and sharing a record 324-run third–wicket partnership with Younis Khan (267). The pair scored a total of 451 runs, which represented 79.12 per cent of Pakistan's total of 570, the second-best in Test cricket in an all-out innings, after Don Bradman (304) and Bill Ponsford (181), who contributed 83.05 per cent of the Australian total of 584 against England at Leeds in 1934.

In India's first innings, Virender Sehwag became the third batsman to pass 150 in the match, blasting his way to 201, but also became the first Indian to end up on the losing side after contributing a double-century. He had held the record for the previous top score in a losing side for India, when he made 195 against Australia at Melbourne in 2003-04.

In the first Test at Mohali, Sehwag (173) was involved in three century partnerships – the first three of the innings – a first for India in Test-match cricket. He began with a 113-run opening stand with Gautam Gambhir, added 103 for the second wicket with Rahul Dravid and then 118 for the third wicket with Sachin Tendulkar.

"Sehwag can change the course of a match with the ease of Moses parting the Red Sea."

Ian Chappell

● Hot on the heels of becoming the first batsman to reach 1000 Test runs for the 2004 calendar year, Brian Lara finished the third Test against England at Manchester with exactly 10,000 career-runs to his credit. He became just the fourth batsman – after Sunil Gavaskar, Allan Border and Steve Waugh – to reach the landmark, doing so in record time. Lara took the least number of Tests (111) and innings (195) to achieve the milestone.

During the second Test against Pakistan at Kolkata in 2004-05, India's Sachin Tendulkar matched Lara's feat in reaching the 10,000-run landmark in 195 innings, becoming the youngest batsman to do so, aged 31 years and 326 days. The Indian ace also became the first batsman to score 10,000 runs in both Tests and one-day internationals.

● Appearing in just his third Test match, England's Ian Bell peeled off a century before lunch en route to an unbeaten 162 and a career average of 297.00. Batting at No. 4 in the second Test against Bangladesh at Chester-le-Street in 2005, Bell struck his maiden century, after previous innings in Test cricket of 70 and 65 not out. By chiming in with 105 runs (57*-162*) in a two-hour session on the second day, Bell became just the sixth England batsman – and the first since Les Ames in 1935 – to score a century before lunch in a Test match.

● Despite seven Test centuries to his credit at the time, South Africa's Graeme Smith had never reached three figures in a one-day international until his 58th attempt when he made a match-winning 105 against England at Port Elizabeth in 2004-05. At the end of the match, Smith had batted in 58 Test *and* 58 ODI innings, and while a century had eluded him until Port Elizabeth, he had an unblemished record when it came to ducks in one-day internationals possessing a clean slate.

Smith's 105 was the first century by a South African captain in a one-day international, putting to rest the anguish of being run out for 99 against Sri Lanka at Centurion two years previously. Two matches later, Smith did it again, batting through the entire 50 overs against England at East London with an unbeaten 115.

● When Steve Waugh reached 100 in the first indoor one-day international, at Melbourne's Docklands Stadium in 2000, the Australian captain's century (114*) was the 500th scored in the shortened version of the game. His hundred came one ball after Michael Bevan (106) had scored the 499th century, the two sharing a massive fourth-wicket partnership of 222.

● Dutch batsman Daan van Bunge, who appeared in the 2003 and 2007 World Cups, hit a 38-ball century for the MCC at Weybridge in 2004. His innings of 121, which included 14 fours and nine sixes, was higher than that of his opposition, the Surrey Under-19s (119), and was the fastest hundred in the history of MCC Young Cricketers. Between the years 2003 and 2005, van Bunge collected 3400 runs for the MCC junior side.

● Opener Don Cherry blossomed during the 2005 County Championship, becoming the first Glamorgan batsman to launch his century-making career with two scores in excess of 150. The left-hander posted his maiden century against Middlesex at Southgate, an innings of 226, and later struck 166 against Gloucestershire at Bristol.

Cherry came within 34 runs of joining a select band of cricketers who began their careers with two double-centuries. The first to do so was Victor Trumper, for New South Wales in 1898-99. His maiden first-class century was an unbeaten 292 against Tasmania at Sydney; his second was 253 against the touring New Zealanders, also at the SCG, later in the season.

● Within his first nine Test innings against Pakistan, India's Virender Sehwag had scored a century, a double-century and a triple. On his debut against his near neighbours, at Multan in 2003-04, he scored 309, made 173 four innings later at Chandigarh the following season, and then 201 at Bangalore two Tests later.

Sehwag became only the third batsman to achieve such a treble, after Don Bradman against England and Walter Hammond against New Zealand. Bradman needed 13 innings to bring up a century, a double and a triple against England, while Hammond required just six goes, posting consecutive scores of 100 not out, 16, 227, 336 not out and 140 against the Kiwis during the 1930s.

● During the calendar year of 2003, Ricky Ponting became the first batsman to score over 1000 runs in the 12 months at an average of over 100. In just 11 Tests, Ponting hit 1503 runs, with six hundreds, at an average of 100.20. In 2005, the Australian captain then became the first batsman to top the 1500-run mark twice in a calendar year, collecting 1544 runs, with six centuries, from 15 Tests.

Ponting began the year of 2006 in history-making style, becoming the first batsman to celebrate his 100th Test match with a hundred in each innings. His dynamic double of 120 and 143 not out in the first Test match of the year – at Sydney – saw Ponting also pass the twin-milestones of 1000 Test runs at the SCG and 1000 runs against South Africa. Previously only five others – Colin Cowdrey, Gordon Greenidge, Javed Miandad, Alec Stewart and Inzamam-ul-Haq – had marked their 100th Test with a century, with Ponting also becoming the first Australian to score a century in each innings of a Test match twice in the same season, having made 149 and 104 not out against the West Indies at Brisbane earlier in the summer.

Ponting came close to topping 1000 runs in the domestic summer alone, scoring 944 with five centuries and a further four half-centuries in the seven Tests of 2005-06. After scoring exactly 100 runs (46 & 54) in the opening Test of the summer, against a World XI at Sydney, he finished the season at the same venue by becoming the first batsman to register five Test hundreds at the SCG. His unbeaten 143 – which contributed to a big Australian victory – was his 21st century batting at No. 3, overtaking Don Bradman's feat of 20 hundreds at this position. The first Australian to hit five Test hundreds in a season, Ponting also slipped into the top ten of Test cricket's highest-scoring batsmen of all time.

● After his first ten innings in Test-match cricket, Mike Hussey sailed past the milestone of 500 runs, to sit at No. 2 on the Australian all-time list, just behind Don Bradman. After scoring one on his Test debut – just as Bradman had done back in 1928-29 – Hussey put together three hundreds in accumulating 595 runs in his first five appearances.

His third century, which took him past the 500-mark, came during the Boxing Day Test match against South Africa at the MCG in 2005-06. With Australia perched precariously at 9 for 248 in the first innings,

Hussey was joined at the crease by the No.11, Glenn McGrath: "**I must admit when Glenn came to the crease and I was on 27, I didn't think I could score a hundred**." Only three other batsmen had been able to reach 100 from such a score, or a lower one, when joined by the No.11 – Australia's Johnny Taylor against England at Sydney in 1924-25, England's Peter Willey against the West Indies at The Oval in 1980 and New Zealand's Nathan Astle against England at Auckland in 1996-97. Hussey went on to 122, with the No.11 making 11 not out, in a partnership worth an invaluable 107. Hussey's contribution of 95 runs in the stand outstripped the previous best in Test cricket of 89 runs by Pakistan's Azhar Mahmood in the world-record partnership of 151 with Mushtaq Ahmed against South Africa at Rawalpindi in 1997-98.

After a partnership of 231 with Matthew Hayden against the West Indies in Hobart a month before, Hussey became only the fourth batsman – after England's Wilfred Rhodes and Alec Stewart and Australia's Reggie Duff – to have taken part in a century stand for the first wicket and the last in a Test match. McGrath also made the record books by becoming the first tail-ender – and only the second after Nathan Astle – to feature in two Test-match 100-run stands for the last wicket, following one scored with Jason Gillespie against New Zealand at Brisbane the previous summer.

MOST RUNS AFTER FIRST FIVE TESTS

Runs	Batsman	Scores	100s	Avge
831	Sunil Gavaskar (I)	65 & 67*, 116 & 64*, 1 & 117*, 124 & 220, 4 & 53	4	118.71
714	George Headley (WI)	21 & 176, 8 & 39, 114 & 112, 10 & 223, 0 & 11	4	71.40
622	Conrad Hunte (WI)	142 & 11*, 8 & 37, 260, 5 & 114, 0 & 45	3	77.75
607	Don Bradman (A)	18 & 1, 79 & 112, 40 & 58, 123 & 37*, 8 & 131	3	67.44
599	K.S. Ranjitsinhji (E)	62 & 154*, 8 & 11, 175 & 8*, 71 & 27, 6 & 77	2	74.88
595	Mike Hussey (A)	1 & 29, 137 & 31*, 133* & 30*, 23 & 58, 122 & 31	3	85.00

MOST RUNS BY AUSTRALIANS AFTER FIRST FIVE TESTS

607	Don Bradman	18 & 1, 79 & 112, 40 & 58, 123 & 37*, 8 & 131	3	67.44
595	Mike Hussey	1 & 29, 137 & 31*, 133* & 30*, 23 & 58, 122 & 31	3	85.00
557	Herbie Collins	70 & 104, 64, 162 & 24, 59 & 32, 5 & 37	2	61.89
541	Michael Clarke	151 & 17, 5 & 39*, 91 & 73, 17 & 7, 141	2	67.63
527	Kepler Wessels	162 & 46, 44 & 1, 47 & 14, 19 & 53, 141	2	58.56
503	Arthur Morris	2, 5, 21 & 155, 122 & 124*, 57 & 17	3	71.86

● With knocks of 103 and 116 against South Africa at Durban in 2005-06, Ricky Ponting became the first batsman to score a century in each innings of a Test match three times in the same season. Following his doubles of 149 and 104 not out against the West Indies at Brisbane and 120 and 143 not out against the South Africans at Sydney, Ponting became only the second batsman after India's Sunil Gavaskar (124 & 220 v West Indies at Port-of-Spain in 1970-71, 111 & 137 v Pakistan at Karachi in 1978-79 and 107 & 182★ v West Indies at Kolkata in 1978-79) to register the feat. Gavaskar took eight years to achieve his three doubles, whereas Ponting needed just eight matches.

● Ian Harvey, who appeared in 73 one-day internationals for Australia but never in a Test, struck the first *two* centuries in Twenty20 cricket. In 2003, he became the first player to reach three figures when he made 100 not out off 50 balls for Gloucestershire against Warwickshire, and made number two the following year with a barnstorming 108 for Yorkshire versus Lancashire at Leeds. Later in the summer, Queensland's Andrew Symonds, playing for Kent, smashed 112 off just 43 balls against Middlesex at Maidstone, his innings including 18 fours and three sixes.

● After 15 years and some 500 appearances at the crease in first-class and major limited-overs cricket, Shane Warne finally scored his first century in 2005, while captaining Hampshire in the English County Championship. Batting at No. 9 against Kent at Canterbury, the 35-year-old Warne smashed an unbeaten 107 off just 81 balls, with 16 fours and three sixes. He reached his hundred in 100 minutes off 72 deliveries, laying to rest his previous first-class best of 99, made during the third Test against New Zealand at Perth in 2001-02.

His maiden hundred came in his 238th first-class match, and in his 321st innings, having debuted in 1990-91. Warne was still a long way off the record of England and Derbyshire wicket-keeper Bob Taylor, who scored his only century in first-class cricket – 100 against Yorkshire at Sheffield in 1981 – in his 744th innings. Having waited so long for his maiden ton, Warne produced another just five matches later. Playing against Middlesex at Southgate, Warne smashed another rapid-fire hundred – 101 off 82 balls, with 12 fours and three sixes.

"We're on TV, so I can't swear."

Shane Warne when told in 2005 that umpire Darrell Hair had missed a no-ball during his 99 against New Zealand at Perth in 2001-02

● Seven years after making his first-class debut, Michael Klinger finally recorded his maiden century against the same opposition which he had achieved his previous highest score. Coming into the Victorian side in 1998-99 as the youngest batsman ever to score a century in Melbourne grade cricket, and as a captain of the Australian Under-19s, Klinger's first three-figure innings in first-class cricket came in 2005-06 when he struck 107 against Tasmania at Hobart.

It was in the same fixture four years previously that Klinger had last had a sniff of a century, when one run away from reaching his goal, his captain Paul Reiffel declared Victoria's first innings closed. Not only was Klinger somewhat cruelly left stranded on 99 not out, Victoria went on to lose the match.

● When Sri Lankan opener Sanath Jayasuriya amassed a formidable innings of 253 against Pakistan at Faisalabad in 2004-05 he shared a ninth-wicket stand of 101, in which his partner scored just one. Dilhara Fernando's single came off his 19th ball when the stand was worth 71, his contribution the lowest by any batsman in a partnership of 100 or more in a Test match. In 2003-04, the West Indies began the third Test against South Africa at Cape Town clubbing a first-wicket stand of 126, but with one of the openers contributing less than 20. The 100-run mark came in 72 minutes off 98 balls, with Chris Gayle (116) hitting 77 and Daren Ganga (17) 16.

● After becoming the first batsman to be run out for 199 in a Test, Pakistan's Younis Khan was heart-breakingly dismissed for 194 in his following match, a world first. Younis' double – at Lahore and Faisalabad in 2005-06 – elevated him into exclusive company becoming the first batsman to score a century in four consecutive Tests against India, and only the fourth in Test history to do so against a particular opposition. After making 147 and a duck at Kolkata in 2004-05, Younis then made 267, 84 not out, 199, 83 and 194 against his near-neighbours. In just five innings, Younis had plundered a record-total of 827 runs, average 206.75. And by scoring a total of 553 runs, average 110.60, Younis became the first batsman to achieve 500 runs in consecutive three-match Test series against a particular opposition, having made 508 runs at 101.60 against India in 2004-05.

Younis and Mohammad Yousuf were in fine fettle as a combination during the '05-06 series, scoring over 700 runs in partnership for the third wicket in the first two Tests. At Lahore, they piled on a record 319 runs, with stands of 142 and 242 in the second Test, for a total of 703 in just three innings. After both made ducks in their next outing together, in the first innings of the third Test at Karachi, the second innings saw yet another century partnership, one of 158.

● The explosive Shahid Afridi struck back-to-back centuries against India in 2005-06, both of which came in under a hundred balls. The first of 103 at Lahore saw him reach 100 in 78 balls, with seven fours and seven sixes, while his second of 156 at Faisalabad was a little more sedate. It was Afridi's first score of 150-plus in a Test match, reaching triple figures off 96 deliveries with 13 fours and four sixes.

By striking a total of six sixes, Afridi became the first batsman to achieve half-a-dozen in successive Test innings and the first to accomplish the feat on four separate occasions. His previous Test century – 122 against the West Indies at Bridgetown in 2005 – also came off less than 100 balls (78).

● As a means of easing his way back onto the game after shoulder surgery, Sachin Tendulkar turned out for the Lashings World XI in England in 2006 and came within two runs of scoring centuries in his first five innings. After making 155 on his debut for the club against a Cambridge University XI, he then hit 147, 98, 101 and 105 in his next four outings: "**This is a great opportunity for me to get back**

into cricket, to get some batting practice and to play matches that will help raise money for charity. I get the chance to play alongside international players, but not in games where every run counts."

A few months later, Tendulkar completed his comeback with an unbeaten 141 balls opening the batting against the West Indies in the 2006-07 DLF Cup in Kuala Lumpur. He became the first batsman to reach the milestone of 40 one-day international centuries, with Sanath Jayasuriya and Sourav Ganguly equal-second on the list at the time, a long way back with 22 hundreds.

● Appearing in the fifth one-day international against South Africa at Centurion in 2006-07, Sachin Tendulkar became the first batsman to reach the milestone of 25,000 international runs. Going into the match with 10,469 Test runs and 14,482 runs in one-dayers, Tendulkar motored his way to 55, his 74th ODI fifty, and establishing yet another first in the game.

● In a one month-period in England in 2006, Victorian spinner Cameron White smashed a world-record score in a Twenty20 match and then bashed a maiden first-class double-century, but both times ended up on the losing side. Captaining Somerset on each occasion, he struck an unbeaten 141 out of 198 for 4 against Worcestershire at Worcester in the Twenty20 Cup, an innings reached in 70 minutes off 70 balls, with 14 fours and six sixes. White reached his century off 55 balls, with 11 fours and three sixes.

The following month and with Somerset facing a huge victory-target of 579 in a County Championship match against Derbyshire at Derby, White led the way with a blazing 260 not out at a strike rate of 105.69. White, a few days shy of his 23rd birthday, faced 246 balls and hit 40 fours and three sixes in his last Championship innings of the summer before he returned home to Victoria. It was the highest score in the fourth innings of a first-class match, burying the previous record of 251 by Hansie Cronje, for Orange Free State against the 1993-94 touring Australians at Bloemfontein.

In 12 Championship matches in 2006, White scored over 1000 runs in the season, his total of 1190 coming at an average of 59.50; while he, and county team-mate, the West Australian, Justin Langer, were the only ones to pass 400 runs at a fifty average in Twenty20 cricket.

● Glen Chapple, who made his one-day international debut in 2006, hit a first-class century for Lancashire in 1993 in world-record time after he'd been promoted from No.10 all the way to the top. Chapple opened the second innings of the County Championship match against Glamorgan at Old Trafford with the Spanish-born No.11 Alexander Barnett, and struck an unbeaten 109 thanks to a succession of full tosses and long hops sent down to expedite a declaration.

After whacking his way to 50 in ten minutes, Chapple brought up his maiden hundred in first-class cricket in just 21. In the 2006 County Championship, Essex opener Mark Pettini reached 100 against Leicestershire at Grace Road in 24 minutes off 27 balls, with 11 fours and ten sixes, all thanks to accommodating bowlers, including opening batsman Darren Robinson, who returned figures of 4.4-0-117-0, conceding a little over 25 runs per over. Pettini finished with 114 not out, all coming in boundaries (12 fours & 11 sixes).

West Australian batsman Murray Goodwin was also the recipient of some so-called 'joke' bowling in 2006, bringing up a ton for Sussex in 25 minutes off 32 balls in the match against Middlesex at Southgate. Out for 156, he reached the 150-mark in 42 minutes off 47 balls, securing 19 fours and 11 sixes.

The quickest authentic first-class century remains a 35-minute effort by Surrey's Percy Fender (113★) against Northamptonshire at Northampton in 1920, while South Australia's David Hookes reached 100 in 34 balls against Victoria at Adelaide in 1982-83.

● When Adam Gilchrist made 104 against India at Bangalore in 2004-05, he became the first Australian wicket-keeper to score a century while captain. Only three others had achieved the feat before him – England's Percy Sherwell and Alec Stewart and Zimbabwe's Andy Flower, who did so on three occasions.

Gilchrist also extended his extraordinary run of scoring centuries on different grounds. His 104 was the 11th Test-match hundred of his career, all of which had come at different venues around the world – four in Australia (Hobart, Sydney, Brisbane, Perth), two in South Africa (Johannesburg, Cape Town) two in India (Mumbai, Bangalore) and one each in England (Birmingham), West Indies (Port-of-Spain) and Sri Lanka (Kandy).

The sequence did, though, eventually come to at end … in the first Test against New Zealand in 2004-05 when he made 126 – his second Test ton at the 'Gabba, a match in which both the No. 7 batsmen made identical hundreds. Earlier in the match, NZ all-rounder Jacob Oram smashed 126 not out, and with Gilchrist responding in kind they provided only the second instance in history of opposing No. 7 batsmen hitting centuries in the same Test. The previous occasion was at Delhi in the summer of 1948-49, when Everton Weekes made 128 for the West Indies and Hemu Adhikari replied with an unbeaten 114 for India.

● Appearing in just his third match, Kent batsman Joe Denley scored his maiden century in first-class cricket, and then scored another in the second innings. Opening the batting with Neil Dexter against Cambridge at Fenner's in 2006, Denley struck 115 in a first-wicket stand of 252, and then posted a second-innings knock of 107 not out in an unbroken opening stand of 184.

● On the day of his 31st birthday, Australian fast bowler Jason Gillespie climbed the absolute dizziest of heights by scoring a record-breaking double-century in a Test match as a nightwatchman. The first player to be dropped after the disappointment of the 2005 Ashes series, Gillespie – in his comeback series – made an unbeaten 201, batting at No. 3, against Bangladesh at Chittagong in 2005-06. He became only the second Australian, after spinner Tony Mann in 1977-78, to score a Test century as a nightwatchman, going on to the double-century mark off a mammoth 425 deliveries: **"This is ridiculous. I was just lucky that the shots came off and I had a bit of a laugh all the way. It's unbelievable. It's a fairytale really. Hansel and Gretel and Dizzy's double-hundred. It's one and the same … absolute fairytale."**

The 200 was Gillespie's maiden century in the first-class game, eclipsing his previous best of 58 – also made as a nightwatchman – for South Australia against Western Australia at Perth in 1996-97. His preceding highest score in all forms of cricket had been a 90-odd in a lower-grade match in Adelaide in the early 1990s. He was only the second batsman in history to have scored a maiden first-class century in a Test match, and then proceed on to 200. The other was Sri Lanka's Brendon Kuruppu, who coincidentally also made 201 not out, against New Zealand at Colombo in 1986-87.

Just the sixth Australian to convert his maiden Test century into a double, and after a painstaking nine and a half hours at the crease, Gillespie achieved something that had eluded a number of the world's greatest-ever batsmen over the years – Mohammad Azharuddin (199), Ian Chappell (196), Richie Richardson (194), Mike Atherton (185*), Desmond Haynes (184), Colin Cowdrey (182), Dilip Vengsarkar (166) and Mark Waugh (153*) were all unable to score a double-century in Test-match cricket. Gillespie ended the two-match series by topping the batting averages with a whopping 231.00, beating Ricky Ponting, who made 191 runs at 95.50, and Hussey, who mustered a total of 242 runs at 80.66.

Australian Financial Review *cartoonist David Rowe's take on the long innings played by nightwatchman Jason Gillespie at Chittagong in 2005-06 and the extra-long innings played by then-Prime Minister John Howard*

● When Indian bowler Ajit Agarkar scored 109 not out at Lord's in 2002, he became the first tail-ender with an average of less than 10.00 to score a maiden century in Test cricket. Coming into the match, his average was just 7.81 from 11 Tests, with a previous highest score of 41 not out and a total of eight ducks. But Agarkar's tale pales into insignificance when stacked up against the case of England batsman Bill Edrich, who scored his maiden Test century with a career-average of 8.00.

Edrich had failed in his first eight Test matches with a total of just 87 runs and a top score of 28. After falling for one in the first innings of the fifth Test against South Africa at Durban in 1938-39 – the famous drawn ten-day 'timeless' Test – Edrich was promoted to No. 3 from six, and responded with his maiden Test fifty, then century and double-century. His knock of 219 came in the longest first-class match ever played, and put to rest a horrid baptism in Test-match cricket.

Marvan Atapattu – the first Sri Lankan to score six Test-match double-centuries – was another to begin his career in disastrous fashion, making one run and five ducks in his first six innings. His maiden century – 108 against India at Chandigarh in 1997-98 – came in his tenth Test, when armed with an average of 10.70. His first double-century – 223 against Zimbabwe at Kandy in 1997-98 – came in his 13th Test, when his average stood at 21.42.

MAIDEN TEST CENTURY WITH THE LOWEST AVERAGE
Qualification: 5 matches

7.81	Ajit Agarkar	109*	India v England	Lord's	2002
8.00	Bill Edrich	219	England v South Africa	Durban	1938-39
10.00	Syd Gregory	201	Australia v England	Sydney	1894-95
10.42	John Parker	108	New Zealand v Australia	Sydney	1973-74
10.70	Marvan Atapattu	108	Sri Lanka v India	Chandigarh	1997-98

MAIDEN DOUBLE-CENTURY WITH LOWEST AVERAGE
Qualification: 5 matches

8.00	Bill Edrich	219	England v South Africa	Durban	1938-39
10.00	Syd Gregory	201	Australia v England	Sydney	1894-95
15.64	Jason Gillespie	201*	Australia v Bangladesh	Chittagong	2005-06
18.76	Robert Key	221	England v West Indies	Lord's	2004
19.20	Wasim Akram	257*	Pakistan v Zimbabwe	Sheikhupura	1996-97

ART & LITERATURE

● Following his release from prison in 2003, best-selling author Jeffrey Archer was spotted at the Lord's cricket ground watching the England-South Africa Test and rubbing shoulders with the likes of Ian Botham and Viv Richards. While in jail on charges of perjury and perverting the course of justice, Archer, who had his membership of the MCC suspended as a result, had purchased £1000-worth of turf from the dug-up outfield at Lord's to cover his garden in Cambridgeshire.

● A massive artwork honouring the greatest cricketers to represent the Indian state of Karnataka was unveiled outside the Chinnaswamy Stadium in Bangalore in 2006. The 600 square-foot fibreglass mural by Pushpa Dravid featured terracotta images of players such as Anil Kumble, Javagal Srinath, Syed Kirmani and Brijesh Patel. The mural also included her son Rahul Dravid: **"I am very proud of the fact that I could create him for the second time ... once when he was born and now through this. He will remain in the memory for hundreds of years for youngsters to see the legends of Karnataka."**

● British novelist John Fowles, whose best-selling works included *The French Lieutenant's Woman* and *The Magus*, was a talented cricketer at his school, later receiving a trial at the Essex club. A fast bowler, Fowles played in the Bedford first-XI in the early 1940s.

● When two cricket fans went to buy tickets for the Australia-Pakistan Test match at the SCG in 2004-05 they were inadvertently given passes for another event. *The Sydney Morning Herald* reported that sales staff had printed off tickets for a production of *Waiting for Godot*, Samuel Beckett's play about futility and boredom, with one of the fans wryly noting: **"That doesn't sound like cricket at all**."

In his younger days, the Irish writer Beckett was himself a cricketer of some standing – a left-handed batsman and medium-pace bowler – who played in two first-class matches for Dublin University, both against Northamptonshire. He made his highest score of 18 in his first first-class innings, at Northampton in 1925, and opened both the batting and bowling in his other appearance, at the same venue, the following summer.

● After a portrait of Shane Warne had been unveiled at Lord's in 2005, Britain's *Sun* newspaper ran a story revealing that the Australian bowler's so-called 'middle stump' had been retouched so as not to offend. The newspaper suggested that Warne's 'googlies' were a little too large in the original. The painting by artist Fanny Rush was her first portrait of a cricketer: **"The MCC wanted him to look, shall we say, a little less masculine. It was a toss-up who I was going to offend – Shane or the MCC**."

Warne became only the third Australian to have his portrait hung at Lord's, after Don Bradman and Keith Miller: **"It's a privilege for me. I feel very proud of the achievement**."

"He is a very powerful and attractive man and I wanted to get that across. From an artist's point of view he was a dream because his face is very symmetrical – which is a sign of beauty and something which all human beings look for in other faces. He has great colours in his face and those eyes are beautiful. The mouth in the portrait is the most beautiful mouth I have ever painted. I'd be nuts if I didn't think he was gorgeous. My girlfriends were jealous and my boyfriends were jealous. Everybody was jealous."

Fanny Rush

Another portrait of Warne was not as warmly received the following year, with *How Is He?* by David Ralph failing to make the cut for the prestigious 2006 Archibald Prize: **"I do wonder if it's about the desirability of him as a subject. I'd love to be able to speak to the judges about it, but unfortunately you don't get any written explanations**."

Fanny Rush's portrait of Shane Warne, unveiled at Lord's in 2005, and former Zimbabwe fast bowler Henry Olonga's portrait of a contemporary, Pakistan speedster Wasim Akram

● A painting commemorating Kent's winning of the County Championship in 1906 was sold at auction a century later for a record £600,000. Albert Chevallier Taylor's *Kent v Lancashire, Canterbury 1906* was sold at auction after the club found itself unable to afford insurance. The oil painting – expected by Sotheby's to fetch £500,000 – was purchased by Andrew Brownsword, whose charitable foundation meant it was able to remain on public display.

One of the game's most famous paintings – Albert Chevallier Taylor's Kent v Lancashire, Canterbury 1906 *showing Colin Blythe bowling to Johnny Tyldesley*

● The internationally-recognised poet Rupert McCall was a surprise part of Queensland's Pura Cup victory over Tasmania at the 'Gabba in 2004-05. McCall, a high-profile

Bulls supporter, was asked by team management if he'd like to carry the drinks, but ended up substituting in the field covering for injured fast bowlers Andy Bichel and Joe Dawes. McCall was positioned at mid-on for one over in the match, which he described as the best experience of his life: "... **wearing a pair of whites lent by 12th man Noffke. Symonds was the bowler, Griffiths the facing batsman – Maher was reciting poetry at second slip – McCall was shitting bricks at mid-on! ... fielded one in Jonty Rhodes-like style, whipped it back over the bails! Batsmen crossed for an easy single.**"

RUPERT McCALL'S ALL-TIME BEST TEST XI

Matthew Hayden (A)
Gordon Greenidge (WI)
Sachin Tendulkar (I)
Viv Richards (WI)
Steve Waugh * (A)
Ian Botham (E)
Rod Marsh † (A)
Wasim Akram (P)
Shane Warne (A)
Dennis Lillee (A)
Joel Garner (WI)

● *Wisden Cricketers' Almanack* was 'super-sized' in 2006, with the book's publishers producing a larger-format edition for the first time in its 143-year history. About twice the size of the normal edition, it was limited to 5000 in number and came with a ribbon bookmark and slipcase.

● British playwright Harold Pinter was asked in 2005 to confirm that he had once said, "**I tend to think that cricket is the greatest thing that God ever created on earth – certainly greater than sex, although sex isn't too bad either.**" He replied that it was meant to be a joke.

"After lunch the Australians, arrogant, jocular, muscular, larking down the the pavilion's steps. They waited, hurling the ball about, eight feet tall. Two shapes behind the pavilion. Frozen before emerging a split second. Hutton and Compton. We knew them to be the two greatest English batsmen."

Harold Pinter on the 1948 Ashes series

● Former England spinner Phil Tufnell took up art in 2005 and sold his first painting in the same week as he began taking classes. British DJ Fatboy Slim forked out £1100 for *Spinning*, described as a 'red, whirling window into Tufnell's soul'.

● Double international Ken Taylor, who appeared in three Tests spread over the years 1959 to 1964, was an artist of some note, whose works featured in a 2006 publication *Drawn To Sport*. While combining cricket with Yorkshire and football for Huddersfield, Taylor was able to pursue his other passion, and gained admission to the Slade School of Fine Art in London, after being accepted by Sir William Coldstream.

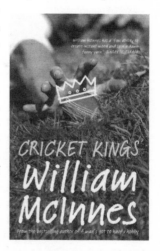

● William McInnes, a Logie award-winning actor of *SeaChange* fame, won plaudits when he put pen to paper and wrote *A Man's Got To Have A Hobby*, a book of childhood memories, published in 2006. The same year saw the release of his second book, *Cricket Kings*, the main character of which is a middle-aged man who plays for the Yarraville Wests fourth-grade cricket team on the weekends.

"When we spoke of literary figures, we spoke of Englishmen. But when we spoke of cricket, we spoke of our own. No Australian had written *Paradise Lost*, but Bradman had made 100 before lunch at Lord's."

Australian writer Thomas Keneally recalling childhood memories of school

TIM HEALD'S ALL-TIME BEST TEST XI

  Len Hutton (E)

  Sunil Gavaskar (I)

  Don Bradman (A)

  Denis Compton (E)

  W.G. Grace * (E)

  Garry Sobers (WI)

  Alan Knott † (E)

  Fred Trueman (E)

  Bill O'Reilly (A)

  Shane Warne (A)

  Dennis Lillee (A)

Tim Heald – author of a number of cricket books, including Village Cricket *and an authorised biography of Denis Compton*

● Dennis Silk, who captained the MCC on trips to North America and New Zealand, forged strong personal ties with two of Britain's most influential literary figures, making several recordings of the poet Siegfried Sassoon which later turned into a BBC Radio special. In the early 1950s, Silk – who scored seven centuries in his first-class career – was introduced to the cricket-loving Sassoon by a mutual acquaintance, the poet and author Edmund Blunden.

"In the years 1910 and 1911 I had 51 innings, with ten not-outs, and an average of nineteen. This I consider quite a creditable record for a poet."

Siegfried Sassoon

● A claim made in a book published in 2006 that Shane Warne had bedded over 1000 women brought a threat of legal action from his estranged wife, and a denial from the cricketer himself. Warne said the notion he had slept with so many women was just one of a number of mistakes in Paul Barry's biography *Spun Out*: "**The 1000 women thing … an exaggeration. There are just so many inaccurate facts in there that are totally untrue. It just looks like articles from other things that have all been put together. I've had seven books written about me and they're all bullshit**."

DAVID FRITH'S ALL-TIME BEST TEST XI

Andrew Stoddart * (E)
Archie Jackson (A)
Don Bradman (A)
Walter Hammond (E)
Garry Sobers (WI)
Mike Procter (SA)
Godfrey Evans † (E)
Ray Lindwall (A)
Bill O'Reilly (A)
Sydney Barnes (E)
Bhagwat Chandrasekhar (I)

Prolific cricket author
David Frith

● Roy Sheffield, who played in 177 first-class matches for Essex, was once arrested on suspicion of being a Bolivian spy. He was arrested and put in jail while working as a cowboy in Paraguay and wrote a book about the incident entitled *Bolivian Spy?* Sheffield scored 85 not out on his first-class debut for Essex in 1929, and after emigrating to New Zealand, played in three first-class matches for Wellington in 1938-39.

● Described by British Prime Minister Winston Churchill as 'a deed of glory, intimately involved in high strategy', the World War II raid on the French port of St Nazaire in 1942, was an event that later became the subject of a painting by an England Test cricketer. The painting, *The Greatest Raid of All*, by former wicket-keeper Jack Russell found a home at the Imperial War Museum in London.

THE NAME GAME

● The rather appropriately-named Queensland batsman Martin Love celebrated Valentine's Day in 2002, by scoring a double-century in the Pura Cup match against South Australia at the Adelaide Oval. It was Love's first first-class century in Adelaide and he shared in a record-breaking third-wicket stand of 296 with Brendan Nash (157), before retiring hurt on 202.

● When Mark Powell made his debut for Northamptonshire in the year 2000, he became the third player with the name M.J. Powell doing the rounds in first-class cricket in England that summer. The other two were Warwickshire's Mike James Powell, and Glamorgan's Mike John Powell, who marked his first-class debut in 1997 with an unbeaten innings of 200 against Oxford University.

● At Mumbai in 2004-05, all ten of Australia wickets in the first innings were taken by bowlers whose last name began with the letter 'K'. Anil Kumble led the charge with figures of 5 for 90, Murali Kartik took 4 for 44, while Zaheer Khan took 1 for 10. The Indian XI included two other players with a surname starting with 'K' – debutant wicket-keeper Dinesh Karthik and batsman Mohammad Kaif. For Australia, Simon Katich was caught by Kaif, bowled Kumble, while Michael Kasprowicz was caught Kumble, bowled Kartik.

● In the first international Twenty20 match contested in Australia, the only batsmen to lose their wickets for the home-side had surnames beginning with the letter 'H'. Australia A's top five in the batting order against Pakistan at Adelaide in 2004-05 were James Hopes, Brad Haddin, Brad Hodge, Mike Hussey and David Hussey.

● With a surname similar to that of Sachin Tendulkar, and a run-scoring appetite to match, a 14-year-old Indian schoolboy rewrote the record books in 2005-06 with a triple-century in a game in Mumbai. Rahul Tondulkar scored an unbeaten 357 for Sule Guruj against St Francis in the Harris Shield, the same schools competition in which Tendulkar announced his arrival with a triple-century in 1987-88. A 15-year-old Tendulkar scored 326 not out in a 664-run partnership with Vinod Kambli, whose competition-record innings of 349 not out was broken by Tondulkar.

● When Madhya Pradesh met Karnataka in the 2004-05 Ranji Trophy at Bangalore, one of the opening batsmen who scored a century was named Sachin, while one was named Barrington. Sachin Dholpure scored 107 for MP, while Barrington Rowland, named after England Test batsman Ken Barrington, scored 283 for Karnataka. Rowland, who possesses the middle name Marquis, beat Arjun Raja's knock of 267 against Bengal in 1990-91 as the highest individual first-class innings for Karnataka.

● Matthew James Wood made his first-class debut for Somerset in 2001 in a match at Bath where he played opposite another player named Matthew James Wood. The debutant Woods made 71, while Yorkshire's Wood hit 124 in an opening stand of 187.

● England's Adam Hollioake named his daughter, who was born in Perth in 2002, after his late brother who was killed in a car accident in the West Australian capital. Bennaya was named in memory of Ben and his girlfriend, Janaya, who suffered serious injuries in the crash.

● When Lundi Xhanti Xhongo made his debut for Western Province in South Africa's Provincial Cup in 2004-05, he became the first player with a surname beginning with the letter 'X' to play first-class cricket. Xhongo marked his first-class debut – against North West at Cape Town – by failing to score a run, take a wicket or take a catch.

● For the third Test against South Africa at Durban in 1930-31, England fielded players from 11 different counties. Four members of the team were named Maurice – Leyland from Yorkshire, Turnbull from Glamorgan, Allom from Surrey and Tate from Sussex.

● Glenn McGrath's father, Kev, put aside his fear of flying in 2005 making his first-ever trip outside of Australia so he could be present to witness his son reaching the landmark of 500 wickets, which came in the first Test at Lord's. Scheduled to join Kev to savour the once-in-a-lifetime moment was McGrath's fitness trainer, Kev, the fast bowler's mother, Bev, and his stepmother, also named Bev.

● When Namibia's Jan-Berrie Burger made his first-class debut in 2004, he joined three other players with the same surname in the side. Opening the batting for Namibia against Kenya in the ICC Intercontinental Cup at Nairobi, Burger played alongside Bernie Berger and brothers Louis and Sarel Burger. All four bowled in both innings, with Louis and Jan-Berrie each scoring 50.

● West Indian Xavier Marshall, one of the few players in first-class cricket possessing a name beginning with the letter 'X', made his one-day international debut against Australia at Melbourne in 2004-05. It was an appropriate city for his initiation, with the Jamaican batsman's middle name being Melbourne.

In 1901-02, England's Sydney Barnes made his Test debut in Sydney. He marked his first match with an unbeaten 26, batting at No.10 and 5 for 65 in Australia's first-innings total of 168. South African bowler Lennox Brown, who sported the middle name of Sydney, also made his Test debut in Sydney, taking 1 for 100 against Australia in the second Test of 1931-32.

● The touring Australians had to count their blessings when they played the Zimbabwe A side at Harare in 2004. They had none, but their opposition did, in fast bowler Blessing Mahwire. Also in the Zimbabwean side was an all-rounder named Innocent Chinyoka, while the wicket-keeper was one Wisdom Siziba.

A SELECTION OF COLOURFULLY-NAMED ZIMBABWEAN
FIRST-CLASS CRICKETERS

	Major Domestic Teams	First-Class Debut
Bothwell Madaufipo Chapungu	Midlands	2003-04
Chamunorwa Justice Chibhabha	Mashonaland	2003-04
Innocent Chikunya	Midlands	2004-05
Romeo Tatenda Kasawaya	Matabeleland	2003-04
Friday Kasteni	Midlands	2004-05
Mbekezele Mark Mabuza	Matabeleland	2003-04
Ngonidzashe Blessing Mahwire	Mashonaland	2000-01
Darlington Rutendo Matambanadzo	Mashonaland	1993-94
Everton Zvikomborero Matambanadzo	Mashonaland	1993-94
Tafadzwa Vintlane Mufambisi	Mashonaland	2003-04
Wisdom Thomas Siziba	Matabeleland	1999-00
Prosper Utseya	Mashonaland A	2001-02

... AND SOME FROM THE WEST INDIES

Omari Ahmed Clemente Banks	Leeward Islands	2001-02
Jaggernauth Buller	East Trinidad	1970-71
Chetwyn Gideon Burnham	Barbados	1964-65
Ignatius Cadette	Windward Islands	1976-77
Kirsten Nicole Casimir	Northern Windwards, Windward Islands	2001-02
Shirley MacDonald Clarke	Barbados	1999-00
Hallam Adolphus Fitzlaurie Cole	Barbados	1894-95
Fish Collins	Trinidad	1882-83
Patrick Woodman St George Evanson	Leeward Islands	1959-60
Linden Aggrey Kaunda Fraser	Guyana	1983-84
Zepton Cyril Greaves	Windward Islands	1972-73
Lanville Allonie Harrigan	Leeward Islands	1988-89
Hemnarine Harrinarine	Guyana Board President's XI	2001-02
Lorenzo Prince Ingram	West Indies B	2002-03
Vibert Charles Mortimore Johashen	Guyana	1973-74
Thomas Zephaniah Kentish	Windward Islands	1976-77
Kyron Gregory Nello Lynch	Trinidad & Tobago	2004-05
Marjoribanks Keppel North	British Guiana	1894-95
Lendl Mark Platter Simmons	Trinidad & Tobago	2001-02
McChesney Venie Simon	Leeward Islands	1985-86
Richard Greville Arthur Wellington Stapleton-Cotton	Jamaica	1901-02
Randy Rommel Thomas	Barbados	2002-03
Jermey Claxton Verwayen	British Guiana	1876-77
Altemont Beresford Wellington	Jamaica	1965-66
Elquemedo Tonito Willett	Leeward Islands	1970-71
Tonito Akanni Willett	Leeward Islands	2000-01

● When Liam Zammit made his debut for New South Wales in 2003–04, he became the first Australian player whose surname began with the letter 'Z' to play first-class cricket in a decade. During the latter part of the 1980s, South Australia's Andrew Zesers and Bob Zadow and Western Australia's Tim Zoehrer all played together in three Sheffield Shield matches.

While Zammit became the eighth Australian 'Z' player to play first-class cricket, there remains to this day, two letters of the alphabet that have not provided a single Aussie first-class cricketer – 'U' and 'X'.

● A rather familiar name re-emerged on the first-class cricket scene in 1990s, with the debut of a Sri Lankan batsman called Bradman Ediriweera. The left-hander, who was born with the names Prince Bradman, made a half-century (68) opening the batting in his first first-class match, for the Colombo club in 1995-96.

● A batsman by the name of Matthew Crease was reported after refusing to leave the crease when dismissed in a club match in England in 1997. Crease was later banned for life on charges of verbally abusing the umpire.

● Chamila Gamage Lakshitha, a Sri Lankan fast bowler who made history with his very first ball in Test-match cricket, possesses as many first names as he does wickets. Born in 1979 with the names Materba Kanatha Gamage Chamila Premanath, Lakshitha began his Test career – of just two matches – by dismissing Mohammad Ashraful with his first delivery in the second Test against Bangladesh at Colombo in 2002.

"Imagine if you got him on a triple-word score in Scrabble."
TV commentator David Lloyd discussing the lengthy name of Sri Lankan fast bowler (Warnakulasuriya Patabendige Ushantha Joseph) Chaminda Vaas

---

● In a move designed to promote Twenty20 cricket in 2005-06, Cricket Australia came up with the idea of players having their nicknames instead of surnames on their shirts. One player, however, was not allowed to use his preferred sobriquet so as not to upset KFC, one of the tournament's major sponsors. New South Wales fast Aaron Bird was refused permission to use the name 'Flu', with the potentially fatal bird flu sweeping various parts of the world at the time.

"I look forward to pictures of the twerps whose idea this was walking round the 'Gabba with 'Plonker' and 'Dickhead' inscribed on their backs."

Guardian *journalist Mike Selvey on Cricket Australia's decision in 2005-06 to use players' nicknames on their shirts for Twenty20 matches, including the inaugural Australia-South Africa clash at Brisbane*

● During the 2006 EurAsia Cricket Series at Abu Dhabi, two India A bowlers with the same surname each took five wickets in an innings in the same match. Test players Rudra Pratap Singh and Vikram Singh bowled unchanged in the 50-overs match cleaning up United Arab Emirates for just 70 in 15.1 overs. R.P. Singh took 5 for 30 off eight overs, while V. Singh took 5 for 30 off 7.1.

● Opening the innings on his state debut in 2006-07, a batsman by the name of Napoleon Einstein had a brilliant match scoring 92, and inventing a match-winning double-century partnership with Murali Vijay. Einstein, aged just 17, shared in an opening stand of 203 for Tamil Nadu against Kerala in a Ranji One-Day Trophy match at Secunderabad.

● When England's Mal Loye opened the batting against Australia at Brisbane in the 2006-07 CB Series, he became the first player named Malachy to play international cricket. A few months previously, a Malachi Jones had made his one-day international debut for Bermuda.

MEDIA WATCH

● During the summer of 1985-86, Australia's Test line-up included three players who would all go on to enjoy successful careers in radio. Occupying batting spots five, six and seven in three of the Tests were Greg Ritchie, David Hookes and Greg Matthews, each of whom pursued media work after their cricket careers had come to an end. Ritchie was a member of the top-rating breakfast show crew on Brisbane's Triple M until his retirement in 2004, Hookes presented a sports show on Melbourne's 3AW, while the effervescent Matthews also joined Triple M, in Sydney, and tried his hand at cricket commentary, including stints on the ABC.

● Richie Benaud reached a unique milestone in 2004 when he became the first person to attend a total of 500 Test matches, as either a player or commentator. Benaud, who made his Test debut in January 1952, reached the 500-mark while commentating on the first England-New Zealand Test at Lord's, and upon the match's conclusion was honoured by Britain's Royal Television Society with a lifetime achievement award: **"His broadcasts bring us unparalleled knowledge and insight – no man is better prepared, never mind the statistician alongside him, providing information, he's already worked out all the information for himself. He also manages to make the modern game as compelling as the old game – every day for this remarkable person is as exciting as the day before."**
After 68 Tests for Australia, Benaud made his television debut for the BBC in 1963, with the England-New Zealand match at Lord's in 2004 representing his 432nd stint in the commentary box.

RICHIE BENAUD'S ALL-TIME BEST TEST XI

Jack Hobbs (E)
Sunil Gavaskar (I)
Don Bradman * (A)
Sachin Tendulkar (I)
Viv Richards (WI)
Imran Khan (P)
Garry Sobers (WI)
Adam Gilchrist † (A)
Shane Warne (A)
Sydney Barnes (E)
Dennis Lillee (A)

● Host broadcaster Channel Nine incurred the wrath of many fans during the 2004 Test match against Sri Lanka at Cairns, when it decided to go with a game show rather than Shane Warne's tilt at history in pursuit of the world wicket-taking record. With Warne perched on 526 Test wickets, and one shy of Muttiah Muralitharan's record, Channel Nine pulled the plug on the final day's play of the second Test and put to air its scheduled 5pm show *The Price Is Right*. The network eventually relented, ditched Larry Emdur and returned to the cricket, but only after the historic moment Warne had taken the wicket of Upul Chandana to equal the world record.

● A massive statue of Shane Warne roaming the streets of London was the centrepiece of a TV advertising blitz that preceded the 2006–07 Ashes series. The ad campaign centred on a group of Australian cricket fans delivering a statue of Warne to the people of England. The 'Big Warnie' campaign was unveiled in London in 2006 with a 28-foot tall replica of the Australian spinner that visited landmarks including Buckingham Palace, Big Ben and Piccadilly Circus.

The 'Big Warnie' statue on the move in London in 2006

● During the third Ashes Test of 2006-07, Shane Warne was seen on Channel Nine's coverage of the Perth Test relentlessly sledging England batsman Paul Collingwood, who had just scored a double-century in the previous match at Adelaide. Warne was suggesting that his 200 was 'all arse', to which on-air commentator Richie Benaud wryly noted: "… **talking of big arses … is that not the pot calling the kettle black?**"

"He is the man. He knows everything about everything."

Shane Warne on Richie Benaud

"He's a fat bloke that can spin a ball a bit."

a caller to BBC Radio in 2006 referring to Shane Warne

● In 2006, *The Bulletin* magazine published its '100 Most Influential Australians' list that included three first-class cricketers. Alongside iconic figures such as media magnate Rupert Murdoch, former Prime Minister Gough Whitlam, feminist Germaine Greer and mass murderer Martin Bryant were cricketers Don Bradman, Shane Warne and Tom Wills. Bradman was described by the magazine's selection panel as "… **the cricketing benchmark that no player will ever meet**", while Warne's on-*and*-off-field exploits were taken into consideration: "**Celebrity sportsmen are routine enough, but Shane Warne stands apart. The soap-operatic rhythms of his life have fascinated the world since his Test cricket debut in 1992.**"

Wills, who appeared in a total of 32 first-class matches mostly for the MCC, Cambridge University, Kent and Victoria, is honoured for his role in the development of Australian Rules football.

● While attending one of her network's official functions in 2006, Channel Nine presenter Jessica Rowe ended up collecting the autographs of a number of current and past cricketing legends. The then co-host of the *Today* breakfast show was present at the launch of Nine's Ashes cricket coverage for the 2006-07 series and took the opportunity to gather some autographs for her husband, former *60 Minutes* reporter Peter Overton: **"Peter is a huge cricket fan. They are all right here, so I thought, 'Why not?' "**

DAVID KOCH'S ALL-TIME BEST TEST XI

Victor Trumper (A)
Arthur Morris (A)
*Don Bradman * (A)*
Greg Chappell (A)
Allan Border (A)
Keith Miller (A)
Adam Gilchrist † (A)
Shane Warne (A)
Alan Davidson (A)
Dennis Lillee (A)
Glenn McGrath (A)

David Koch – co-host of Channel Seven's breakfast show Sunrise

---

● During his knock of 123 in a one-day international against Pakistan at Ahmedabad in 2004-05, Sachin Tendulkar sent a six flying over the fence that knocked a television cameraman to the ground. The six, struck off leg-spinner Danish Kaneria, landed on the head of the cameraman as he tracked the flight of the ball towards him. First-aid staff applied an icepack before he was assisted from the ground for further medical attention.

● A television interview with Stephen Fleming in 2006 in which he called former team-mate Mark Richardson an 'idiot' was later revealed to be a set-up, but only after the NZ captain's comments were reported around the world. It was a joke set up by the pair for airing on a TV show co-hosted by Richardson, who had 'interviewed' Fleming after the fourth day's play of the first Test against the West Indies in Auckland.

Martin Crowe, former Kiwi great, and Sky TV's executive producer of cricket, was forced to issue a statement clarifying what had really happened: "**The interview was a spoof in which Stephen has a crack at Mark about his commentary. It was scripted and not real, although it has appeared on the internet as a news item.**"

Richardson: *OK, thanks. Good luck.*

Fleming: *Thanks mate* [interview ends]. *Yeah, you're an idiot, that's ridiculous, seriously that's just ridiculous. Two things ... you've forgotten who your mates are, some of your comments in the changing room? And the other thing is you're just an idiot talking about scoring rates and picking up the ... uh ... the tempo of games ... you were one of the most boring players to watch and from what I've seen so far in your commentary position is crap. You're forgetting who your mates are mate, about six months ago you were with us.*

● Dermot Reeve, who appeared in three Test matches for England in 1992, was forced to resign from his position as a Channel Four television commentator in 2005 after admitting to a cocaine addiction. The Hong Kong-born Reeve revealed he went on air during the 2004 Lord's England-New Zealand Test while under the influence, conceding he had no recollection of seeing the ball over two days: "**I had to watch the match video to hear what I said. No one seemed to notice much difference, they just said I was my usual self, but more chirpy – and kept doing Imran Khan impressions off-screen. They said it was the funniest commentary they had ever heard.**"

"Before I joined Channel Four, I played for a team that won f**k-all for fifteen years."

> *Mike Atherton accepting an honour at the 2006 Royal Television Sports Awards on behalf of Channel Four's winning commentary team*

● Michael Davie, an Australian journalist who was a one-time deputy editor of *The Observer* and editor of *The Age* in Melbourne, is credited with taking American funny-man Groucho Marx to his first cricket match, at Lord's, which elicited a most famous one-liner. When asked by Davie what he thought of the game so far, Marx is said to have replied: **"It's great ... but when does it start?"**

Davie was also a highly respected cricket reporter, covering the 1958-59 Ashes tour for *The Observer* and the Brisbane tied Test against the West Indies in 1960-61 for *The Times*.

● The start of the historic Bangladesh–Australia Test match at Chittagong in 2005-06 was held up in unusual circumstances when a group of journalists occupied the pitch in protest at local police assaulting a photographer who'd been denied entry to the ground. Another contingent of police arrived later in the day, which resulted in more beatings and some journalists seeking refuge in the Bangladesh dressing room to receive first aid.

"The first incident occurred after the photographer refused to show his identity card and an argument ensued. The second time, a group of journalists and photographers attacked two of our senior police officials and our personnel retaliated."

Chittagong police chief Majeedul Haq

The following day saw Adam Gilchrist staging his own mini-protest, and a highly unusual, but effective, one it was. The Australian wicket-keeper is one known to gee up his team-mates during play with his rather distinctive voice often heard beaming through stump microphones. But the usual cries of "Bowled, Shane" etc, were replaced with a few special messages during the second day's play.

Gilchrist was heard to shamelessly plug a number of the team's, and his own, sponsors – a plan devised by the players to try and force TV broadcasters to turn down microphones during play. In their previous series, in South Africa, the players had come under fire with allegations of sledging – some of the Australian players, including Mike Hussey, were incensed, complaining that stump microphones had been turned up, and left on, to catch them out: **"From a player point of view, the disappointing thing is that we weren't told they were on the whole time. We were under the impression that they were only** on for certain periods or they only broadcast certain bits that were said. It is difficult, because you do get emotional on the field and there are going to be things said and done. Some things certainly aren't appropriate for young listeners."

"One for the boys at Tavelex. Come on."

"Plenty of energy from a Milo Energy Bar."

"Phone home on 3 Mobile."

"Keep it well-oiled with Castrol, boys. Come on."

Adam Gilchrist's free plugs for sponsors during the second Test v Bangladesh at Chittagong in 2005-06

● *Test Match Special* commentator Henry Blofeld came close to making his Test-match debut in 1963-64 when a depleted England side sent out an SOS to the journalist who was covering the MCC's tour of India. Blofeld – who scored a first-class century (138) for Cambridge University against the MCC on his debut at Lord's in 1959 – was asked to act as a stand-by with many players in the Test XI sidelined with illness leading up to the second Test in Bombay: **"I don't care if** [Colin] **Cowdrey and** [Peter] **Parfitt are flying out as replacements. If I make fifty or above in either innings, I'm damned of I'll stand down for Calcutta!"**, he said tongue-in-cheek. In the end, 'Blowers' was not required, even though England only used ten men, with Micky Stewart contracting dysentery on the first day and appearing on the scorecard as 'absent ill'.

● In 2005, listeners to the BBC voted a 'blooper' featuring Brian Johnston and Jonathan Agnew as the best piece of sports commentary of all time. During the 1991 Test match against the West Indies at The Oval, Agnew had attempted to describe Ian Botham's freakish hit-wicket dismissal by saying **"… he just couldn't quite get his leg over."** Their fit of giggles as they tried to compose themselves and continue the commentary received a resounding 78 per cent of the vote, followed by a description of the 2003 rugby World Cup and the TV call of the 1966 soccer World Cup.

● ABC Radio clocked up a noteworthy double-century in 2006 when commentator Jim Maxwell called his 200th Test match. Maxwell, who began his commentary career alongside Alan McGilvray in 1977, attained the milestone at the MCG Boxing Day Ashes Test match, the one in which Shane Warne became the first bowler to reach the target of 700 Test wickets: "**I'm just a conduit to take the cricket to the fans. I suppose 200 Tests is a milestone of sorts, but cricket is a sport that lends itself to longevity.**"

● Two of the longest-serving Channel Nine cricket commentators share the same birthday. Richie Benaud and Tony Greig were both born on October the 6th, Benaud in 1930, Greig in 1946.

● Former Australian batsman Dean Jones was sacked as a commentator by the Dubai-based company Ten Sports in 2006 after referring to the South African batsman Hashim Amla as a 'terrorist' during TV coverage of the second Test against Sri Lanka in Colombo.

When Amla, the first South African of Indian descent to reach the national squad and a devout Muslim, took a catch to dismiss Kumar Sangakkara in the first innings, Jones – unaware he was live on air – said: "**The terrorist has got another wicket.**"

Jones' comment prompted a wave of complaints and he was dismissed virtually on the spot: "**It was a silly and completely insensitive thing to say and, obviously, it was never supposed to be heard over the air. I am truly sorry to have caused offence to anybody and the last thing I intended was to be disrespectful. Everyone needs to get away from perpetuating the myth, publicly and privately, that beards associated with the Muslim faith are somehow suspicious, and I intend to do exactly that. The irony is that I am great friends with most of the Pakistan team and they are all Muslims. I have no end of respect for the Muslim faith – that's why I'm so sorry at making such a stupid comment. It does not represent who I am, how I think or what I believe. I will be the first person to apologise to Hashim as soon as I get the chance, and I will assure him that prejudice against anybody, on any basis, is unacceptable and not something I will ever condone.**"

"We work in a news room or commentary box, so we have to be careful of what we say. You have to assume that the microphone is always on. There will be some network somewhere who will be on live even when there is a break."

Indian commentator Harsha Bogle

Despite his sacking by Ten Sports, Jones was picked up shortly afterwards by the Australian Southern Cross radio network, trumpeting that he was in hot demand: "**Two other networks have been after me, but I won't say who.**" He also sought to clarify his 'terrorist' comment, suggesting he was talking about someone else: "**In the long run, I wasn't even really referring to him** [Amla]. **What was my comment? And who got the wicket? Amla got the catch, Nicky Boje was the bowler. Just listen to the comment. The terrorist got a wicket. Who got the wicket? I'll leave it up to you to work out who I was referring to.**"

DEANO – YOU SAY IT BEST WHEN YOU SAY NOTHING AT ALL

crowd banner during the 2004-05 India-Australia Test at Nagpur
referring to commentator Dean Jones

"We just have to be careful what we say about [Zimbabwe President Robert] Mugabe. I've got no big deal about him. I'm just there to watch the cricket and I don't give a rat's arse what he does about his country."

Dean Jones, the TV commentator

● BBC commentator Edward Bevan had a smashing time calling a Twenty20 match at Cardiff on 2006 when a cricket ball crashed through the commentary-box window. As Glamorgan batsman Richard Grant hit a six during the match against Gloucestershire, Bevan noted: "**That's coming towards us**." After the sound of breaking glass, Bevan was heard to say: "**It's come through the commentary box!**" No one was seriously injured, although the scorer received a small cut to his arm.

● The Roshanara Club in Delhi hosted its first first-class cricket match in 17 seasons in 2004-05, marking the occasion by barring all spectators.

The Ranji Trophy match between Delhi and Andhra Pradesh was only the tenth first-class game at the ground since its first in 1926-27 and saw the police called in to remove journalists from the venue on the second day. Authorities defended the bans, saying Roshanara was a private club and any admissions needed to be regulated.

● Australian Test selector Merv Hughes received a public dressing-down from his employers Cricket Australia in 2006 after he was heard by all-and-sundry swearing at a journalist during a cricket match in Queensland. Hughes had taken exception to a newspaper article written by Brisbane *Courier-Mail* reporter Ben Dorries, and confronted him outside the press box at Cairns during the Top End cricket series. Hughes let loose with a string of four-letter words, and was yelling so loudly that even the players on the field heard the former fast bowler's tirade.

"I didn't like to be friendly with rivals. I wanted them to feel the heat. And I didn't like reporters because you people think you know everything."

former West Indies fast bowler Curtly Ambrose

"I am not talking to anyone in the British media. They are all pricks."

Australian captain Allan Border at a press conference
at Hove during the 1993 Ashes tour

● The Pakistan cricket team at the 2007 World Cup was banned from speaking in English at news conferences. A team spokesman said the ban was imposed to stop players being misquoted, and by speaking in their national language, Urdu, could help promote Pakistan as a tourist destination.

● Indian captain Rahul Dravid was made guest editor of the country's biggest-selling English newspaper *The Times Of India* in 2007, and one of his first deeds was to move cricket from the front page. He also relegated stories about movies to lesser prominence: "**There are far more important things to be written about**."

ALL CREATURES GREAT & SMALL

● A Victorian country cricketer claimed a hat-trick on his A-grade debut in 2005-06, just two days after suffering a potentially fatal snake bite. Fifteen-year-old Grant Place had been cleaning up around the nets on a practice night when he was bitten: **"I never saw it. I didn't know I had been bitten at the time but about an hour later I looked at my ankle and saw it had swollen up."**

After spending some time in hospital, the leg-spinner bit back, cleaning up three Noorat batsmen in a rare hat-trick on his A-grade debut for Pomborneit in the South-West Association competition: **"The first ball of the over I got hit over mid-wicket for six. It wasn't looking good ... the third guy didn't even know it was a hat-trick."**

West Indies batsman Brian Lara takes a break with a snake while on tour of Australia in 2004-05

● A stray dog that disrupted play in the third Ashes Test at Nottingham in 1993 was later adopted and named after Merv Hughes. While fielding, Hughes had taken it upon himself to get the canine off the ground when all other attempts to shoo him away had failed. Hughes got on all fours and managed to win the confidence of the pooch, which was eventually taken off the field by Michael Slater and handed to a steward on the boundary. After the dog's plight was seen on TV, more than fifty people rang the local RSPCA to offer him a home. The successful applicant later named him Merv.

● During the first-class summer of 1963 in England, wandering dogs on the pitch resulted in two instances of four-run penalties. In a West Indies tour match at Hove, Sussex's Ian Thomson was awarded a four when a shot off the bowling of Alf Valentine was 'fielded' by a black dog, which took the ball over the boundary. It happened again two months later to another England Test player, Northamptonshire's wicket-keeping captain Keith Andrew. In the County Championship against Hampshire at Southampton, Andrew had his score in the first innings increased by four when one of his shots was intercepted by a stray dog.

● Leicester Spring appeared in three first-class matches for Auckland in 1936-37 as a medium-pace bowler, capturing five wickets with a best innings-return of 3 for 28. In 1953, he purchased his first racehorse, Rising Fast, which won nine races out of 11, including the 1954 Melbourne Cup.

● Former Australian batsman Mark Waugh, a keen punter, but one who's allergic to horses, was a keen observer of the 2006 Melbourne Cup at Flemington, where a horse trained by his wife was one of the starters. Mahtoum, which won the 2005 Sydney Cup, was Kim Waugh's first runner in the big race. Ridden by Corey Brown, it finished a credible sixth with a take-home prize of $110,000.

"I'm not much of a horseman. To be honest, I was pretty scared of horses when I first met her. I'm a bit better, but I wouldn't really trust myself with a million-dollar horse."

Mark Waugh

● On the same day Andrew Flintoff made a duck in his first innings of the 2006-07 Ashes series, his horse was beaten in a meeting back home at Towcester. The England captain's horse, called Flintoff, was set for victory, but was pipped at the post by Principe Azzurro. A correspondent in *The Times* newspaper remarked: "**I'm not sure what would bother Andrew Flintoff more: that his racehorse came second or that his thoroughbred bowlers look like such donkeys**." Australia declared both of its innings, at 602 for 9 and 202 for 1, to win the opening Test by 277 runs, handing Flintoff his second defeat in just a few days.

"From our point of view the people criticising now are the ones who run with the foxes and hunt with the hounds. All we can do is run with the fox."

England coach Duncan Fletcher explaining the problems of selection after losing the Ashes in 2006-07

● Worcestershire coach Steve Rhodes was dogged by a number of telephone calls during a County Championship match against Leicestershire in 2006 from people wanting to buy kittens. An advertisement for pussycats had been placed in a local newspaper by the county's New Zealand import Lou Vincent.

● Something fishy occurred during a match in the English Cricketer Cup in 1986, when an Old Cliftonians batsman was almost hit by a mackerel. The fish, purloined by a seagull from a nearby zoo, was dropped by the bird as it flew over the ground.

● Just a week after sustaining a broken finger in a 2006-07 Pura Cup match, Australian opener Matthew Hayden was attacked by a dog. Hayden was jogging during a visit to his parents' property at Kingaroy in Queensland when he was unexpectedly bitten: "**It was a vicious attack. I was out for a leisurely run. You are always a bit shocked by that sort of thing, but I was more disappointed than anything**."

● A rabbit whose tail caught on fire caused an estimated £60,000 damage to cricket equipment at a club in England in 2004. Groundsmen at the Devizes cricket club in Wiltshire had lit a pile of branches and leaves, apparently setting fire to a rabbit which scarpered into a nearby shed containing equipment used for the care of the club ground. Two local fire engines and 11 firemen attended the blaze, but were unable to save the shed, its contents … or the bunny. Philip Flowers, from the Wiltshire fire brigade, commented that he had never before fought a blaze caused by a burning animal: "**We're 99 per cent confident it was the rabbit that caused the fire. It was either burnt to a cinder or it escaped through a small hole in the corner of the shed – but I imagine it perished and went to bunny heaven**."

● A second-XI cricket match was brought to a halt in England in 2005 after a rampaging bull jumped a fence from a neighbouring paddock and began chasing players and spectators. The game between Derbyshire and Leicestershire was held up for about 30 minutes.

"I think one of the bulls got amorous with a cow or perhaps another bull. I am not sure about the sexual orientation of bulls."

Derbyshire 2nd-XI coach Karl Krikken

The most idyllic of scenes – a village cricket match in England

EXTRAS

● Sri Lanka's Arjuna Ranatunga created history in 2000 when he became the first cricketer to represent his country in its first *and* 100th Tests. Ranatunga made his debut in Sri Lanka's inaugural Test, against England in 1981-82 as an 18-year-old, and celebrated his country's 100th Test match in 2000 against Pakistan in Colombo.

● Ashley Ross, a former Victorian cricket official, took coaching to a new high in 2004 when he came up with a training document entitled *Phone Sex, Masturbation and the Real Deal: Cricket Training as It Has Always Been*. Employed as a development manager and technical advisor by New Zealand Cricket in 1998, Ross was asked to review his novel coaching methods by chief executive Martin Snedden: "**It's certainly not the angle we would usually take on coaching and it's fair to say I'm not comfortable with it**."

● Essex fast bowler Ashley Cowan, who once toured the Caribbean with England but failed to gain international colours, lapped it up in 2006 with a benefit year partly sponsored by an adult entertainment venue. Essex club official Greg Landsdowne was quick to support the concept of a lap-dancing club, called The Cave, getting behind the fast bowler: "**There are a variety of events in a benefit year ... some of an adult nature and some for all the family. Ashley's 'Cave Nights' will cater for the more mature end of the market**."

● In 2004, British financier Nigel Wray came in at No.485 in the *Sunday Times* 'Rich List' with a fortune estimated at 85 million pounds. In the same year, a former batting partner of Wray's, Justin Langer, together with

Matthew Hayden became the most profitable openers for Australia in Test cricket history. Back in 1988 as captain of the Old Milhillians cricket club in England, Wray had taken a young Langer under his wing and nurtured a budding star, doing so with the same vigour that made him one of England's leading businessmen: "**I had to tell Justin straight that if he wanted to play for Australia, he needed to make some serious decisions. He wasn't fit enough, he wasn't tough enough mentally, his attitude wasn't quite right and he wasn't working hard enough at his game.**"

Wray fulfilled a promise to Langer that if he ever made the grade, he would fly to any destination in the world to witness his Test debut, and was part of the crowd at the Adelaide Oval in 1992-93, when Langer scored a half-century (54) against the West Indies: "**Nigel is a multi-millionaire. It's funny how we clicked. I can never thank Nigel enough for changing my attitude … I'm a fanatic and a batting junkie thanks to him.**" Wray was also present at Langer's farewell Test match, against England at Sydney in 2006-07.

● An overly enthusiastic cricket player had to be rescued after a mishap in India in 2006 when he got stuck in a well. Alok Patra was visiting some relatives in Mahisbatan and joined in a game of street cricket when a ball was sent into a nearby well and was the only one brave enough to go down and retrieve it. He was rescued by firemen, and by all accounts, was relatively unscathed.

● A helicopter disrupted proceedings between a Babington team and Ditcheat in Somerset in 2005 when it landed in the grounds of a hotel where the match was being played. The chopper had been called in to transport an injured hotel employee to hospital.

● A diamond-and-gold-encrusted cricket ball, made in Sri Lanka, was brought to Australia in 2004 to celebrate the opening of a jewellery store in Melbourne. The ball – the only one of its kind in the world – was made with 2704 diamonds and an 18 carat gold stitch.

● Granny Scholz has a special, and undeniable, place in cricket history, being the first person to get Don Bradman out. She was the midwife who delivered Bradman on 27 August 1908 in a small private hospital situated in the front room of a cottage in the New South Wales town of Cootamundra.

An application to have the Bradman birthplace – at 89 Adams Street – officially recognised as a property of national significance was rejected by the Federal Government in 2004. In the same year, Adelaide's Burnside City Council resubmitted a proposal that Bradman's private residence in Holden Street, Kensington Park – the home where he died in 2001 – be granted heritage-listing, a move that was always strongly resisted by Bradman.

A club cricket match in progress between Old Sydneians and I Zingari across the road from one of Don Bradman's childhood homes at Bowral in New South Wales

● During the 1996 World Cup, Holland's team included two players with an age difference of nearly 29 years. Nolan Clarke, born on 22 June 1948, and Bas Zuiderent, born on 2 March 1977, both made their one-day international debuts against New Zealand at Baroda. Clarke remains the oldest-ever player to appear in a one-day international, aged 47 years and 257 days in his final match.

The 2004 Asia Cup, staged in Sri Lanka, also featured two players in the same team with an age difference in excess of 25 years. The Hong Kong XI that played Pakistan at Colombo included Rahul Sharma, born on 14 September 1960, and debutant Nadeem Ahmed, born on 28 September 1987 – an age gap of just over 27 years.

● In the Border-Free State match at East London in 2002-03, West Indies import Vasbert Drakes was listed as 'timed out', only the third-such instance in first-class cricket history. Drakes, though, could be forgiven for his tardiness in making his way to the crease, for he wasn't even at the ground when the match started – he'd been delayed on a flight in Sri Lanka with the West Indies team.

Andrew Jordaan was the first player dismissed in this way, with his demise coming in the Eastern Province-Transvaal match at Port Elizabeth in 1987-88. Not out at the end of the day's play, a heavy overnight downpour of rain prevented him reaching the ground on time the following morning and was subsequently given his marching orders.

The fourth 'timed out' dismissal at first-class level took place in 2003 and was similarly unfortunate. Nottinghamshire bowler Andrew Harris had suffered a groin injury during an early-season match against a Durham University XI at Trent Bridge and was just a bit too slow as he limped out to the middle, with his team already in a match-winning position at 542 for 9. Harris had only agreed to bat with team-mate Chris Read closing in on a century (94*), and was so sluggish he hadn't even reached the playing field when he was given out.

DISMISSED 'TIMED OUT' IN FIRST-CLASS CRICKET

Andrew Jordaan	Eastern Province v Transvaal	Port Elizabeth	1987-88
Hemulal Yadav	Tripura v Orissa	Cuttack	1997-98
Vasbert Drakes	Border v Free State	East London	2002-03
Andrew Harris	Nottinghamshire v Durham University Centre of Cricketing Excellence	Nottingham	2003

● When Pakistan hosted the West Indies at Indore in 1990-91, both countries introduced one new player to the ranks of Test-match cricket. Masood Anwar took three wickets for the home side in his one and only Test, with the other debutant being one Brian Lara, who would go on to scale the twin peaks of 100 Tests and 10,000 runs.

● Picked as one of the best cricketers in the world to take on Australia in a one-off Test match in 2005, Brian Lara not only failed to click with the bat, he also collected the unwanted record of being the 'biggest loser' of all time. The Australia-World XI 'Super Series' Test at Sydney resulted in a big win for the reigning world champions, handing Lara his 55th Test-match defeat and the record previously held by England's Alec Stewart.

With innings of five and 36, Lara finished the match with a total of

4695 Test-match career runs – and a whopping 12 centuries – in a losing cause, streets ahead of Stewart, who made 2993 runs in his 54 defeats. At the conclusion of the third Test at Adelaide later in the summer, Lara had clocked up 5000 runs in a losing cause.

MOST RUNS BY A BATSMAN IN A LOSING TEST MATCH				
351 (221 & 130)	Brian Lara	West Indies v Sri Lanka	Colombo	2001-02
341 (142 & 199*)	Andy Flower	Zimbabwe v South Africa	Harare	2001-02
303 (176 & 127)	Herbert Sutcliffe	England v Australia	Melbourne	1924-25

● During the summer of 2005-06, as many as three players celebrated their 100th Test appearance in the same match. The first Test against New Zealand – played at the appropriately-named venue of Centurion – saw South Africa's Jacques Kallis and Shaun Pollock and Kiwi skipper Stephen Fleming all complete a century of Tests. Fleming marked the match with a duck, while Kallis and Pollock celebrated their country's 100th Test-match victory.

● Northern Districts batsman Mark Bailey, who played cricket at the 1998 Commonwealth Games in Malaysia, only played in a single one-day international, in which he was not required to bat or bowl and didn't take a catch. His only taste of the big time came in a quarter-final of the 1998-99 Wills International Cup against Zimbabwe at Dhaka.

England's Jack MacBryan famously played out his Test career without having to bat or bowl, when his sole appearance – against South Africa at Manchester in 1924 – was ruined by rain.

● Duncan Fletcher, who coached England to Ashes glory and to the No. 2 spot in the world Test rankings of 2005, enjoyed a successful career in systems management, devising Zimbabwe's car-registration system. As a player, Fletcher famously captained Zimbabwe to a shock victory over Australia at Nottingham in the 1983 World Cup. Leading the side in Zimbabwe's maiden one-day international, Fletcher top-scored with 69 in a celebrated 13-run victory.

● Apart from the usual array of books and DVD's, as well as CDs, philatelic items, watches, tankards and calendars to cash in on England's 2005 Ashes victory came the release of a commemorative rose. Named 'Sweet Victory', the patio rose was limited to 10,000 in number, with former England captain Mike Gatting celebrating its release by planting the first rose in the Harris Garden at the Lord's cricket ground.

Former England skipper Mike Gatting with the 2005 'Sweet Victory' Ashes rose at Lord's

"Have you ever smelt the perfume of a rose? When you smell a rose it really gets you back living in the mould."

former Australian opening batsman Justin Langer

● An English-born schoolteacher based in the United States claimed a world record in 2001, when he batted for 24 hours and faced over 12,000 balls. Stephen Speak, a second-grade teacher at a school in California, undertook the marathon batting performance with just two 15-minute breaks, receiving most of the deliveries from a bowling machine: **"They say some people are born with a silver spoon in their mouth, well I was born with a cricket bat in my hand."**

Another teacher set an unusual cricketing-related world-first two years later, when 60-year-old Doug Robertson paid a visit to each of the 18 English county cricket-ground headquarters in 18 days. Rain on one of the days prevented him watching play at each of the venues, but his feat raised £6000 for charity.

● Michael Jeffrey, Australia's Governor-General between 2003 and 2008, is a former club cricketer who managed a few wickets as a swing bowler for East Perth. Sir Michael's cricketing days were cut short, though, when he injured his shoulder in a parachuting accident.

"As a youngster growing up, firstly in the goldfields, and then in Cannington, an outer suburb of Perth, Western Australia, I enjoyed a stable family life. My four loves were cricket, the bush, fishing and school cadets. Kids would come for miles around to play cricket."

Australian Governor-General Michael Jeffery

MICHAEL JEFFERY'S ALL-TIME BEST TEST XI

Gordon Greenidge (WI)
Barry Richards (SA)
Don Bradman (A)
Sachin Tendulkar (I)
Viv Richards (WI)
*Garry Sobers * (WI)*
Alan Knott † (E)
Shane Warne (A)
Richard Hadlee (NZ)
Dennis Lillee (A)
Glenn McGrath (A)

● Five first-class cricketers in the New Zealand city of Dunedin blamed a 'haunted house' for a spate of injuries that forced them out of the game at exactly the same time during the summer of 2005-06. Otago players Greg Todd, Aaron Redmond, Neil Broom, Jonathan Trott and James McMillan had all taken up residence in a former nursing home for the terminally-ill that had been converted into a five-bedroom townhouse. Over a period of just two weeks, all five suffered various injuries, with Todd breaking his right knee in a bowling mishap, Redmond dislocating a knee, while the others were sidelined with serious muscle strains. Trott also claimed that pieces of furniture and other items mysteriously moved about the house during the night.

"These injuries have been a shocker. It's just too bizarre. It's ironic because at the top of our house is a medical Red Cross. It's like an ambulance cross on the roof. It's all a bit spooky."

Otago's Aaron Redmond son of Rodney Redmond, who famously scored a century and half-century (107 & 56) in his only Test match, against Pakistan at Auckland in 1972-73

● On England's tour of India in 2001-02, Andrew Flintoff claimed he'd been shot at while fielding during a one-day international at Delhi. The all-rounder said the entire incident had been swept under the carpet by authorities:"**I felt something hit me and, looking down, saw pellets on the ground. You expect to have plastic bottles thrown at you when you are playing on the sub-continent, but you don't expect to be shot. I think I should have made more of a stand because I wasn't there to be shot at. We explained it away as the crowd just being overexcited at the time, but I wasn't sure about that at all**."

The claim was rejected out-of-hand by Chand Khanna, a senior official of the Delhi & District Cricket Association:"**If such a thing actually happened, why did the England team keep quiet about it? No one told us a thing then or after the tour. He can't be serious**."

● Indian all-rounder Robin Singh played in over 100 one-day internationals, but only ever appeared in one Test match. Singh was given his one and only Test cap at Harare in 1998-99, a full ten years after his one-day international debut. In all, he appeared in 136 one-dayers, achieving two five-wicket hauls and scoring one century, a neat 100 against Sri Lanka at Colombo in 1997.

Singh had appeared in 60 ODIs before making his Test debut, while Australia's Ian Harvey played in 73 matches and never played in a Test. Conversely, England batsman Mark Butcher appeared in 71 Tests, but never got the chance to play in a one-day international. And Justin Langer, who retired after 105 Tests in 2006-07, only appeared in eight ODIs.

● Justin Langer marked his 100th Test match without scoring a single run after being cracked on the helmet from a thunderbolt sent down by South Africa's Makhaya Ntini. Facing up to the opening ball of Australia's first innings in the third Test at Johannesburg in 2005-06, Langer copped a bouncer to the side of his head and left the field, taking no further part in the match: **"It was like Lennox Lewis whacked me."**

In his very first Test match – at Adelaide in 1992-93 – Langer was felled by the West Indies' Ian Bishop, who was also present at the Johannesburg Test working as a commentator for broadcaster SABC.

"As a five-foot-nothing top-order batsman, I have had my fair share of hits on the helmet."

Justin Langer

● A club cricketer was knocked unconscious by a wayward-flying hang-glider during a match in England in 1997, but recovered to come back and bowl later in the innings. John Hague was the unlucky player, who was fielding at the time, in the match for the Horncastle club in Lincolnshire: **"I nearly didn't play because I'd woken up with a migraine. Being biffed in the head by a hang-glider was all I needed."**

● The oldest man in Britain Henry Allingham paid a visit to The Oval in London in 2006, the first time in 100 years he had attended a game of cricket at the famous ground. Mr Allingham, who was one month shy of turning 110, recalled that the last match he had watched at The Oval featured one of the game's true legends: **"I saw W.G. Grace that day. You could always tell who he was by his long beard, but I can't remember how many he got."**

England's oldest man, Henry Allingham, who was 109 when he watched the Surrey-Gloucestershire match at The Oval in 2006

● Played in temperatures that regularly dip to minus ten degrees, an annual ice cricket tournament began in Estonia in 2004 on a frozen lake in the capital city Tallinn. Played on a pitch carved into the thick ice of Lake Harku – and without the aid of matting – the contest turned 'international' in 2006 with the

launch of the 'Ice Cricket World Championships', that featured players from countries such as Australia, India, South Africa and Finland.

● On the same day that a massive earthquake and series of tsunamis devastated southern Asia on Boxing Day 2004, two of the countries most affected by the disaster suffered defeats in one-day internationals. Bangladesh marked its 100th match with its first-ever victory at home, defeating India by 15 runs at Dhaka, while Sri Lanka suffered a seven-wicket loss on the same day against New Zealand at Auckland. The Sri Lankan players returned home shortly after the NZ tour began, with several players incurring substantial property losses.

● In the same season that Glenn McGrath played his 200th one-day international, the Australian fast bowler also made just his 20th appearance in a limited-overs match for New South Wales. His 'landmark' 20th match came in the ING Cup against Victoria in Sydney in 2004-05, and since his debut in the 1992-93 season, McGrath, at the time, had never once been required to bat.

● Mark Taylor earned plenty of kudos in his first outing as Australia's one-day international captain, by claiming a 14-run victory, and the man-of-the-match award. Filling in for an injured Allan Border at the SCG in 1992-93, Taylor (9) bombed with the bat – as did most – in a rain-affected duel against the West Indies, but won plaudits for his leadership, and value in the field, where he took four sharp catches at slip.

● An English cricketer showed absolute dedication to his cause during a village match in 2006, where he continued to bat despite suffering a heart attack. Jim Young was playing against Bishop's Stortford in Essex when he experienced stabbing pains in his chest and dropped to his knees. But instead of leaving the crease, he continued batting taking his score from 32 to 44 before retiring: **"The old runs were a little bit lacking, but I was having a good game and found it too easy. I was getting sixes and fours and was really feeling good about my game. Then I got this pain down my chest. At the time, it seemed the right thing to carry on. I knew I was close to my first 50 of the season, so I suppose that motivated me. But one of the guys noticed I was struggling and told me to retire because it was not worth it."**

The 57-year-old stayed on at the ground and even returned to the crease, but ran out of partners, finishing unbeaten two runs shy of his maiden half-century of the season. An ambulance then took him off to a local hospital where he underwent surgery: **"I think I was a bit of an idiot really. I should have stopped straight away because it could have finished me off there and then."**

● Despite occasional bursts of heavy rain and the obvious dangers of a sausage sizzle, a nudist group paid tribute to Australia's war dead in 2006 with an inaugural 22-player-a-side game of cricket at a beach in New South Wales. The event, staged on Anzac Day, attracted up to 200 nudists to Tyagarah Beach at Byron Bay, with one participant admitting nude-cricket did have its drawbacks: **"This is my way of showing I'm thinking of the Anzacs ... the only problem is I don't have anywhere to pin my father's medals."**

The event had begun on a much smaller scale in 2001, when two ex-servicemen, both nudists, dreamt up the idea of an Australia versus Kiwi cricket match to remember their fallen comrades.

● The Ashes fever of 2005 that gripped Australia and England was also felt in war-torn Iraq with a series of special 'Desert Ashes' matches held in Al Muthanna province. The first match was played on the opening day of the first Test at Lord's, a limited-overs contest between Australia's Second

Cavalry Regiment and the Light Dragoons. The game was played on a coconut matting pitch in boiling hot weather, with the Australian soldiers scoring 220 off its 25 overs before shooting out the opposition for 102.

⬤ Tensions in the Middle East disrupted Israel's participation in the European Cricket Championships held in Scotland in 2006 with one match cancelled and others shifted to safer ground. The Israeli army incursion into Lebanon in the deadly conflict over Hezbollah prompted local protests against its national cricket team with their opening match against Jersey at Glasgow abandoned and other fixtures transferred to the security of a British airbase.

"It is unthinkable for the Israeli cricket team to play in our backyard while these acts of aggression continue to take place."

Federation of Student Islamic Societies spokesman Faisal Hanjra

---

⬤ A casual conversation about cricket sparked an eleventh-hour bid, albeit a failed one, in 2005 by Australian Guantanamo Bay detainee David Hicks to escape US-backed terrorism charges. In a discussion with his American lawyer Michael Mori, Hicks was asked how he felt about England's success in the Ashes series: "**He** [Hicks] **told me he'd never felt very partisan about the Ashes and wouldn't mind much if England took the series because his mum had never claimed Aussie nationality and still carried a UK passport. My jaw hit the floor. I asked him: 'Do you realise that may mean you're legally a Brit?' We both knew that the implications of that could be stunning**."

Unlike the Australian Government, the UK shunned the US Military Commission process and was successful in bringing home nine British nationals detained at the Guantanamo Bay facility. Although David Hicks was granted British citizenship, the Blair Government shunned his bid for freedom, on the basis he was an Australian citizen when captured and detained.

● One of the suicide bombers responsible for the London public transport bombings of 2005 was, by all accounts, a promising cricketer. Twenty-two-year-old Shehzad Tanweer, described as an 'awesome batsman and medium-pace bowler', was seen playing cricket at his local park in Leeds on the eve of the bombings which occurred on the same day that England defeated Australia in a one-day international at Headingley.

A year later it was claimed that Tanweer's love of cricket had possibly thwarted an ambitious al-Qaeda plan to wipe out the Australian and England cricket teams in Birmingham. The directive had allegedly been for the London transport bombers to get jobs at the Edgbaston cricket ground leading up to the second Ashes Test match and to then pump the deadly gas sarin into the team dressing rooms. But, according to Britain's *Sunday Times* newspaper, Tanweer said 'no' to the plan, and the other option – the bombing of buses and train stations in London – was taken up instead.

"Most of us knew it was just a mickey-take, but there is that 'what if?'-thought in the back of your mind."

Yorkshire captain Craig White after a man with an Osama bin Laden mask and a backpack strode out to the middle of the pitch during a one-day match against Warwickshire at Scarborough in 2005

● London transport police claimed to be on the ball in 2006 when they pulled up a Londoner and cautioned him of the dangers of carrying a cricket ball in public. Chris Hurd was stopped by a police officer near Lord's and told that the cricket ball he was holding was a 'potentially lethal weapon': **"She was completely humourless and inflexible, and showed no understanding of my excitement about the Ashes. She confiscated the ball for most of our conversation, gave me a verbal warning and said she was being very lenient."**

● As part of increased security in the United States, post-September 11, cricket bats were banned from American aircraft cabins in 2002. Also on the list were baseball bats, brass knuckles and cattle prods. In the same year, an American cricket fan had the bomb squad arrive at his home to investigate what was deemed to be a suspicious package. It turned out to be a copy of the 2001 edition of *Wisden Cricketers' Almanack.*

● The 6th of August 2006 provided a watershed moment in cricket history, signalling the first time ten countries were seen in international matches on the same day. Sri Lanka was playing South Africa in the second Test at Colombo, England and Pakistan were in action in the third Test at Leeds, Zimbabwe hosted Bangladesh in a one-day international in Harare, Scotland played The Netherlands in a one–day international at the European Cricket Championships in Ayr, while Canada was up against Kenya in a ODI in Toronto.

● Festive cheer was in short supply in 1997 with a one-day international played on Christmas Day at Indore lasting a mere 18 balls. The match between India and Sri Lanka was called off after the two captains – Sachin Tendulkar and Arjuna Ranatunga – suggested that the pitch was too dangerous.

● Essex batsman Alastair Cook, who was born on Christmas Day, made his England Test debut in 2005-06 in place of Marcus Trescothick who was also born on December 25. For Cook, all of his Christmases came at once, hitting a century and a half-century (60 & 104★) in the match against India at Nagpur. At 21, he became the youngest England Test debutant to score a century.

Another late scratching from the Indian tour joining Trescothick – who cited so-called 'personal reasons' for his withdrawal – was an injured Simon Jones, who was also born on Christmas Day.

● An English club cricketer was banned for six matches in 2001, when he stripped off during a match in Oldham. The 19-year-old Saddleworth all-rounder Andrew Long performed an impromptu streak, jumping over the stumps, after saying he became bored watching his team-mates batting in the match against Bolton.

● Within a week of minnows Ireland eliminating Pakistan from the 2007 World Cup, a current and former official from each side died in Jamaica. Pakistan's coach Bob Woolmer was found dead in his Kingston hotel room just hours after the defeat, a death that turned into a murder investigation. Soon afterwards, Robert Kerr, a former president and chairman of the Irish Cricket Union, died of a suspected heart attack.

"World Cup 2007 will be forever remembered for this [Woolmer's death]. My personal opinion would have been to stop, but knowing Bob he would have wanted this to go ahead. Bob was an extremely professional man, was an extremely soft person ... gave his life to cricket and probably paid for it."

former South African bowler Allan Donald

"We have lost a good coach and a good person. Woolmer was a fatherly figure to all of us and we have lost our greatest supporter."

Pakistan's then-captain Inzamam-ul-Haq

"Death threats ... I've had a million of them. They don't faze me. It's a part of the job."

Bob Woolmer

● Coming into his seventh Test match, England's Sajid Mahmood had played in seven innings and scored 77 runs. He completed the first innings of the match, against Australia at Melbourne in 2006-07, with a duck, and later a pair. At the same time, his best bowling return in a one-day international was 3 for 37, while his best in any one-day match was 4 for 37, and his best in first-class cricket 5 for 37.

● Shane Warne marked his 37th birthday in 2006 with a trip to hospital after earlier receiving an honorary doctorate from a British university. Test cricket's leading wicket-taker was awarded the special degree from the Southampton Solent University during Hampshire's Pro40 match against Worcestershire at the Rose Bowl. Decked out in traditional academic dress, Warne received his doctorate from university pro-chancellor Glyn Tonge: **"As arguably the greatest bowler who has ever lived, Shane Warne is highly deserving of this honorary doctorate. His sporting success is an inspiration to all. We felt it was only fitting to break with tradition and confer this degree at the Rose Bowl, the home of Hampshire cricket, in recognition of the huge contribution he has made not only to international cricket but to the success and popularity of cricket in the Hampshire region."**

Later in the day, a bloodied Warne had to attend a local hospital after being hit in the head by a bouncer, courtesy of West Australian import Matt Mason. Batting at No. 3 for Hampshire, Warne top-edged a ball between his visor and the grille of his helmet, and went off to the local hospital for treatment before returning to the ground and resuming his innings: **"It was a short one … I was in a good position to hook it, but it zipped and bounced a bit quicker."**

"I am officially the spin doctor now. By law I can call myself Dr Shane Warne now, or Shane Warne PhD."

Shane Warne

"My mother was a teacher and she used to tell me when I was a young man, 'Mikey, I know you love sport, but I want you to remember one thing: you've got to get a piece of paper behind you.' Well, now I have."

former West Indies fast bowler Michael Holding on receiving an honorary civil law degree from the University of East Anglia in 2006 for his contribution to cricket

---

● During the summer of 2008-2009, an auction took place for a day's fishing with Australian all-rounder Andrew Symonds. The winning bid was $8000 – paid for by Symonds, so he could go fishing by himself.

FERENCES & CREDITS

BOOK REFERENCES

The Cricketer's Quotation Book – David Rayvern Allen (Robert Hale Limited, 1995), *Who's Who of Cricketers* – Philip Bailey, Philip Thorn and Peter Wynne-Thomas (Guild Publishing, 1984), *The Latham Diaries* – Mark Latham (Melbourne University Press, 2005), *The Complete Who's Who of Test Cricketers* – Christopher Martin-Jenkins (Macmillan, 1987), *Quick Singles: Memories of Summer Days & Cricket Heroes* – Christopher Martin-Jenkins and Mike Seabrook (J.M. Dent & Sons Ltd, 1986), *First-Class Cricket in Australia: 1850-51 to 1941-42* – Ray Webster and Allan Miller (Ray Webster, 1991), *The Complete History of Cricket Tours at Home and Abroad* – Peter Wynne-Thomas (Hamlyn, 1989), *Wisden Cricketers' Almanack* (John Wisden & Co Ltd, various years), *Wisden Cricketers' Almanack Australia* (Hardie Grant Publishing, various years).

MAGAZINES

Cricinfo Magazine, Cricket International, Cricketer, The Cricketer, Inside Cricket, Wisden Cricket Monthly, The Wisden Cricketer.

NEWSPAPERS

The Age, The Australian, The Canberra Times, The Daily Telegraph, Herald Sun, The Sun-Herald, Sunday Telegraph, The Sydney Morning Herald.

WEBSITES

www.abc.net.au/cricket, www.bbc.co.uk/tms, www.caribbeancricket.com, www.channel4.com/sport/cricket, www.cricbuzz.com, www.cricket.com.au, www.cricinfo.com, www.cricketarchive.co.uk, www.cricketzone.com, www.howstat.com.au/cricket, www.lordstaverners.org, www.rediff.com/cricket, www.rupert.mccall.com.au, www.sify.com/sports/cricket, www.thatscricket.com, www.worldcricketcentre.com.

PICTURE CREDITS

Rae Allen, Australian Broadcasting Corporation, Australian Rugby Union, Jason Barry, Graeme Bell, Hamish Blair, Nick Branson, Brisbane Broncos, Bunburys Cricket Club, Andrew Campbell, *The Canberra Times*, Channel Nine, Channel Seven, Channel Ten, Nicole Cleary, Andrew Cornaga, Digicel, Rob Duong, Empics, Eve Vocal Trio (www.evevocaltrio.com.au), Mark Fletcher, Frankston YCW Cricket Club, David Frith, Grafik Lab, Hachette Australia, Ron Haddrick, Tim Heald, Hodder Moa Beckett, Irish Cricket Union, Ian Jennings, Victor Keegan, Kent County Cricket Club, Lashings Cricket Club, Bill Leak, Lord's Taverners, MCC, Rupert McCall, McGrath Breast Cancer Foundation, Jim Maxwell, Elaine Mayson, Mukta Arts Limited, Mat Murphy, National Missing Persons Helpline, News Limited, Office of The British Prime Minister, Office of The Governor-General of Australia, Henry Olonga, Keith Page, Photosport, Michael Picht, Postcards From The Sledge (www.postcardsfromthesledge.com), Geoff Pryor, R&R Publications, Alan Robertson, David Rowe, Seán Ruane, Fanny Rush, Sanitarium, Shanghai Cricket Club, Six & Out, *The Sun-Herald*, Thejas K. R., Darren Waters, Weston Creek Cricket Club, Rob Wilmshurst.

Every effort has been made to trace copyright owners. If, however, there are any omissions, apologies are extended and any acknowledgements will be made in any subsequent edition.

PERSONAL THANKS

Julian Abbott, Keith Andrew, Marcus Kelson, Connie Liu, Rupert McCall, Anna Warren.